Europe

Asia

Africa

Equator

Indian Ocean

Australia

Cape Town

Cape of Good Hope

Lady Pepperell

Roaring Forties

Cape Leeuwin

Tasmania

Sydney

New Zealand

Kerguelen Islands

Westerlies

Prevailing Westerlies

Southern Ocean

Antarctica

| Kilometers | 0 | 1000 | 2000 | 3000 | Km. |

| Statute Miles | 0 | 1000 | 2000 | 3000 | Mi. |

30 45 60 75 90 105 120 135 150 165 180

Degrees East Longitude

THE
Mooneshine
LOGS

THE
Mooneshine
LOGS

FRANCIS STOKES

SHERIDAN HOUSE

First published 1994 by
Sheridan House Inc.
145 Palisade Street
Dobbs Ferry, NY 10522

Library of Congress Cataloging-in-Publication Data

Stokes, Francis.
    The Mooneshine logs / Francis Stokes.
        p.   cm.
    ISBN 0-924486-67-8
        1. Sailboat racing.   2. Sailing, Single-handed.   3. Stokes,
    Francis.   4. Sailors—United States—Biography.   I. Title
    GV826.5.S76   1994
    797.1'4—dc20   94-25389
                                                              CIP

Design by Jeremiah B. Lighter

Photos by the author unless otherwise credited
Boat plans in appendix courtesy of Robert H. Perry
and William Garden/Mystic Seaport Museum

Printed in the United States of America

ISBN   0-924486-67-8

Because we love bare hills...
And were the last to choose the settled ground.

W. B. YEATS

CONTENTS

Introduction

THESE ARE TALES of modest adventure, suitable for middle age. They are drawn from my sailing logs of fifteen years, spanning earlier days of solo ocean sailing and the special times for those who were there. Much has changed since I made my first intrusions on the ocean; nearly a generation has passed. Solo Atlantic crossings are now commonplace, and the singlehanded and shorthanded races have evolved, at least in the larger classes, into high-technology and big-budget athletic contests. Old expectations of crossing times have been shattered (and some of us have been made to look foolish in the process).

Happily, the oceans are out there, and unchanged, offering the extraordinary gift of loneliness and a multitude of beauties for those who dream of empty places. I write of racing here, and a lot of my sailing has been in the course of races. I should say, however, that I am not really a racing sailor, certainly not a good one. As I look back, I see that I must have used the organized races as excuses to make my breaks with the land. I must also confess that once into a race I took pleasure in the competition and special delight if I arrived ahead of selected rivals. There are many rewards of a personal nature in crossing an ocean in your own boat. If you manage to beat a certain other skipper in the process it's even better.

I have had more than my share of good fortune in the sailing events that I entered, and also with the sailors and others met around the world. This writing is by way of small repayment, but also with the thought that it might encourage at least a few to sail the oceans in their own small boats. I hope also to please "an old man on a winter night" as Yeats said, and here I pay my respects to the many books of the sea that have instructed and inspired me. I do believe I was imprinted early in life, like a young duck, with scenes of the sea from books.

My intention was not to write a book of instruction, certainly not a book on seamanship, because others are far more qualified. (I am probably tied to land in more ways than I would care to admit.) In a larger sense this is a how-to piece. I have attempted to explain a state of mind that takes leave of the land; describe certain oceanic scenes that fix in the memory; and, finally, convey, however inadequately, the quiet rewards you bring home from the sea.

If this is a how-to book, I hope the reader will also find it a why-not book. Or, as the late Abbie Hoffman said, "Don't bullshit. Just do it!"

one

Lady Pepperell off Cape Town (photo courtesy Barbara Lloyd).

Crazy Jane

*J*UNE 14, 1970. IT was the first night at sea in *Crazy Jane*, after departing Barnegat Light, New Jersey with her destination Plymouth, England. I slept for brief periods, and when I awoke it was to disbelief and wonder at finding myself alone on the water. Light from a partial moon was glancing off the waves; *Jane* moved easily with the mild south wind, and the only sounds were of flowing water. Each time I stirred myself to look out it was like waking in a strange room. Part of the old self had been left behind, and good riddance.

Twenty years later this memory remains fresh. I have often thought how selfish this solo sailing is, since no one else is there to share it. If this is selfishness, so be it; solitude sharpens the experience and the memory. You store these things away, and like money in the bank they add something to your sense of security.

This voyage had a number of beginnings. In early March of that year my boat had not yet been delivered, but the intent to sail the Atlantic had been declared, and the prospect was beginning to gnaw at my insides. A late winter northeaster was blowing. I thought that I should have another serious look at the ocean, and so took leave of the office using some excuse now forgotten and drove down to Manasquan Inlet on the New Jersey coast. Manasquan is one of three "all weather" inlets on the New Jersey coast and is protected on north and south sides by rockpiles extending well out from the beach. A strong ebb tide was running and caused the incoming waves to rise into row on row of gray monsters—to my eye—in the failing light. It was a thoroughly dismal and threatening scene. I worked my way out on the rocks to an iron tower which I grabbed with the thought of leaping upwards if necessary. Confidence was ebbing with the tide.

My wife, Nancy, had accompanied me to the New York boat show in January of that year. We boarded several of the sailboats exhibited in the well of the hall, and I would sit in the cockpits and survey the craft for suitability as if I had great knowledge of the sea. As we sat on a 30-foot Cal I said, "This one will do." And that was that. (My wife has always thought that I am a better sailor than I am.)

I wonder whether our decision-making process may be more a matter of chance than rationale. The really big choices like buying a house, or even getting married, are likely to come from some stray whim of fate. Leaving such things to Fortune might not be such a bad idea anyway.

This sailboat was designated the Cal 2-30, being the second 30-footer introduced by this manufacturer. She was designed by Bill Lapworth, who was famous at the time for his Cal 40, which was then winning races. This was shortly before the new IOR rule began to influence sailboat design, some say detrimentally. The Cal 2-30, I thought, had good lines for a sea boat and was adequate structurally. It was notable for a radically chopped off reverse transom, which gave it a controversial look. Even as a loyal owner, I would never nominate it for a beauty prize.

I wrote to Bill Lapworth seeking assurance that his fin keel and spade rudder together with that fat exposed transom constituted a reasonable approach to an Atlantic crossing. He kindly answered my foolish questions with cryptic marginal notes on my letter, and I felt (somewhat) reassured. With hindsight, I would not have chosen a boat with a deck-stepped mast, which pretty well assures the loss of the rig if one wire stay breaks. It also had a large mainsail with a boom so long that anything other than a well-controlled jibe might cause the boom to foul the backstay with potential for disaster. Nevertheless, it was a good, fast boat. I have now lost track of her but assume she is still a good, fast boat somewhere on the Chesapeake Bay. There is a sister ship in

Annapolis, and I have experienced small pangs of appreciation when I see it.

Other seeds for the Atlantic voyage had been planted in July of the previous year. I then owned a Cal 25, a fast, happy sailboat, tender in a fresh breeze. It is not a boat to take very far offshore. By chance or by fate I conceived the idea of sailing in her by myself from the New Jersey coast direct to Montauk Point on Long Island. It is about 130 miles from Manasquan to Montauk and not a daring voyage by any measure. We called this boat *Margalo* after a character in E.B. White's *"Stuart Little."* Margalo was the small bird with dreams of flying north.

My little trip in *Margalo* was memorable for being my first night offshore alone. I motored out of Manasquan Inlet, the six-horsepower outboard engine shoving us through the exaggerated inlet swells and into the last of a sunny afternoon on the ocean. I had the impression that powerboat people were waving excessively, as if I was starting out on a real voyage. I stayed at the tiller, vainly trying to get the boat to self-steer while the shore and finally the lights on shore faded away. Then I attempted to sort and identify the confusing light patterns of navigation aids on the Long Island coast at night while the vast loom of New York City lights remained an unsettling presence in the west. I felt vulnerable to be out there at all. There was a tendency to edge toward the shore, deviating from that direct compass line to Montauk. As a result I spent some hours sailing and motoring parallel to the beach the next day while lack of sleep turned a sailbag on the foredeck time and again into a mysterious unknown crewperson. I rounded the point under Montauk Light with night falling and felt the lift of gray Atlantic swells passing under me as I sailed by the buoy marking Great Eastern Rock. I couldn't have been more pleased if I had just completed some grand voyage of exploration.

Two days later I sailed home via the Long Island Sound. It was a blustery southeast day, winds to 25 knots. This time, with double-reefed mainsail, a small jib sheeted flat, and the tiller tied off, I managed to fly down the Sound, passing everything (I thought) while sailing "hands off," just like Joshua Slocum. I wonder if anyone before or since has as successfully sailed a Cal

25 the length of Long Island Sound with no hands. This is a boat that had repeatedly embarrassed me by flitting around like a butterfly when it was supposed to be lying docilely at anchor like other boats.

The remainder of this voyage was something of a let-down as I motored through New York in heavy rain. The East River that day had everything unsavory in it and on it, and indeed I read later that a body had been fished out. Nevertheless, I had completed a singlehanded voyage to remember.

That fall I went to Goldberg's Marine store in Philadelphia and came home with a Plath sextant.(These were not so expensive at the time.) "What do you think you're doing with that thing?" was the predictable response on the home front. But I would go down to the beach and practice bringing the sun down to the horizon—a pretty easy exercise, of course, when sitting in the sand. I also bought a book on celestial navigation and then a second book to help explain the first. Between the two of them I thought I could manage.

To unravel further the reasons for my travels I would have to probe my psyche deeper. I sometimes said that it was to get away from politicians, and there is more than a little truth in that, though I should have realized that politics in the broad sense is as the air we breath: There is no escape.

I have often regretted my birthplace in a small land-bound New Jersey town. Forebears had come from England, claiming religious persecution. Conditions in England were terrible, it was said. "The cities were dangerous, the roads impassable, and ruthless tax gatherers were abroad in the land." To all of which we can only say amen. Family histories have tended to add more luster to these honest people than can be known for certain, reaching back into pre-history with such descriptions as: "We believe he must have been close to the court." I would prefer to think they had admitted to at least some spirit of adventure. We do know that our immediate settler was a baker, that his group sailed up the Delaware River and landed in the mud of what is now Burlington, New Jersey. I have faulted them for passing the high ground and deep water where now lies Philadelphia. Three hundred years later we suspect that Philadelphia cousins still look down upon us from their heights across the Delaware. I was born just eight miles from the site of the original landing, which I think shows a certain complacency: those who arrived later had to move on.

I most certainly despaired of the dreadful hours spent as a young lad examining the carpet in the Quaker meeting house, carpet that was chosen for its very plainness and the fact it would never wear out. Seeds of protest sprouted in that room, and what a disappointment I was to good people there. Did I ever lift my head from carpet studies and actually listen to the earnest messages delivered by elders dressed in gray? Or would it have made any difference in the end? Serious matters of Doctrine pass, as do other fashions, but life goes on. "Quaker Gray is a gray like no other. It is the gray that is left after that color has been drained of all life, and cheer, and hope," thus wrote a cousin years ago. Old family diaries tend to bear this out, but through generations the genes become the typical human stew of promise versus reality that is life. I have merchants, and Quaker saints, and drunkards, and artists, and even a few sailors to draw upon.

My great-great grandfather was a captain in the China trade, though he felt it necessary to find respectability ashore before his conscience would allow him to marry. I have a logbook written in his even hand, still legible after 170 years. In it are sailing directions for the Indian Ocean and the straits leading to the South China Sea according to season. In the same book he wrote the method for obtaining longitude by lunar distances and the extensive tables needed for these unbearably tedious calculations. The modern sailor must be humbled by the accomplishments of such men. I have now sailed some of the same waters, and it is a small achievement compared to theirs—but I am pleased to have followed them in my way.

Henry Hudson appears at the base of one family tree in my possession. He explored the New Jersey coast in the year 1609, even describing the charms of Barnegat Bay and its perilous exits to the sea. But on his next voyage he and some loyal crewmen were set adrift, like an early Captain Bligh with his men, in eponymous Hudson's Bay, and were never heard from again. Time has

hidden these dreadful events: one account had it that the true
mutineers were killed by Eskimos, but when the remnants of crew
finally arrived back in England they were never punished. Hudson's ship, *Discovery*, survived to make three more voyages to the
ice.

Joshua Slocum, who knew something of mutiny, at sea and
also at home, says he slept easily on the *Spray*, knowing that all
was well up forward. "There was no dissension amongst the
crew." And that is as good a reason as any for sailing alone.

FORTUNE SMILED ON that first voyage of *Crazy Jane*. I must
have chosen well the departure date of June 14 because I experienced virtually no headwinds on the entire crossing. At the time
I thought this must be the perfectly normal condition on the
Atlantic in June. I have since learned that is not the case, and even
then I realized that maybe I had unfinished business with this
ocean which should be attended to later on if opportunity presented. Meanwhile, life would be the mix of work and family,
roughly translated as time vs. money, that is the Catch 22 of sailing. This first trip was made on stolen time, which perhaps contributed to the sense of illicit freedom on the water.

It would please me to think that this account might encourage another to try some unlicensed freedom out there.

My boat was delivered in April to the Lippincott Boatyard,
which was located by a muddy cut off the Delaware River north
of Philadelphia. A sailboat with five-foot draft will exit this cut
only at high tide. I worked evenings and weekends at projects I

thought would be useful, such as adding a small chart table and trying to guess where unwanted water might enter. She was a very typical fiberglass boat of this rather early period in the fiberglass revolution. "Frozen snot" was a term still heard, but I would reply that boatbuilders only used wood until better material came along. The interior was Clorox-bottle utilitarian since competition at the shows had not yet forced manufacturers into creating their versions of proper yacht decor. I remember inspecting my aluminum mast extrusion, judging its weight against others in the yard. Mine appeared to be the thinnest of all comparable spars, one more small worry to store in the back of my mind.

In early June I moved the boat to a small yard in Toms River off Barnegat Bay to await the arrival of the Aries windvane steerer from England. And here began my association with Nick Franklin, mastermind of the Aries vane that has helped me over a good many oceans. The singlehanded races of the sixties had encouraged development of these essential devices for short-handed sailing. The Aries is a species of vane gear called, in the ponderous British manner, "servo-pendulum," meaning that a little wind power harnessed considerably more water power to steer your boat in a direction relative to the wind. The voyage of *Crazy Jane* would never have taken place without it.

Nick Franklin had arranged the shipping with his usual attention to detail, and I watched nervously as the designated container was unloaded at the port on Staten Island. I carried my device to the boat, where it was installed just a few days before departure, but the narrow waters available to a sailboat with five-foot draft and the shifting winds on the river prevented any real testing. The afternoon before appointed departure day I ventured the 12 miles down the bay to Barnegat Light with one friend on board. We ignominiously fetched up on a mud bank somewhat short of our goal and had to call on assistance from a passing powerboat. (I never employ the term "stinkpot" because of occasions like this.) The Barnegat Inlet area is rife with mud flats on the bay side and shifting sandbars on the sea side. A long journey is taken a few steps at a time, and just then the hazards of Barnegat Inlet appeared as awful as the ocean itself.

I had been embarrassed by interest of the press in what I thought of as a private enterprise. At that time and place it was considered newsworthy for someone to sail the ocean alone, though it certainly had been done many times before. I began to get peculiar advice through the mail from unknown persons who must have sensed a fellow crazy. I wondered if there wasn't a lonely fellowship of misfits out there, reaching out to me. Newspaper accounts picked up on the vast stores of liquor (greatly exaggerated) I reportedly was loading. Despite the fact that most of our antecedents had to have arrived by water we seem to have turned our backs to the sea. I was identified as a strange one.

There were more spectators on hand for the departure than I was comfortable with. Taking graceful leave of wife and five children is daunting enough without onlookers. I would have to appear competent and in charge as I left the dock, raised sail, and negotiated the inlet. All of this was far more the immediate cause of nerves than contemplation of the voyage; time enough for that later.

That year the buoyed channel in the inlet ran for some distance parallel to the beach. I had to motor into the wind, but hoisted the mainsail for appearances. This was to be a sailing voyage, after all. After passing close to the familiar lighthouse I saw a knot of spectators on the beach. There was a final glimpse of family there while I held *Jane* to what I hoped was the channel. With some relief I faced the ocean when the inlet was finally cleared. You anticipate this time of relative quiet; the preparations can be hectic, and goodbyes are always difficult if not guilt-ridden. But now is the time to relax a little, lay out the course, and tidy up for sea. It has not always worked this way; other times there have been sleepless first nights in full foul-weather gear and anxiety.

My log for the first days at sea sounds tentative, only slightly worried but unsure of many things: I haven't checked the compass; I have two watches, they don't agree; my first sun sights are wildly off; I have to get used to holding on; there are shipping lanes to cross. "I'm not lonely, but a bit apprehensive over the length of the journey ahead . . . the mind can't take in the number of miles to England."

The weather here was kind to me. My confidence would have quickly drained had the weather decided to test me. I had seen very little of any ocean at that time, not even from the deck of a ship. My only readiness for rough weather was from books, especially the fearful photographs of storm waves in Adlard Coles' *"Heavy Weather Sailing."* But here I was enjoying a mild southerly breeze, and moving steadily on course at good speed. This must be the Atlantic in June, I thought, and all was well.

The logical eastbound sailing route from our East Coast ports parallels the routes shown on pilot charts for commercial shipping. One sails east for 1100 or 1200 miles to approximately 48 degrees west longitude before bearing left or roughly northeast for England. This plan carries you south of the tail of the Grand Banks where the warm Gulf Stream impinges on the cold Labrador current. (Farther north you are assured of fog and the possibility of icebergs, and one usually opts for sunshine on the eastbound passage.) If you trace off the great-circle course from this point on your Mercator chart it develops a graceful curve, taking you north more quickly, but actually saving only about 20 miles over the rhumbline or straight route on the Mercator chart. Whether sailing north a little sooner also places you in the path of storms is another small worry. There is 600 miles of northing to be made on this route—but why rush it? Pilot charts, which in 1970 cost just 50 cents, are still one of the world's great bargains, containing a vast amount of information for the mariner, gathered from captains over 150 years at who knows what cost. Among the bits of advice here are the frequency of gales for the month in each five-degree square of the oceans. This tends to be reassuring for these routes in June because the gale percentages shown are quite low. Later editions of the pilot charts have a notation to the effect that these gale predictions are skewed to the low side because they are based on ship reports, and ships use weather advisories to route themselves around predicted bad weather. Small sailboats, usually not enjoying that option, take what comes, and it has been my experience to endure more gales than would be expected from the charts. Of course, one man's gale can be another man's fresh breeze, and at that time I had little but the Beaufort windforce descriptions to guide me.

I don't think I am alone in being led onto the ocean from both curiosity and fear. If you want to see and understand the ocean you know there will be gales sooner or later, and you worry. Now that I have seen quite a few gales and some storms I still am anxious when bad weather is on the way, but I also have a stock of confidence to draw on. On this voyage there was much to be experienced for the first time, and that realization was added to other sensations as the sandspits of New Jersey disappeared.

Other active concerns for my well being were (1) staying on the boat, and (2) avoiding collision. These are of immediate and general concern to all singlehanders. You only have to visualize the boat sailing off, leaving you to swallow water in its wake, to understand what might be called the ultimate loneliness—"the ineradicable loneliness of death." Nightmare scenarios abound. You quickly appreciate the need for good technique with safety harness and tether. Early mornings on this first voyage would find me, figuratively, on my knees in thankfulness for passing another day safely attached to my boat. On subsequent trips I have put this business of the harness in perspective, and many times I have moved forward on deck minus tether. I have sometimes wondered just what my thoughts would be should the boat sail on without me, hoping that I could muster a smile. I am reminded of a friend who was adjusting lines at the stern of his boat and lost his balance. Thinking quickly, he managed to land squarely in the dinghy he was towing, but the sudden load snapped the painter, leaving him to rock in the dinghy while his boat sailed off. Luckily, this was on the Chesapeake Bay, and he was able to hail a passing motorboat.

Sailors are lost off boats whether crewed or solo, and I don't mean to treat this lightly. My point is that the utter necessity of staying with the ship becomes another part of accepted routine, and therefore loses its awful immediacy. You relax somewhat while remaining vigilant. One thinks of the sailors working high in the rigging of sailing ships in centuries past without harness or personal flotation device. Or lawyers, in those days.

The subject of collision at sea is tricky. Singlehanded sailing has been criticized by certain authorities as a violation of the accepted rule requiring a lookout at all times. The Royal Western Yacht Club at Plymouth, which has sponsored the best-known Atlantic races, responded by limiting the overall length of competing yachts to 56 feet and later to 60 feet, on the theory, I suppose, that we would not sink shipping, and that seems reasonable. We would also hope not to be a nuisance to people earning their living out there while we sailors are vacationing after our fashion. A question that never will be answered satisfactorily is whether our friends in ships are also keeping their 24-hour watch. Most do, of course, but even then there is a very good chance a small sailboat would not be seen. Not many years ago we had the example of the *Exxon Valdez,* which may serve to put the matter of watchkeeping on small sailboats into perspective.

Some have employed mathematics and the laws of probability to calculate the chance of collision on an Atlantic crossing. Figures like one in half a million or one in a million sound reassuring, but we know of too many actual collisions and close calls to have any faith in these predictions. I have become more wary of encounters rather than less as I have grown older, and now regard collision in its various forms as a major reason for care. In 1970 *Crazy Jane*'s defenses were rudimentary. Her running lights were typical of the time, which meant inadequate even for inland waters. I had a wire mesh radar reflector, designed for lifeboats, which was cumbersome to deploy, and there was no radio or other means to communicate. I did not know Morse Code and could not signal by flashlight. Times have changed, and I would not set forth in that manner again. Still, on a typical west-east crossing it is easy to go for 10 days without seeing a ship, especially if you successfully stay some miles clear of expected shipping lanes. You can convince yourself that you are quite alone. It is also true that you are fooled into thinking you see more of the ocean than you actually do from the deck of a sailboat. The horizon may be four miles off; you might see a ship at eight miles. Some ships will overtake you quite slowly; others, especially container ships moving at 20 knots or better, can come over your horizon while you are down for even a brief nap. The truth is that you can be unpleasantly surprised by a ship at any time. The continental shelves and fishing banks are home to fishing trawlers, and there is no relaxing at all there. The western approaches to the English Channel form a giant funnel for cargoes to and from Europe, making those waters a dubious place for sound sleep. Short naps and careful time management are your best choices here.

There are objects other than ships to collide with. We have all heard tales of the semi-submerged cargo containers wandering the seas like Flying Dutchmen. The original Dutchman was to wander until he found a woman who would be true, and good luck to him. Most of these containers, we can hope, are also mythical. We know there is lumber out there, and trees, and I like to remind my multihull sailing friends of the 1200 telephone poles reported lost off the deck of a ship in the Gulf of Mexico. There is an astonishing record of multihulls in the transatlantic races coming to grief by hitting some unknown objects. As a monohull sailor, I might be tempted to speculate that perhaps their boats are simply coming apart. On the other hand, we have seen more whales in recent years, and one French multihull man was heard to say, "there are too damn many whales!" Whales, in fact, ganged up on and sank a 30-foot monohull in the 1988 Atlantic race. We don't know whether this was calculated revenge or merely hooliganism on their part. But I am happier if I don't see whales from my boat.

I did not think seriously of these things on those first nights, and probably slept too soundly in my quarter berth, lulled into a sense of well-being by the sound of water flowing by just inches from my ear. I was becoming attuned to the sounds of my boat. This awareness becomes a form of natural instrumentation that serves as status report on your ship and the weather. You soon learn to judge boatspeed by sound or even the feeling of bubbles under your feet when standing in the cabin. Changes in windspeed or direction are also identified by a change in motion, and it can range from the most subtle to an uproar in the rigging. Whatever is happening, when you are alone you know you are on call 24 hours a day—but it quickly becomes an enjoyable routine.

The Gulf Stream is shown on most charts as turning east in a smooth wide curve, so that in sailing due east from New Jersey you won't encounter it until the fifth or sixth day out. That is just as well because the warmth of the Stream almost always disturbs the weather. Often it is spotted from a long distance off by towering clouds, and sometimes lightning. That lightning may be a very long way off but is never reason for cheer. The Gulf Stream, of course, is continually shifting its course, and by the time one encounters it east of New Jersey it more nearly resembles a rampant garden hose covering a huge expanse of ocean. It throws off warm eddies to the north which are like large clockwise doughnuts, typically 50 to 100 nautical miles in diameter, and cold eddies to the south which wheel anti-clockwise. All of these currents disturb wave patterns depending upon wind direction. The common result is uncomfortable going, but occasionally there may be the unusual wave called "rogue" when you are looking for a scapegoat. You may get a glorious lift in miles from the favoring current, and other times you can be dismally set back, and I have experienced both. All this is quite unpredictable unless you have more immediate knowledge of local current patterns than I ever did. You can plan your route with care, but don't underestimate the role of luck.

On the fifth night out I was surrounded by amazing columns of black cloud intermittently highlighted by a full moon. Polarized light from the moon on clouds and waves presented an exaggerated image in sharp black and whites, like an Ansel Adams silver print. The difference is that it is real this time, not darkroom tricks, and it's printed on your mind. I knew this was the Gulf Stream. The going was rough, but we were making good time, 600 miles run, and no turning back now. You are actually in this current the rest of the way to England, though it loses identity and is called the North Atlantic Drift. The pilot chart shows orderly green arrows, an artist's rendition, indicating a half-knot eastbound current which would mean 12 free miles each day. That would be hard to prove, especially by the shaky celestial navigation on *Crazy Jane* that year.

The unsettled character of the weather in this area affected by the Gulf Stream brought my first gale experience on June 20, the seventh day out. I was being introduced to the business of ocean sailing by incremental stages. At least my log appears to have a cheerful air, if slightly forced: "Now I'm using storm jib alone, with Aries steering downwind in the night. I can't see what's going on . . . the ostrich effect . . ." And the next morning: ". . . this is what we're here for. Ran all night under storm jib while I got several hours sleep in my quarter berth with only a few drips. Awake at 0415 and found it quite light, which shows this is the longest day of the year. I hope this longest day is not too literal. Endless chaos outside my windows. I hope I am right with my jib. If it works it's right . . ."

As I look back on that early morning I can recall those waves. They were indeed gale waves and just a bit unusual for that area of ocean in June. The tactic of running off with storm jib was an impromptu performance then, but is a preferred option that I have employed successfully many times since.

Francis and *Crazy Jane* were now almost 800 miles on their way to England, with mutual confidence developing.

TIME HAS ALWAYS passed easily for me at sea. I slipped into a pleasant routine of eating, sleeping, and reading—those preferred vacation pastimes. This was time stolen from the cares of work which only added to my delight and the feeling that this was some extraordinary holiday. But there were the messy sail changes to be made, and the nights of rolling without wind and terrible banging aloft. Some days there was endless fiddling with the self-steering and sail combination to achieve something like the desired course. Since this was a vacation I was determined to keep the hand steering to a minimum. On this trip I believe there were less than three hours total spent "hands on." I have since come to terms with sitting long hours at the helm, and even those hours become enjoyable.

Without a radio transmitter I was incommunicado, which had its positive side since this trip was to be an essay in self-sufficiency. I have used ham radio since 1980, and that opens a whole new world, but I am glad that I have had it both ways. I could almost recommend to anyone planning a first lone voyage that they do so without that electronic tie to land, for it is a tie. Having said that, I confess to amusing myself daily with such short-wave broadcasts as I was able to hear on a small battery-powered receiver. In 1970 the Japanese electronic invasion had barely begun; progress in communications has been truly astounding in the intervening 20 years. One cannot say the same for the content of the AM shortwave broadcasts I have followed over this period. There is a continuity in the political struggles of our species, bloody and otherwise, that may be depressing or reassuring according to your philosophy. Conflicts in the news in 1970 are still conflicts in 1990. "All things are born through strife" said Heraclitus 2500 years ago, but out here you may turn off your radio if you don't like contemplating the great human experiment.

I have generally kept logs by way of a journal in addition to the navigation scribblings. Perhaps it is a substitute for talking to yourself. There is no doubt it is of more interest to the logkeeper than anybody else, but since it is hard enough to please anyone in this world, I think you may certainly set about pleasing yourself with good conscience. That said, I offer these log excerpts with the hope that they accurately convey my voyage. Some may perceive a lightheadedness as I run down the miles to Plymouth. I do admit to being quite immersed in my reading at times, and there was always that growing anticipation of landfall which is one of the enduring pleasures of voyaging. With so much that is new to be taken in and made your own it must be all right to engage in some foolishness.

> *June 21, Day 8.* A sight this afternoon under wild conditions tends to confirm the noon position. Where is all this south wind is coming from . . . and fog? If it blows any harder I will change to the storm jib. You would have to be crazy to row across this ocean.

My onboard reading had included the Chay Blyth-John Ridgway account of their crossing by rowboat just four years earlier. I often thought of them, with incredulity, as I watched *Jane* reel off her miles through this tossing waste. Their goal was one degree of longitude per day, weather and blisters permitting. I was doing three, and gaining weight.

> *June 22, Day 9.* 0630. A ship! A large westbound freighter three miles to port. I prefer to think there is nothing I can possibly run into out here. 0645, and it's gone into the mists . . . I'm lingering over a third cup of coffee. Time to relax, do nothing . . . like one long Sunday afternoon at home. It's a day of fog, some rain, gentle wind and easy motion. I'm drying matches over the Aladdin heater. It's time to move the clock ahead one hour. I dislike losing the hour. The surface of the sea is gray but as you look deeper it becomes an inky blue, perhaps because the sun is trying to burn through overhead.
>
> At 1700 the water really has changed color to a violet blue, like the ink we used as schoolboys, now out of fashion. Visibility is low again, and one has a nagging fear of ships. I opened the radar reflector, but it is a clumsy device.

Early the following morning came a startling encounter with the Canadian naval vessel *Saskatchewan*; here was a misty-green warship bearing down on me a thousand miles from land. The first thoughts were "My God, what have I done? I'm not supposed to be out here . . . something must be wrong at home . . ." I had to have been self-centered indeed after just 10 days alone. It happened they were merely curious, and sailors lined the rail with cameras. I thought they might signal by flag or lamp, exposing again my unfitness to be out there. Instead, they came close enough to pass a position via voice while I tried to appear nonchalant and spilled my coffee in the cockpit. I also thought the latitude given was low and wondered if they were lost. Then I was alone again with the roaring southwest wind and rough seas. But I was determined to work hard at the navigation this day if conditions permitted—one has to have faith in one's own work. Later I was conceited enough to call the position given me 34 miles off. Landfall 2000 miles ahead would be the final test for me and my Plath sextant.

> *June 24, Day 11.* The mind can't truly absorb a blue like the blue of the ocean this afternoon as I look deep alongside the boat. The sky, the water, and perhaps the reflected blue of my hull reinforce each other. It's topped off by the white of breaking waves. Sunglasses spoil it and I leave them off. My cabin is so filled with sunlight, fresh air, and quiet this afternoon it's like a house at the shore. The sounds of water outside most resemble the gentle rhythms of mild surf at the beach.

Twenty years later and after quite a few Atlantic crossings I can look back on that afternoon as a special time. Water has not had quite that intensity of Gulf Stream blue or the winds and waves been so complimentary. I think that memory serves well after 20 years, and I am not overpraising nature here on my first time out. It was another of the memorable days I enjoyed on that crossing for which I hope I have paid sufficient respects to my good fortune.

Crazy Jane had now turned the corner at 47 degrees west and would follow a great-circle course 1780 miles to the Scilly Isles. With following winds it is relatively easy to follow the curve of this track. I was preoccupied with my eastbound mission, and probably gave little thought to the problems faced on sailing west. The fact is, you are easily lulled into complacency when sailing off the wind and sliding effortlessly down waves. If you turn and sail uphill it becomes a vastly different game. But that would be in the future.

A single chart covers the width of the Atlantic, 3000 miles reduced to the span of three feet. A hundred miles is covered by one fat thumbprint, so that even a good day's run for a small sailboat seems like mighty slow progress across the world according to your chart. I would spend many hours staring at that chart, pricking off daily runs and anticipating days to follow. There is always the temptation to count miles before they are run and to guess the date of landfall.

June 25, Day 12. I opened a fold of the chart last night and found the Azores just over the eastern horizon— meaning I could be there in seven days. An intriguing idea but will have to save it for another time. I have figured out the date of arrival in Plymouth and having been this foolish may as well be dumb enough to write it down. It's to be July 11. We have averaged 125 miles a day so far with mostly favorable winds . . . a good day for rowing as the southwest "trade wind" continues, although lighter. It's equally fine indoors or out on these sunny days. A coincidence this morning: I was lying in bed dreaming or imagining and saw a ship astern. When I got up half an hour later there it was, three miles off but identical to the ship in my dream.

June 27, Day 14. I was up early with the missionaries on shortwave this morning after a sleepless night of wind and rain. All noises are intensified at night; I worried about the poled-out genoa. Then the steering vane fouled on the radar reflector, causing us to luff up with a terrible banging. I threw open the hatch, pinching a finger. Finally at 0300 I stowed the spinnaker pole and eased things somewhat. (It's getting light by then.) Now

I'm watching the telltale compass swing through half a circle and wonder if I should shorten sail to the small jib or storm jib.

June 28, Day 15. Last night, with a dying west wind I gave up and hove to as the only way to manage some sleep. Otherwise the light swell keeps the rigging in an uproar and sleep is impossible. And this with a vang and foreguy on the boom and shock cord on the sheets. Then I found my boat surrounded by a mass of what appeared by flashlight to be brown jellyfish. I had blundered into one of nature's ritual orgies, but why here in the middle of the ocean, which is three miles deep at this spot? There was no moon, and the stars stood out in the blackness with a peculiar penetration. The undulating outline of the Milky Way seemed close at hand; water and sky were one, with no horizon.

1900. This is near the widest part of the Atlantic, and it resembles a deserted Barnegat Bay on a gray day. There is little or no swell, and we are moving at just 4.5 knots with only the mainsail. For some reason the course is steady with mainsail alone in these light conditions. It looks like a quiet night with the ocean to ourselves.

Looking at my log entries for these days I can visualize the large, lazy high pressure that often dominates mid-ocean in summer. One looks for help from the pilot charts which show tantalizing westerlies of Force 4 and 5 with a tiny percentage of calm. So much for averages; the distance sailor learns patience or engages in another sport. Resignation comes harder if you are racing and think your immediate competitors have been more clever finding wind. I had no competitors and no fixed schedule that year. What was the hurry? It was gale anxiety—the fear of being caught out. I kept looking to the sky in the west.

June 29, Day 16. My world is circumscribed by fog this morning. With a little imagination you could be any-

where. The barometer is high and rising. I hope it fore-
tells a change in the weather.

1700. 16 miles run since noon. It is so quiet you can
see the track we have made a quarter-mile astern. Pur-
poseless clouds give no hint of a change. I lowered the
jib to save wear.

June 30, Day 17. 0530. It's the Dead Sea. 60 miles run
since yesterday noon with no visible change in the
weather. This day offers no promise of change. A little
blue shows through insubstantial clouds. Somehow the
boat stays more or less on course, and slow progress is
made at cost of chafed sails and nerves. When the wind
is at its best I can hear the low sound of water passing
the hull.

My two watches were not reliable so I would tune in most
mornings to shortwave radio for a time check. In the early mornings and in the evenings all the clamor and importuning of our
world were drawn into my small radio. One listens in detachment.
I am simply an observer, I think. Have I always been just an
observer?

July 1, Day 18. Low-lying slate-colored clouds make a
gray Atlantic dawn. A long break in the clouds to the
east lets the early light touch the water—it could be
dreary or promising. I love the long swells that roll up
astern about an eighth of a mile apart. There were dis-
agreeable noises in the rigging most of the night as the
wind dropped. I left the sails on because we were moving, and slept rather well in spite of it.

0730. Fog. 3.5 knots.

0815. My God. I was startled to hear a foghorn close
at hand. Up with the radar reflector; then prepared the
engine to make a fast move if needed. Now the ship has
passed. The horn reverberates several seconds after the
blast. Is it an echo off the fog, the waves, the imagination? This is the first sign of a ship since June 25. My

isolation is illusory. Now we're in the cross-waves from the ship.

0930. I keep hearing foghorns. They originate somewhere between the ears.

1030 and it's just clear enough for a sun sight. The ocean is . . . empty.

July 2, Day 19. It was another tiresome night of mischief in the rigging. I let the mainsail take the beating this time. We are behind even yesterday's pace. Wind freshened at dawn, and I put a jib out on the pole. Now we're down again. That's the way it goes. I try to imagine more guts to the clouds today, but they come and go impotently.

Here's a notable milestone: We've passed the fold in the chart. Now I am looking at Europe instead of North America; closing a gap instead of opening one. At 1400 we've been overtaken by a breeze and are running at six knots. I have hopes for a real change at last.

1600 and the wind is off—and fog . . . Finally, it's clear again and we have a truly fine afternoon. I believe it is a change. Wind is southwest, on the quarter, and I spend time in the business of sailing. Now I'm finishing these notes to a variety of noise from the radio and some good music. We are moving well—I can tell by the feeling under my feet. I haven't thought about it much, but I'm beginning to realize the excitement of the first landfall. On to the Scilly Isles.

July 3, Day 20. There was an embarrassing encounter with an unknown steamer at 0030 this morning. I woke up for a routine look around and saw lights of a ship astern, always a shock or annoyance when you haven't seen anything for several days. Worse, they shut off their engines when half a mile abeam and signalled by Aldis lamp. I could only wave my flashlight in return, and feel defeated. I don't know who was more surprised by the affair. One really wants to be left alone. Later, fog closed in again . . . Fog all morning, and I'm frankly jumpy. There is nothing like staring into fog to make you start seeing and hearing things. Distant airplanes which normally you don't hear become possible ships. I can see jet trails overhead despite fog at sea level.

I didn't realize it at the time, but this ship was employing the insistent Morse "A" sign—short-long, short-long—meaning they wanted to initiate contact. In that black night it seemed especially menacing, revealing my fraudulent status as mariner. What was I doing out here anyway in the sailor's world? In this day of crowded VHF channels and our own readiness to grab the microphone, it is easy to forget that in 1970 the VHF radio was not yet in general use. Oh, how we love to talk. There is no turning back now to the old ways, though, and the old signalling skills will be lost.

That year the electronics on *Crazy Jane* consisted of one depthsounder. I used the admirable Thomas Walker taffrail log, which had an integral generator connected to a speed dial. This apparatus was a minor nuisance but did its job well, just as it did for old Slocum. I have carried it on subsequent travels as a redundancy. It might even serve a grandchild someday in that way.

By July 4 we were 850 miles from Plymouth—less than 1000 miles! Even a small boat can chew away at 1000 miles! It might take a week, and a week goes by quickly. I was eyeing my predicted arrival on July 11, but the winds remained light.

July 5, Day 22. A delicate balance of wind, sails, and vane kept us going through the night. The heading is roughly 90 degrees magnetic while the sea kindly closes over the crooked, dancing track. I slept for nine hours with only two brief lookouts. The water has been wonderfully luminous the last two nights. Every breaking wave, the ship's wake, and the log line glow with white light. The BBC World Service gave us John Dowland madrigals this morning, and all too short. Then an excerpt of Billy Graham speaking from the Lincoln Memorial left an uncomfortable reminder of affairs in the U.S. Somehow reports of ancient hatreds in Northern Ireland project the human condition—timeless, insoluble problems that only show the stubborn resilience of the species.

. . . Just waiting for the fog to lift. Twenty men are missing in the English Channel this morning after a collision in fog. Seven Great Shearwaters are swinging in arcs close by, flying so close to the water that their wing tips flick to clear wavelets.

I am enjoying a piercingly blue afternoon after the fog of the morning, a common pattern lately. A new wave of clouds seems poised on the western horizon while the morning gloom disappears to the east. "And fair needs foul I cried."

After supper we are still running our almost silent five knots under a sky turning gray and increasing swell from the west.

The quote above and lines below are from Yeats, and the original Crazy Jane from whom my boat took its name:

> *I am tired of cursing the Bishop*
> *(Said Crazy Jane)*
> *Nine books or nine hats*
> *Wouldn't make him a man.*

I have now chosen names for six boats and so far have eschewed the wretched sea-going puns of which the English language must be a fertile source.

The following day, July 6, must have been a time of small accomplishment or perhaps too much rolling, for I find Lawrence Durrell poems copied into my log. This is a sample, and I would not vouch for my state of mind or the content.

> *The foxy faces*
> *Of Edwardian Graces*
> *Horse faces full of charm*
> *With strings of beads*
> *And a packet of seeds*
> *And an ape-tuft under each arm!*

I was overdue for the change of weather that came the next day.

July 7, Day 24. An early start today. Awoke at 0330 to increasing racket and went on deck to reef the mainsail. I watched the sunrise at 0415 through a narrow slit in clouds on the eastern horizon. There is mist, rain, and a strong southwest wind. The barometer has been slowly falling for two days and reads 29.80.

A typical gale of the North Atlantic summer was on a track to pass north of us, though I was lost in my usual state of worry and ignorance. The mainsail was off, then on again just in time for the next squall. I was looking at daylight now through seams in this poor sail. These were the days before simple slab reefing; I would go forward with a crank to roll in more reef, and the deeper the reef the greater the bag in the remaining sail. This was also the era of undersized winches. *Jane* had only woefully small single-speed winches for her genoa sheets. I didn't know any better and returned home with the sailor's "winch elbow" as a reminder that our bodies are contrivances of breakable sticks and string. In a more perfect modern sailor's world all winches would be over-sized and self-tailing.

White water was flying this day; I couldn't even sit down without holding on, but for some reason decided to sort and repack supplies. I blamed Chichester's account of his first Atlantic crossing for my excess of stores: "100 eggs, 100 potatoes, 100 bottles of grog . . ." 100 bottles of grog? It was an outburst of nervous energy as we approached land, even though I thought we were 400 miles off. When the sun poked through briefly in mid-afternoon I took a quick sight, which can be a foolish pursuit in gale conditions.

July 8, Day 25. I was up at midnight and dressed for the deck, and then changed my mind—a case of exaggerated sounds in the night. The barometer is 29.35 and steady this morning. I've been out jibing and getting back on course as the wind veers to northwest and blows harder.

Will the wind hold long enough to allow arrival in Plymouth on Saturday the 11th?

I never tire of watching seas build up over the stern and then slide under. Breaks in the clouds give an after-the-storm look to the world. The difference in latitude shows. I would not expect a sea and sky like this at home in July.

The barometer is rising this afternoon and with it the wind, which seems to flatten wavetops. We are overpowered with my small jib and take rather a beating, but I will leave it on. The speed is seven knots and up to eleven knots surfing down waves. The sky is a mixture of blue and cloud as in the mountains after a snow squall. Waves are now longer and higher, and there is a fragment of rainbow in the southeast.

I was pressing on here and careless of my mast and rigging. It's a state of mind—only 200 miles or so from the Scilly Isles, and you sense the end of the journey within reach. I hope I appreciated at the time that this was a glorious tailwind. Had it been on the nose, or anywhere near on the nose, which could easily have been the case, the situation would have been vastly different. Neither *Jane* nor I were ready to do battle upwind, but I don't remember giving that a thought at the time, as if these westerlies were some kind of right. Besides, I was in a hurry now to get there.

July 9, Day 26. Gannets are flying today, indicating the British Isles are near. These wonderful birds have an angular aloofness as if they belong to the geologic past. The wind is moderate, but there is a large uncomfortable sea which makes the daily routine difficult. Now a windshift to the west is giving the usual problems of control. I am writing this after lunch, running wing-and-wing while the compass swings between 60 and 120 degrees. A small freighter is passing, the first sighting today. I would have expected more traffic here in the approaches to the English Channel. Last night I passed three fishing vessels arrayed on our course a few miles apart. I stayed in the cockpit watching them for quite a while, well bundled against the cold wind, which seemed to be fresh off the Greenland icecap.

It's hard to get good sunsights, mainly because the waves hide the horizon. You try to catch the sun while the boat is on top of the swell, but there may be waves between you and the true horizon, and all the while you wedge yourself to keep your balance. By then the boat may have turned, and the sun hidden behind your sail. I'm making excuses for possible problems today. We are about 130 miles from the Scilly Isles and 120 miles south of Fastnet Rock on the coast of Ireland. I have been listening to soft voices on an AM station in Ireland. England must be there because I have heard English humor on a BBC channel.

It was time to say goodbye to a companion here, and I heaved my empty Chivas Regal bottle into the gray water of evening twilight as a kind of offering.

July 10, Day 27. Landfall today? The early morning position is about 50 miles from Bishop Rock. We are plunging ahead in good form with a southwest breeze, some blue overhead, and a varied cloudscape. And no fog . . . thanks. In the night lights of ships appeared on all sides. My mental alarm clock failed, and about 0130 a huge shape passed less than half a mile to starboard. I assume they were keeping a better watch than I. Now the sea is empty again.

I was aiming for Bishop Rock Light, the lonely stone tower that rises from a tiny islet in the sea at the south end of the Scillies. On this morning I was blessed with sun and a following wind. I commenced filling my plotting sheet with lines of position marching toward the Bishop while scanning the ocean ahead for anything poking above the horizon. Through it all, there was the wonderful exhilaration—I had crossed an ocean, almost!

A log note at 1000 tries to sound sober as I tell myself I won't see anything till noon. But at 1100 . . . "I see something . . . it's

Bishop Rock. 1115 . . . I see a bit of low-lying land. Changed course to 120 degrees to skirt tidal overfalls shown on the chart south of the light."

And that was the landfall. How lucky I was that day with sun and visibility to make it easy. At 1300 I was a few miles due south of the light. There was a small celebration on board, a beer and a Fig Newton. A mist had now settled over us, but on the main island of St. Mary's I could see fields and inviting cottages. There were fearful rocks in the foreground whose names, Daisy and Gorrigan, I will forever remember. After 27 days of pure ocean only, the sight of real rock is startling, and off-lying dangers the more awful.

I now had to get serious again about sailing. There was drizzle and mist and the wind fell light. I tried to set a new course of 90 degrees for Lizard Point, 45 miles away. But *Jane* was reluctant to leave the Scillies, and twice I found her bow pointed back at Daisy. I did not realize that a small, tough nut of a depression was on its way until rains came and a south wind built quickly. Easy coastwise piloting became lee shore paranoia as visibility dropped and the wind blew up to Force 7 with gale force gusts. Visions of rocks mixed with the excitement of being there at all. An outbound freighter passed close to starboard, the bow plunging and tossing off spray. I felt lightheaded as a young lad who has read too many sea stories, but the image of that ship is still fresh in all its salty detail.

Lizard Point Light is a powerful three-second flash visible for more than 20 miles, though it can be obscured by local conditions. I commenced watch for the light while working nervously offshore, uncertain of currents or leeway. I was unsure of my boat in these conditions and whether she could work at all to windward in gale winds. Then came that blessed relief when the light showed itself in clouds off the port bow. How green I was at this landfall business! I tried to take a bearing on it with my hand-bearing compass, but the wildly swinging card made it useless. I was now energized to wash pots and clean the toilet while my boat plunged and I kept a smart lookout for traffic. Lights of six or more vessels are often seen at once here, and trawlers are entirely unpredictable as they ply their nets.

Four miles off the Lizard the wind fell away. I was left working sails for two hours, and watching trawlers. All was black with little wind, and we rolled while the lights showing our relative positions appeared to move through three dimensions. One seemed determined to run me down; my pose as an ocean sailor was wilting there under the flashing Lizard.

But at midnight the cold front came in from the northwest; *Jane* revived, and I set a course for Eddystone with the jib and reefed main. There is an illusion that once past Lizard Point you are in protected waters, and it often happens that Atlantic swells are left behind, even though the approach to Plymouth is a very wide open bay. This night the northwest wind had little fetch so that I had a beam reach with fresh wind and flat seas. The remaining hours of darkness were spent below looking through the ports at flying foam. Speed is always enhanced in the dark, and I am left with the memory of a final, wild dash to the finish. Clouds broke away, and the northeast sky showed signs of dawn by 0230. I adjusted Aries to steer between Eddystone Light and the Hand Deeps, with 12 miles left to run.

It was now Saturday morning, and sunny. Small boats with an unmistakable English look were coming out from Plymouth for a day of fishing. I flew the American flag, as if to call out: Look. Look at me! No one paid attention. Plymouth Sound is framed by Rame Head and the Staddon Heights, whose green slopes meet the water, and it is beautiful when set off by early sunlight and blue of the water. Why, I thought, did my forebears ever leave this sparkling island to settle in New Jersey? A friend had filled in a composition book with poems for my voyage. The final entry was, of course, Shakespeare:

> *This precious stone set in the silver sea,*
> *Which serves it in the office of a wall,*
> *Or as a moat defensive to a house*
> *Against the envy of less happy lands,*
> *This blessed plot, this earth, this realm, this ENGLAND!*

THERE WAS NO SHORTAGE of real news in July 1970, such as a war in Southeast Asia. But various accounts of my trip had gone out over the wire services, perhaps as a diversion from usual realities. I was receiving kind notes, as if the writers thought they were connecting with a free spirit. In this they were wrong, of course. I had returned to family and business, tuition and taxes. Freedom is relative and probably best taken in small bites.

This was just three years after Francis Chichester had completed his round-the-world voyage in *Gypsy Moth IV*. He was not the first to circumnavigate alone, but he in effect rediscovered the practice for small boats. He certainly was the first to combine his adventure sailing with the art of public relations. He gracefully gives all credit for this to Lady Chichester, but that, too, may have been a part of his persona.

I give high marks to Francis Chichester. I remember the feeling of excitement at the time he left Sydney, bound for Cape Horn, and how we followed his progress across the Pacific with a certain anxiety. Despite the endless complaints, I think he understood better than most that life is a struggle, and is meant to be so. "It's the effort, not the success that is worthwhile," he said, and practiced it better than most. When he writes at the beginning of one of his books, "I love life," one believes it. Perhaps I feel indebted to Sir Francis because I bear the same given name. For obscure reasons my name derives from a colonial bricklayer; I had spent 40 years looking for another role model of that name. Francis Drake, though a circumnavigator, was too much the buccaneer. Saint Francis was out of the question.

For whatever reasons, in 1970, my voyage caught the interest of the American news machine. I became known as a sailor, which was only partially the case. I was introduced to television in a small way and found how unsatisfactory that medium is when you try to explain a personal and private experience within the terrible time imperatives of the advertising spots. If the matrix of these shows is the advertising, I was useful only as filler. I had the temerity to turn down an appearance on one Philadelphia station and experienced the near wrath of the producer, leaving me to feel small and ungrateful.

I cannot say I did not secretly enjoy my 15 minutes in the sun. It was useful in that having found myself in the news for little reason, I am now most content to be ignored. At the same time I stored away some personal confidence—long overdue, one might think, at the age of 44.

For a shy person, another terrifying prospect now had to be faced. I was asked to appear as speaker by desperate entertainment chairmen. Me, speak in public? I think of our late sailing friend, Jim Crawford, who must have crossed the Atlantic 14 times, claiming "stark terror" on facing an audience. I shared that terror and remembered a survey showing that some fear speaking in public more than death. Now I have faced figurative death in front of audiences, and I know that it does get easier. When the real thing comes that, too, may be easier.

My sailing has led to other public encounters where the personal dignity of the lone sailor was confronted by the absurdity of the occasion. Mine was the least athletic body at a celebrity sports benefit for the March of Dimes, held at an opulent hotel-office complex rising from swamp near the New Jersey Turnpike. At dinner I found myself staring at the enormous roastbeef hands of the football lineman on my right, and at the astounding shoulders of the distance-swimming woman on my left. We were to make appropriate presentations to the assembled dinner guests and thereby warm their check-writing fingers. My turn came immediately after the "Raging Bull," Jake LaMotta, whose boxing career was built on losing to Sugar Ray Robinson, and who took this occasion to go on at some length in a sort of stand-up comic routine. How was I, the despair of all my school coaches, to rescue the image of the singlehanded sailor from this? Quite a bit of money was raised for the March that night, though I have wondered if I earned my dinner.

On another occasion I was a "presenter" at the New Jersey "Governor's Awards" ceremonies. This was a carefully choreographed affair to reflect credit on the State of New Jersey and, in particular, its governor. Indeed, the governor performed a little dance on stage that night. I was paired with Rocky Aoki, the restaurateur and powerboat masochist, to introduce the winner of the Transportation Award with appropriate sweeping gestures. I have no idea now who that was, and the world has forgotten. I do remember thinking what a strange country I lived in, as I mingled backstage with anorexic ballerinas. What this had to do with sailing by yourself is anybody's guess.

I made another mistake about this time involving television. It is difficult enough to walk away from an encounter with this medium with your dignity whole. If you are a sailor, or worse, a yachtsman, it is doubly difficult. Media types in general are amazingly removed from things nautical, and often appear baffled by those who actually like to sail. I had been deprived of evening television entertainment and didn't know what company I would be keeping when asked to do a segment on a magazine show with local producers competing for air time. These pieces are shot ahead of time; your night on the air comes later, based on somebody's perception of timely interest. I supplied film footage I had taken of my boat rolling through gray seas near Cape Horn, and wonderfully salty, I thought. When my night came I was squeezed between Mr. T. of "The A Team" with his fur vest, gold chains, and Mohawk, and an Olympic pole vaulter who had achieved notoriety for underwear ads featuring his body. In truth, it was a very fine body. How is a middle-aged sailor to compete with that? I was mercifully saved from humiliation in my home town because the Philadelphia station substituted for my slot a local artist who had created a new school of post-modern art: he was throwing buckets of paint into the wash of a jet engine to be blasted onto a white screen.

The above is offered as a caution to future sailors in case you are called before the cameras some night when real news is scarce.

I left *Crazy Jane* in England, the vacation over. It was time to fly home and get in harness. But first I had to arrange shipping for *Jane*. After some phone calls it was decided that I would sail to Southampton, where Camper and Nicholson's would build a cradle and see that *Jane* was loaded on a freighter. Nancy had flown to meet me, so the two of us set off down the Channel and had a glorious overnight run, passing the Needles guarding the Isle of Wight in early morning and bursting into the Solent. By then a stiff northwest wind was blowing, so that the last miles motoring past Calshot Spit and into Southampton Water in the teeth of it were a trial by stinging salt spray—*Jane* had no protective cockpit dodger. Camper and Nicholson's were most obliging, and included a tour of the works by our tweedy host. We also engaged a shipping agent to tend to arrangements before departing for Heathrow and home.

Months later *Jane* showed up in Baltimore where I had arranged to meet her with a boat hauler. The plan had been to return to that muddy cut on the Delaware whence we had started. I would be, like Slocum, returning to that spile in the mud at Fairhaven where he had launched the *Spray*. Alas, the cradle Campers had built came from old bits of wood and scrap metal and was showing a definite list to port. We decided to risk a 30-mile overland voyage to Annapolis instead of the longer trip to Philadelphia, while I followed in my car expecting the cradle to collapse on every curve. But *Jane* survived, and I was thereby introduced to the genial river pirates of Annapolis who prey on yachtsmen. I was paying $20 a month for winter storage which seemed a lot of money at the time. Occasionally I would fall behind on my rent and receive a reproving letter beginning, "One of my unpleasant duties . . " etc. Obviously the pirate had been looking at my cradle and knew he had a potential deadbeat on his hands.

I knew that I was truly back home. Hands-off freedom on the high seas was in my past for now.

Mooneshine—The First Voyage

THERE IS A TIME to sleep and a time to make money. In the summer of 1975 money was the essence. I spent long days and nights amid the crash of bottles and cans at my factory. But I also had a few sailing magazines to help my mind travel elsewhere. Ads began to appear for a new sailboat that was to be called the Valiant 40. These were only drawings of her lines. There was no Hull No. 1. Yet factory bedlam was encouraging escapist dreams, and I began to associate this boat with the singlehanded transatlantic race scheduled for the next year. Another ad came out, full page this time. "She's Here!" it said. There was to be a Valiant at the Newport, Rhode Island sailboat show in early September. I drove up to the show . . . But she wasn't there. Any sensible person would have altered course at this point. But wait, there was to be another show at Stamford in two weeks. It would surely be there this time. I drove up from New Jersey once more and foolishly brought a checkbook. Never take your checkbook to a boat show.

A Valiant was secured to the dock stern-to. This was not an ordinary stern but designer Robert Perry's tumblehome canoe stern. I walked past several times, then left and returned an hour later to look again. And again. That stern, which became a Robert Perry signature, was actually based on old designs, specifically *Helga Dansk*, a handsome traditional yacht still in service. In fact, she won a Bermuda Race several years later, but that was due to the vagaries of handicap rating rules. Nevertheless, she was a handsome sailboat, and the tumblehome stern has proven durable aesthetically as well as structurally. The guiding principle behind the Valiant was to combine the classic appeal of an older design with an efficient underbody—the Valiant has a fin keel and a large skeg-mounted rudder located well aft for good control. This was not a new idea, but the Valiant was one of the first serious cruising boats of the fiberglass generation to emphasize lively sailing characteristics. It also gave the impression of strength, and being a family-type person bordering on the timid, I thought it might be a good choice for my entry in the solo race.

Nathan Rothman, the entrepreneur behind the Valiant, was at the show, wearing a beige suit of modish cut and fine shoes that looked uncomfortable around boats. We held a conference on the foredeck. The price was going up, he said, and I would have to assure myself of a production slot. A check for $2000 would take care of that. As I mentioned earlier, we lurch and blunder to those really important decisions. I drove home minus $2000.

I had now sent off my entry for the OSTAR which was the slightly grating acronym for Observer Singlehanded Transatlantic Race, sponsored by the Royal Western Yacht Club at Plymouth and the London Observer. To make this entry official I had to complete a 500-mile qualifying cruise by March 15. Conditions off our East Coast can be messy at that time of year; with that in mind I elected to have the boat delivered to Dion's Yacht Yard in Salem, Massachusetts. My cruise would be out of Salem, skirting Cape Cod and Nantucket Shoals, thence southwest to the Delaware Capes, being 500 miles, more or less. This questionable strategy necessitated weekend commutes to Salem from New Jersey when my boat was finally delivered in January. It had been trucked from Bellingham, Washington, and had disappeared briefly in a Wyoming snowstorm, but finally it arrived in Salem with a cockpit full of snow. It was also foul with diesel soot.

The commissioning process was not a complicated one since electronics were simple, and the basic sailing hardware was in place. The standard Valiant deckplan showed lines and winches worked from the cockpit, convenient for the shorthanded crew. As I look back on this project now I see myself as just a little overwhelmed by both the size of this boat and the transatlantic voyage in prospect. I pushed ahead, mustering what confidence I could from travels in *Crazy Jane*, but I could well have used advice from experience.

I had not confronted the self-steering arrangements, at least for the 500-mile qualifier, and had only a small Tillermaster electric steerer on board. This was sending a small boy to do a man's work, as I soon found out. Shortly after the launch I went for the maiden voyage around Salem Harbor with Jack Cuddire of Valiant Yachts, who had helped in preparations. There was exhilaration in the power of this new boat, but also a small lump in the stomach when I sensed the forces at work as fresh gusts from the land breeze reached across the harbor. Tillermaster was making significant cries for help, which I chose to ignore. An injector stuck when we cranked the Westerbeke to return to the dock; a fearful noise of hammers and iron arose from this engine, and we shut it down. We would dock under sail—no problem for two sailors. But the keel caught on a marine railway, leaving my new rig leaning precariously over the dock with a rapidly receding tide. Lines were thrown, winches plied, disaster averted. I was now ready for my 500-mile cruise.

The problem of a name for the new boat had now to be addressed. I had been reading Samuel Eliot Morison's volumes on the European discovery of America, and especially the voyages of John Davis, the admirable and stalwart Elizabethan navigator. In 1585 he had explored the west coast of Greenland with two small vessels, *Sunneshine* and *Mooneshine*. Greenland Eskimos were introduced to pipes and dancing of English sailors on the decks of *Mooneshine* in what must have been an early case of culture shock in this hemisphere. Even though, as I tell my wife, I have danced my last dance, my boat became *Mooneshine*.

The 500 miles were a wintry experience. How soft we sailors are who wait for spring to launch and put our boats up in the fall, while fishermen earn their living on the water year-round. I was revealed as one of the recreational sailors. There may have been romantic visions of battling Cape Horn gales as I tied stops on the mainsail with freezing hands, but these hands reminded me of their abuse for several weeks after.

It was sunny but cold as I left Salem at 0700 on March 7. Two friends from Valiant were there to see me off, with final advice on navigating the rocky ledges off Marblehead. We were the only craft in sight as I rounded Marblehead and set a course to clear Race Point on Cape Cod. I made a first call to the Coast Guard on my new VHF radio, which had crystals for four channels installed. The radio check was by way of reassurance for a somewhat nervous skipper. (The Coast Guard does not welcome radio check requests these days—there are far too many of them.) Now the wind was building from the southwest and soon was blowing near 25 knots. Fuses began to blow inside Tillermaster. Each time I would extract the small screws to remove the cover and expose the fuse, hands freezing, boat pitching. Luckily, after the third fuse it died altogether, never to exhibit life again, ever. I started experimenting with sheet-to-tiller steering. Log excerpts reveal a naive ill-preparedness:

> 1600. 2nd reef in mainsail.
> 1700. Replaced staysail with storm jib.
> 1800. Windspeed cups blow away. Radar reflector up. Something is wrong here. It isn't blowing *that* hard.
> 2000. Some rain and snow and also stars. Temperature 36 degrees.
> *March 8.* 0100. The weather sheet torn from tiller. Dropped both jibs and steered by hand. Too cold. Took off main at 0230 and am lying ahull. Very rough.

I was drifting south in the Great South Channel between the outer shore of Cape Cod and Georges Bank. By luck, and certainly no management on my part, that was my intended course. I even passed close to a buoy in the early morning and thought I knew where I was. I began sorting things out on deck, including the great Gordian Knot of jib sheet and spinnaker halyard. The sheet had escaped through want of a stopper knot and grappled furiously with the halyard while I was giving in to the cold and wind of the night before. Things were now looking up, but snow was predicted for the next day and, sure enough, the wind veered northeast that night. The next day:

> March 9. 1000. I'm getting a signal on the radar warning. It is snowing with visibility less than a mile. Temperature 29 degrees.
>
> 1200. Making up to 8 knots. Visibility very low in fog and snow. More radar signals. I have been on deck tending to a loose shroud where a cotter pin was missing.
>
> 1400. Heavy going. Temp. 30 degrees. Snow.
>
> 1600. Seemed prudent to heave-to. I have sheeted the storm jib flat to windward (port tack), tiller lashed. All secure on deck.

The heavy table in the main cabin had not been installed and lay as a potential flying object on the cabin floor. I crawled into the V-berths of the forward cabin and thus spent the uneasy hours with vague awareness of the confusion outside. On one lookout there were lights of three trawlers arrayed in a kind of formation against the storm and not far to starboard. I called out on the VHF in some alarm, but there was no answer. We were disconnected lives passing in the night.

By 0730 the next morning I was able to raise some sail while the wind moderated, and my storm jib functioned as a steering device though large waves made the course erratic. By evening I was drifting in unaccustomed silence as the wind had gone light. My turning mark was to be Delaware Light, a large navigational buoy off the coast of Delaware, but overcast prevented sights. I drew some wild lines on my chart from radio bearings on broadcast stations, which only showed again the frustrations inherent in this medium. Well, you can't get too lost in the gentle arms of the larger New York Bight, and the following day, March 11, there was sun and a sailing breeze. This day started early with an unheralded comet low in the eastern sky with a reddish upright streak as tail, like a red squirrel. Then there was a battery scare as the engine refused to start. A hydrometer check showed dismal readings despite my efforts at recharging.

I had plenty to learn, including much about lights and batteries and alternators as found on boats. More accurately, I learned not to take these things at face value, and not to assume that boatbuilders knew best. In the mid 1970s recreational boatbuilders were learning too, which may be a kind way of saying they should have known better. I believe now that my background as operator of a food factory was valuable preparation for solo voyaging. I knew tools, and pumps, and wiring. I knew the pressure of perishable crops and breaking machinery while temporary help might walk off the job. I learned to anticipate what might go wrong and to listen automatically for sounds that might indicate trouble. In short, I knew how to worry and how to stay up late. Welcome to the singlehanded life.

The final log entries are happy ones. It was clear, and I knew well the lights off Cape May while the moon and smooth seas made easy sailing down the last miles. To make certain of my 500 miles I sailed north past Cape May after rounding Delaware Light, then tacked off North Wildwood to double back and enter Cape May Inlet. I picked up a mooring off the deserted Cape May Yacht Club at 0100.

There were now six weeks for final preparations before the departure for England. I cannot honestly say whether *Mooneshine's* first cruise had enhanced or diminished my confidence. I remember one afternoon in early April when I had somehow agreed to take two decidedly non-seafaring couples for a sail. It was a bright, cold day with a hard northwester of early spring. They assumed that I was entirely competent no matter what the conditions. I knew better and feared disaster. I was much relieved to find when we drove to the boat that the northwest wind had practically emptied Cape May Harbor. We left *Mooneshine* resting in the mud of her berth and retreated to a restaurant. It was a successful outing afterall; my good fortune continued.

Mooneshine—The Atlantic 1976

I REALLY WANTED to sail the OSTAR. It was to be the fifth running of this quadrennial event, and interest was high. We all knew the names associated with earlier races—Chichester, Tabarly, and Colas. You have to do this before you are too old, I told myself, before you get your heart attack or your cancer. I was 50, and old enough to see over the horizon. Besides, I knew from days in *Crazy Jane* that I had not really seen the Atlantic.

American sailors in this race have the interesting problem of getting their boats to Plymouth and ready for race committee inspection by the end of May. Some sail their boats over the previous summer and lay them up, thus avoiding the early season crossing in April and May. Pilot charts clearly indicate the ameliorating weather on the Atlantic as June approaches. I say you could miss some useful gale experiences should you choose to avoid sailing in the early months. Since any crossing is a major investment of your time, and maybe emotion, there may be some small tinge of regret if you can't report at least one gale. The days of fine weather become a blur in time; a great gale will be remembered.

Mooneshine's departure from Cape May was set for April 23rd. My son, Whitall, then 13, was to accompany me. I don't know how this happened, or why his mother ever permitted it, but as I have said earlier she thinks I am a better sailor than I am. He was to take time off from school with the proviso that he keep a journal for English class. For history we would tour London and gain appreciation for the origins of our culture. As it turned out we probably failed the school on both counts, since much of his voyage was spent in a mild state of nausea, at least sufficient to inhibit writing, or so he said. My efforts as tour guide in London also fell short. Westminster Abbey and the Tower did not speak to a 13-year-old who had just bounced and rolled across an ocean. In spite of failure in an academic sense I believe our trip paid in ways less easy to define. Six weeks of eighth-grade schooling, after all, will likely disappear in the prevailing fog of the educational process. Besides, we are talking about Middle School—a device promulgated by harassed educators to replace the maligned Junior High School, as if mixing adolescents and pre-adolescents were an improvement. Thus I have justified this piece of parental irresponsibility. Four years later we were to repeat it.

In reading over my log for this Cape May-to-Plymouth crossing I see I had much to learn. I needed a stern mate to order timely sail changes. I also could have used wise counsel early on about sail inventory. I did not have the small working headsails that I sorely needed for the return passage against the westerlies, or a third, deep reef in the mainsail. My cutter rig needed running backstays. I would have all these now, and more. It takes money, of course, but also the knowledge of experience. Five hundred miles is not enough to teach you about a new, larger boat. I did not have a good feel for the amount of sail to be carried. Here we were, leaving on April 23rd, aiming east toward the Gulf Stream, with gales lurking off our coast as they always are that time of year.

My log is sparse for the first few days. I was not into the rhythm of it, and may have been uneasy in the stomach. I am generally free of that malady, though background nervousness creeps into the gut. There were headwinds; I was carrying on too long with the large genoa. At 640 square feet this is an overpowering sail in anything approaching 20 knots of wind, since the Valiant, like most modern boats, likes to be sailed on her feet. All this time Whitall was quietly dealing with his stomach. On April 27, the fourth day, we encountered a gale. I was slow to realize it because we were running with it, a basic lesson I knew but had ignored.

From the log that morning: "0400. Lying ahull. Took down the yankee in 40-knot wind. Wouldn't steer under bare poles. Aries is finished. I arrived just in time to see the oar shaft slipping through its bearings and the gears already gone. The oar shaft is bent."

We were 460 miles offshore. Whitall was seasick, and the waves were huge. I didn't know if I could encourage *Mooneshine* to self-steer all the way to England. Whitall said no when I asked him if we should turn back, so I set about making the best course I could for the rest of that day. The only thing to do was sheet my small storm jib flat using both sheets, and lash the tiller amidships. We were headed very roughly downwind at about four knots while the wind blew all that day at 30 to 40 knots. "Largest waves I have seen," says the log. I felt like an irresponsible father indeed when Whitall told me he had looked out on deck in the night and found himself alone on the boat, he thought. The spreader lights were on, but I was out of sight, buried on the foredeck under the jib I was clumsily trying to secure.

We didn't learn until we reached England that we had been about 50 miles north of Phil Weld and his crewman, Bill Stevens, who were at that time making a new life for themselves in Phil's inverted trimaran, *Gulfstreamer.* Whatever this was, a gale or a storm, the waves were large and unpredictable thanks to the Gulf Stream.

When you are becalmed you think the wind will never blow again; if it's blowing a gale you can't believe it will ever ease—thus the impatient sailor complains. But the next day's log reads: "Sunny today with moderate northwest wind. By afternoon the sea has smoothed, and we move easily at 6.5 to 7 knots. Sheet-to-tiller steering is working well."

Several things were working to our advantage with the steering. First, the configuration of the boat's underbody encouraged good control. I was using the 60-square-foot storm jib from *Crazy Jane,* which was happily matched as a steering sail for my 40-foot boat. I hoisted this in place of the staysail on the inner forestay of the cutter rig with a weather sheet from this jib led to the weather side of the tiller via blocks. (I was lucky also to have a tiller rather than a wheel, although that had been a matter of economics rather than foresight on my part.) Pressure from the weather sheet was balanced against loops of shock cord. I would use one, two, or three loops according to wind strength, or the cords could be moved back and forth on the tiller itself in infinite adjustment of the moment arm. On some points of sail this arrangement worked as well or better than Aries. But later, after Aries was rehabilitated in England, I learned a new appreciation for the convenience of that machinery as compared to my rope and rubber bands.

We were now moving east roughly along the 39th parallel and receiving some handsome daily lifts from Gulf Stream currents. At one week out we were approaching 900 miles but still chasing *Crazy Jane* for the equivalent time at sea. It may be that in April we encountered winds more evenly distributed around the compass. We had certainly had a share of headwinds and also calms. On May 3 I thought that we were safely past the corner of drifting ice south of the Grand Banks and made my left-hand turn onto the great-circle course for the Scillies. With 1700 miles to go I was beginning to acquire a sense of ease.

From the log on May 4: "If not pressed too hard this boat has an easy, cushioned motion. With afternoon sun streaming through the hatches and a good book it can be very peaceful at 7 knots." That may have been the case in the cabin, but working the foredeck with *Mooneshine* surging down waves and the considerable noise of tumbling water beside me, I would become more conservative. I often carried two reefs in the main and would receive those serious, knotted-brow looks from Whitall. I was definitely under pressure here and knew it. Those looks meant, "More sail, Dad!" And so we pressed on. As if he was in a hurry to get back to school.

Now the daily runs were stretching out in good westerlies. We had gained two days on *Jane*. The log for May 10: "Good sailing until 0300 when the wind went light and backed toward west. Such a banging as *Mooneshine* changed her angle into the waves that even Whitall woke up. At 0630 I poled out the yankee, and we have been going well all day as the wind has picked up. I have a clumsy time with that 18-foot pole. It took half an hour to rig it and to shift the jib, which has a terrible tendency to wrap around the forestay." Years later I am still dealing with spinnaker poles. My most recent pole is shorter, but of course, I am older. I now happily use a roller-furling jib and wonder why I resisted so long. This new furling gear is admirable and usually minimizes foredeck battles. *Mooneshine*'s sailhandling was entirely basic. Her yankee, which was the standard working jib, was a big sail since her cutter rig has a large foretriangle. I mention this as possible excuse for inefficiencies encountered in handling my ship.

The log contains notes on the seabirds that roam this ocean and are seldom seen near shore. The ocean hardly seems complete without them, though it's an impersonal relationship. With the occasional exception of fulmars, our lives barely connect. It has to be a one-sided affair: their presence may fulfill my image of the ocean world, while I mean nothing to them. So I salute the jaegers, fulmars, arctic terns, skuas, and shearwaters of the North Atlantic. Less appealing are the Portuguese men-of-war that originate in the Gulf Stream and make their summer's journey in the wide Atlantic. They are small in April and May but grow as the season advances. Some years they are there in such alarming numbers that one worries they may take over the oceans, and what a world full of anger that would be. I picked one off the deck with only a bread wrapper between me and the squirming purple tentacles. It felt warm, as if there was terrible rage there, and probably there was at landing on my deck. Other times, when becalmed, you watch them and imagine they are sailing faster than you are, the raised bladder flopping on one tack and then the other.

By May 11 we were making rapid progress toward England. I was marking off days until landfall, but also beginning to think of the return voyage: "Clouds thickened by late afternoon and we ran for a couple of hours with double-reefed main only. The course holds well with storm jib to tiller. After supper I raised the jib, and we are making good time as the westerly flow continues. Whitall is in the cockpit watching the waves for Mt. Everest or the Matterhorn. It has been difficult to obtain accurate sextant sights because of the almost continuous rough going. We have it easy sailing downhill here. Coming back will be very different." By noon that day we were just 291 miles from our landfall. And closing.

Bishop Rock came up on schedule. The weather being fine I thought to give Whitall a closer look. It was a sunny afternoon with a west wind and easy swells as we edged in toward the tower. Then I glanced behind and saw angry waves curling over the stern as if about to drop into the cockpit. I was trespassing here where the chart warns of tidal overfalls and quickly retreated south, with one more small lesson learned.

Easy sailing through the night brought us into Plymouth the next morning where we tied up at the customs mooring buoys. At 22 days this has remained my fastest crossing, but we were quickly put in our place by Walter Greene, who had just crossed in his small multihull in 16 days. And there beside us was *Cap 33*, a 53-foot trimaran resembling a great orange spider. We had hardly secured *Mooneshine* when an even larger trimaran, *Spirit of America*, arrived from California, sailed by a delivery crew. *Mooneshine* had come to race against these? What had I done?

OSTAR 1976

T HE OBSERVER'S TRANSATLANTIC race was peaking in 1976. No one took time to think of it then, but this piece of the yachting scene could not be repeated. As in nature, our affairs move in cycles; the OSTAR was ripe that year. Most of the 125 boats that made it to the starting line were now rafted against the rough walls of Millbay Inner Dock in a scene of colorful confusion. There was a lower size limit of 25 feet, and a few craft barely met that requirement. There was no upper limit. It was up to the French, of course, to test the limits. This was the year of *Vendredi Treize* at 128 feet, and Alain Colas' magnificent 236-foot schooner *Club Med*. The disparate craft were divided into just three classes, named in honor of noteworthy vessels of the previous races. Class distinction between monohulls and multihulls would come later. I was to be in the Gypsy Moth Class, which included boats from 38 feet to 65 feet. Obviously, I was not there to win, but simply to participate.

In my spare time I would launch my Avon dinghy to row among the boats. Some multihulls looked fragile, made of wood and wire, like World War I airplanes. Others were huge in my eyes. I was rude enough to row under the wing of 70-foot *Kriter III*, a French catamaran. I had watched her enter the docks the day before with a crew of unsmiling Frenchmen. It was a dark afternoon; these were grim men on a black-hulled boat, here to do a job. On the English, if possible, I thought. It belied the bubbly image of its Champagne sponsor. We all ran to watch the arrival of *Club Med*. Too large for the Inner Docks, she was tied along-side a pier with four majestic masts towering over all. Again there were the unsmiling French while at the stern waved the largest French Tricolor I had seen. This was serious business. Colas him-self was hobbling painfully from a dreadful anchoring accident the year before, and *Club Med* had been his dream while recovering from that injury. The French immediately set about making life difficult for the English race committee by requesting that satellite navigation be permitted on *Club Med* in contravention of race rules of that era. The original concept of purity precluded many electronics in this race, and of course, all boathandling was by manual labor only. In my own purity I had never heard of navi-gation by satellite in 1976.

Here I met for the first time many of the solo sailing types who have enriched my sailing years. It may be a paradox, but I believe the main reason I joined subsequent races is that I have valued the friendships gained. We may sail alone, but in port you feel the bond. It is a shared outlook or understanding, or so I like to think. We sail for our private reasons; in my case I have had deep appreciation for the assorted beings who turn up again and again for these lonely events. It is a loose band indeed. You may meet four years later, but the intervening time is quickly forgotten.

Tony Lush was in Plymouth that year for the OSTAR. He had arrived the summer before in his garage-built yacht, *One Hand Clapping*. Tony has an innovative turn of mind and had designed a junk rig for his craft. This is the sailplan that has set a number of records for slowest passage in upwind battles such as this. Aes-thetically speaking the rig was a satisfying match for the chunky hull. There was a prominent smokehead for the cabin stove which reminded me of the Toonerville Trolley, a daily cartoon in the Philadelphia papers that only I am old enough to recall. I met Tony often enough at later races that it seemed perfectly logical that we should meet again in the Indian Ocean in November, 1982.

I would be racing against another Valiant. Everett Smith and his wife, Charlotte, were on hand to call down to us from the custom pier on our arrival, and also to offer pointed remarks on our rolling sailor's walk once ashore.

Many others were there who would turn up again through the years. One thinks it must be a small world of sailors. I looked down at Blondie Hasler's *Jester* which was tied in a corner of the Docks and beset by the loathsome trash that accumulates around docks the world over. Normally God flushes twice a day, but the gates of this basin were opened only at high water. *Jester* was now sailed by Michael Richey, navigator, writer, and oenophile, and was to participate in every OSTAR through 1988. She did not finish every race, but with her junk rig she set some impressive records for time at sea, and accumulated enough seagoing adventure for several lifetimes. *Jester* had been a constant force in the history of the race since 1960.

Another guiding force was the Royal Western Yacht Club, as none of this would have happened without their hard work and patience. Some of the lonely sailors are fractious as noted above, and one has to salute long-suffering race committees. The Club and City of Plymouth also produced some memorable send-off functions. There was good food and drink, together with some serious and some comedic oratory. Sailors were left shaky for the imminent start of the race.

The start is a time of nerves, or weight in the stomach, according to your constitution. Exit from the Inner Dock was timed for high tide when the gates could be opened. I waited my turn as towing boats peeled off the yachts one by one to pull them through the entrance and into the harbor. Spectators, bless them, lined the passage and cheered us through. It was a continuation of the interest and good will of the hundreds who had come to Millbay to see the yachts through the preceding days. The tow was dropped and I was on my own, hoping there were no foul-ups as I raised sail. Overhead, airplanes and helicopters were raining down noise while I picked my way through hundreds of spectator craft. Now Henri of Henri-Lloyd clothiers came by on a power-boat. I knew he had eyed my Goldberg-issue foul-weather suit back at the dock and found it inadequate. "Keep dry!" he called out. Thanks.

This was June 5th, a Saturday. Moderate winds at the start grew lighter; *Mooneshine* was not at her best. I changed the yankee for the big genoa and knew I was losing more time. The course was more south than west and toward the Lizard, which I thought should be the shortest way home. The first log entry was at 1915 with 48 miles run: "Here comes *Club Med.* I'm ahead of her, for God's sake." I was, but the next time I saw her was upon my arrival in Newport.

One hopes to move out quickly here, away from land and shipping, even away from other competitors. Early next morning I was ghosting toward the Scillies. *Cap 33* was drifting across my bow, and if I hadn't taken over from Aries we would have collided. I was unable to rouse the skipper, Tom Grossman, by shouts, and he continued sliding off to the south. Naturally, he too was in Newport when I arrived. It wasn't until nine o'clock that evening that I finally said goodbye to Bishop Rock. By this time we had begun to receive a gift of a southeast breeze that continued through most of the following day. I could think seriously now about the job at hand.

Reading these logs now, almost 15 years later, I am struck by how clearly certain scenes are remembered. It is not true that it's always the happy times that are stored in memory. I was beginning the long bash and discovering the shortcomings in my preparations. I couldn't shorten sail to an effective combination for beating into the 25-knot westerlies which are so typical. Too much angle of heel and *Mooneshine* would slide off wavetops, with leeway eating away at westward progress. The sea hides this in its trackless way so that you don't get the bad news until the next navigational fix. I had little protection from spray in the cockpit. A Valiant is dry as seagoing sailboats go—little heavy water comes aboard, but that does not include the stinging spray that flies in tough windward work. Now my interior comforts were tested also as seawater found its way through the cockpit lockers and thence into my living space. I was squatting in the galley with sponge and bucket. My carpet was ruined! Why was I out on the Atlantic with carpet? Misplaced expectations of comfort, but also cost considerations. The log entry for Saturday, June 12, is typical:

> Banging into Force 6 is tough. Fortunately the southwest wind allows me to make a good course. I went out to reef the main this morning and found six sail track slides torn loose. More serious, there is chafing damage at the headboard. I will not attempt repairs until it is quieter. The damage must come from feathering into strong winds. I will have to be careful as it is possible I would lose use of the mainsail. I am now using the yankee alone and moving well, although it lacks power in handling the waves. I have been bailing the cabin of water that comes in the engine room vents. The port water tank has broken loose from under the settee and is pressing into the cabin and pushing into the table legs.

A typical OSTAR day!

I was fortunate in carrying detailed charts prepared by Terrence Shaw of the Royal Western that showed the daily positions of competitors in the 1972 race. I would spend hours comparing my progress against certain 1972 boats, *British Steel,* for example, and so far I was even! This was a real morale builder when otherwise there was little cheer. I started listing improvements needed for the next race.

Thus ended week one. It was also typical that this day should end in flat calm by 2200 and that I should spend the night rolling in fog with no wind. *British Steel* was moving ahead of me. I didn't realize it then, but I was to continue my education the next night:

> *June 14.* 0100. I am lying ahull. Last night too little wind, tonight too much. I don't have the right headsail for 28-30 knots. The yankee is too big, and I can't take the chance of damaging it with 2000 miles to go. Likewise, I'm cautious with the main because it's weakened at the head. While this was going on I spoke to a crewmember on a Russian ship that was in my path and waited for me. He wanted to know if I spoke Russian. I

asked him to report me to Lloyds of London, but he mis-
understood and proceded to work up a position for me.
We parted friends. Meanwhile, the water tank worked
further out into the cabin like a giant hernia, and I can't
push it back.

The BBC has a special weather broadcast at 0330 for
the race. They report a Force 12 storm at 48 degrees
north, 50 degrees west in addition to gales in other
areas. My winds are Force 7, and I hope I am not going
headlong into a gale.

Of course, I was sailing into this gale. I did not realize the
reach of a major storm and did not recognize that the waves I saw
were part of the storm system. I had been working my way out to
30 degrees west longitude, which I had fixed in my mind as a significant mark of my progress. Now I was to spend three days just
climbing back where I was on the 14th.

The log here has an edge of cheerfulness, but I may not have
been honest with either the log or myself. The truth was I was
anxious.

Noon. A lot of blue sky is headed my way, and it's enor-
mously welcome. It's blowing like hell, and the sea is
magnificent . . . It's nice to have the sun, but I watched
the wind gust to 53 knots and took in the staysail. Now
lying ahull. I would enjoy this a lot more if I weren't trying to get to Newport in 25 days. I think I made a big
mistake in not going farther south.

There was some sun but no easing of the wind. Seabirds were
grounded, so to speak. I watched them ride easily on the backs of
the green waves with the wind pressing their feathers flat. They
were quite at home; I was enjoying dithering indecision. I had
been standing in the galley when I felt myself lifted half onto the
galley counter as a wave swept under me. We monohull sailors
develop an instinctive dependence on the lead in our keels. Now
there was the danger of capsize as lying ahull among those very
large waves became precarious. In the cockpit I adjusted Aries to

a course just off downwind and pulled a tangle of warp out of the cockpit locker, just staring at the mess. We had all read of towing warps in tough conditions. I looked at the tangle of rope; I watched the waves and *Mooneshine.* It was a mismatch, I decided—200 feet of $3/4$-inch nylon line would have little effect on 11 tons of boat in those seas. I dropped it back in the locker and settled for the storm jib while Aries steered. In this way *Mooneshine* sailed quite happily into the night, but toward Scotland. The log says: "A revolting development. I'm headed 60 degrees under storm jib . . . Main concern now is to avoid damage to rudder, tiller, and Aries."

I was taking the easy way, but running away. Later we learned that Eric Tabarly in *Pen Duick* was doing the same in his 76-foot ketch. The difference was that he was farther west and thus nearer the storm center. Of course, he knew what he was doing.

Now came a blunder, too stupid for explanation. I was lying on the starboard settee about 2200 reading *"The Picture of Dorian Gray."* I had often used the Optimus kerosene burners on the galley stove to warm the cabin a little. That night I was also drying clothes. *Mooneshine* must have been riding smoothly enough down the big seas for I gave way to sleep, because the next thing I knew I couldn't breathe. Choking black smoke had filled the cabin down to the level of my nose. I ducked aft to the companionway hatch for air and then returned to stamp out embers on the galley sole. Dangling polypropylene had somehow reached the burner flame or fallen to the stove.

It's hard to accept that you've done something so spectacularly careless. It hurt that I had done this to my beautiful boat. Fire had crazed the port over the stove and burned the overhead. Teak was charred and the stove a mess. Sticky grime had coated the entire interior, forepeak to aft cabin. There was the chemical smell of burned synthetics. *Mooneshine* sailed on for Scotland.

The cleanup was penance. I worked all night with bucket, sponge, and detergent. By morning light I saw I still could not sail, but thought it was safe to lie ahull. That would at least slow the ride away from Newport. Looking at the waves that day I saw

Mooneshine as in a valley while hills marched unceasingly on us from the direction of Newport. Two thousand miles of hills, I thought. It was most disheartening. That day, too, was spent in cleaning my mess. In late afternoon I raised the staysail and reefed mainsail and attempted to sail but progress was discouragingly slow against the confused waves. They were no longer dangerous, but it was not *Mooneshine*'s ocean.

By noon on the following day winds were again Force 8. I found myself lying ahull again for two hours. Another gale. How could this be? What's going on here? It's June, isn't it? I was struggling once more with the water tank. In sliding into the cabin it had sheared off its drain line and drinking water sloshed in the bilge. Everything was wet by that time—sleeping bag, bunk cushions, clothing, foul-weather gear. I thought also of my ancestors in their ship, *Kent,* exactly 300 years earlier, making their move to the new world. No record of this voyage survives, but we are told they sailed for reasons of conscience. How much better to be here for adventure, the romance, the race. What race? I was still working out to 30 degrees west longitude, and when the sun permitted sights on June 17 I found I was 50 miles behind my dead-reckoning plot.

Banging into an annoying head sea trying to keep from going further north. Last night was worse with almost too much wind for the yankee, with no main. Bumpy, noisy going with visibility less than one mile. I got up to listen to the 0330 weather broadcast, wondering whether to eat breakfast or go back to the bunk when the radar alarm beeped. When this goes off the source has to be close. I rushed to the hatch and there was a brightly lit freighter bearing down on me less than a quarter-mile off. We were approaching obliquely, and I passed a couple of hundred yards off his stern. Actually, there was almost no time to take evasive action had it been necessary, and the whole thing was over in what seemed like moments. I raised him on the radio. Not surprisingly, he hadn't seen me on radar. That is the first sign of a ship in days. I went back to the bunk and didn't wake till 0830.

That's the way it is with ships. If I had not had the radar warning device we would have passed unawares. I would have slept easy, thinking I had the ocean to myself.

By June 19 I was still 650 miles east of St. John's, Newfoundland and wondering how I was to get south and across the Grand Banks. The log showed 1730 miles, though we were still far less than halfway. Now came a blessed change as the wind went into the north. *Mooneshine* elected to go south with all sails flying. The ocean was oddly smooth, but a cold, steely gray. All I knew was that I had a free wind, the first since June 7. I could look out the hatch without spray in the face. The course on my chart made an abrupt left turn as I took my chance to move south, and also made my gamble on future winds. One could dignify the choice and call it strategy. I also wanted to see less of the Banks fog. Whether it was strategy or cowardice I was still moving south on the 22nd:

The Atlantic is tough this summer. I continued south all night with staysail only. I was able to get a sun line this morning putting me near 43 degrees west, which pleased me because we don't point well under that small sail. More clouds came in and it was blowing Force 7 with gusts to 40 knots by noon. I lay ahull for a while and repaired sail hanks and tightened shrouds. The staysail sheet parted twice, and I had to change to the heavier genoa sheet. I tacked to the west, then was headed by a windshift. Now the course was northwest, back to the Banks.

It has cleared (this is late afternoon) but the barometer is falling slightly, and it's blowing right out of the west. The sea is in lumps, we're going six knots, and leaping off waves. I was sitting on the bunk with a cup of coffee. Without warning I was weightless, two feet in the air. A crash and goodbye coffee. The kerosene lamp landed in the sink.

We were now closing in on the Grand Banks and the fog that lies to the east of the banks due to the cold Labrador Current. I would cross the tip of the Banks at about 43 degrees north. And here seawater markedly changed color to a green-gray as the depthsounder found bottom at 200 feet. It seemed strange to see scoters, the diving sea ducks, out there with the great shearwaters.

1930.195 feet on the depthsounder and the water is even lighter in color. Still the fog, and *Mooneshine* is finding her way better than I could. I have been on deck only to repair sail hanks. There are now only two of the original lashings. I am using monel wire as the only thing that holds . . . I have 1000 miles to go if I am permitted the desired course . . . I have been on deck twice in the last hour (it's now midnight GMT) with Radar Check and foghorn. Trawlers crossed close ahead. It's a nervous business in 50-yard visibility.

June 26. More alarums during the night. I could hear the clank of diesel engines . . . I am thoroughly anxious to move off the banks. Rain came at 0900 and seemed to help clear the fog. Suddenly I could see a mile . . . Now it's closed in again. The radar beeper had me on deck again, and I took in the main for a second time because it's blowing too hard. And, I'm being headed . . . This is an unusual day and has kept me busy. The southwest wind, Force 7, veered all the way to northeast, Force 7, in less than an hour. Large, steep seas had built up unusually fast from the southwest, so it became exceedingly rough as the wind shifted. I reduced sail to reefed main alone, more because of severe motion than wind-strength. Even so I lost more woodwork below as the starboard water tank broke loose . . . It's getting messy in here. The temperature dropped to 45 degrees. It doesn't seem like June at all. We are now almost running before the northeast wind, a rarity on this voyage, while waves are still marching in from southwest. Water is squeezing into my wiring and put out the chart table lamp. Thus ends the third week.

Things now began to improve. My strategy, or luck, was working. "It's looking better and better. I have a 10-knot tailwind . . . the first sooty shearwaters . . . must be approaching home waters . . . Peeling away the miles this afternoon with an easterly wind that has come back to life. We are making up a little of the lost time, and I think of Newport arrival on Saturday."

I began to hear bits of race news. *Club Med* had been reported 200 miles out of Newport. *Pen Duick* was one of 67 boats unreported for at least a week. (That included *Mooneshine*.) I had 630 miles to go from my noon position. This was the 24th day. Could I still be in the race? A wonderful appetite for Newport was sharpening. Where were all those obviously fast boats—*Kriter, Cap 33, Spirit of America,* and many, many others? Thus began a week of delicious speculation. I felt I was in the groove for Newport.

June 29. We have now travelled 40 miles in the last 8.5 hours over placid water. At the moment we are making 5.5 knots and the water is so undisturbed you can see the wake trailing astern for hundreds of yards. Porpoises appear at the bow. It's an extraordinary sight to look down on them almost within reach through the clear water.

June 30. The light breeze held all night to my surprise because it has no visible means of support. I adjusted lines at the tiller occasionally during the night to compensate for changes in wind strength, but have not touched the sails. I am on the most favorable angle to the 7- or 8-knot breeze for best speed. My piecemeal strategy is working for now. This cutter rig with the large genoa and double slot working is effective for these conditions.

There was sun here and blue water south of Nova Scotia. This should be the pipeline to Newport, I thought, and kept looking for other sails, but saw none. I was also close enough to land that AM broadcast radio was reaching out with traffic reports, talk shows, weather reports. You realize that nothing changes just because you happen to have been in another world for a month.

Georges Bank was coming up. There is fog and the trawlers, but it's on a more manageable scale than the Newfoundland Banks. More important, you are almost home.

> *July 2.* I slept too well, but a radar beep had me clawing at the hatch. *Mooneshine* was threading her way between four trawlers with no problem, but I stayed up. A remarkably steady breeze held us on course for Nantucket Light Vessel. I tried to monitor progress through the fog by depthsounder . . . Now the wind has fallen into a stupor . . . Usually it's enough if I scream at the wind when it drops off, but that didn't work this time. There is still fog and rain and a lumpy sea that slows us. I am determined to make 120 miles today, which would put me in a position to reach Newport before dark tomorrow night. I have a very large curiosity to see who is there . . . Much confusion clearing Georges Bank and entering Great South Channel. The wind went light and right in my face. Thick fog clings to the sea, but with blue sky overhead. There is a whistle buoy, but is it 10 miles south of its position on my chart?—or am I 10 miles north of where I should be?. . . I trusted my own piloting, ignoring the buoy. I am skirting the south limits of Nantucket Shoals . . . I am being headed again and forced into shallower water . . . 15 miles and I will be clear of Davis South Shoal . . . the wind is too light, barely making 5 knots despite my light-air combination.

> *July 3.* 0200. This is near total frustration. Every time I make a move I am thwarted by the wind . . . It is now light and contrary and I am drifting south . . .

If I had known then that a young Frenchman, Alain Gabbay, was just a few miles ahead of me in his 38-foot boat, I would have been even more exercised. Instead, I slept for three or four hours when I should have been working the boat, and awoke to sunshine and a building southwest breeze. I aimed *Mooneshine* to pass between Block Island and Martha's Vineyard. "I still haven't seen a sail, which is a good sign. They can't all be here already. I heard a fisherman report a singlehander, but it sounded like *Mooneshine.*"

The landfall was Point Judith. I altered course for Brenton Tower as the wind began to fail in early evening. We crawled toward the finish line, just managing to squeak over before it died altogether. A cruising multihull out of Newport with three aboard was waiting there—not for me especially, but out of curiosity to look for wandering racers. I dropped my sails in something of a heap and gratefully accepted a tow to Goat Island. I had been out 28 days.

*M*OONESHINE WAS THE 11th boat to arrive in Newport that year. My time of 28 $^1/_2$ days would be slow indeed for subsequent races. Eric Tabarly in *Pen Duick* was the winner in 23 days, 5 hours. *Club Med* finished second but was pushed back to third by a time penalty imposed for accepting assistance in a stop in St. John's. An extraordinary performance by Mike Birch put him third in *Third Turtle*. "You're third, *Turtle*" he was told on coming to the dock at Goat Island.

Eric Tabarly had been, as usual, self-contained and radio silent. No one knew his whereabouts, or if he was safe, until he was spotted on the morning of his arrival silently tacking back and forth in Newport Harbor. I remembered watching *Pen Duick* maneuvering under sail in crowded Millbay dock. Eric had a crew that morning, but all was accomplished cleanly and in complete silence.

I found myself in third place in the Gypsy Moth Class. For that I owe Walter Greene my special thanks. Walter had sailed his *Friends of New England* to eighth place overall. Whitall and I had been on hand for his arrival in Plymouth and watched the ritual of sleeping bags, cushions, and clothing being dragged up for drying (optimistically) in the dampness of Plymouth. By comparison, I thought I had crossed in an ocean liner. He had intended to sail in the Jester Class, but when his boat was measured by the committee it was found to be 38 feet, 2 inches—no problem for Walter, who is a boatbuilder, and he sawed off the offending inches. By this act he reserved my third place in Gypsy Moth. I would go to London and receive a trophy. Normally one would not go to London to pick up a prize for a third-place finish, but this was hard won and kind of special.

The weather that year had taken its toll. The storm of June 14 had done the most damage among the larger boats because they were farther west and caught the worst of it. I prefer to think that storm was unusual for June in the North Atlantic. It was a storm of the type that meteorologists now describe as "Atlantic Bombs," and are far more common in the winter months. We know there can be storms every month of the year, but we look at pilot charts and think the ocean looks pleasant enough in June and July. It's those averages again; 125 boats had started, and my friend, Tony Lush, was the last official finisher, in 75th place. He had taken the Azores route, and as a result had had ample time to develop his suntan in the Azores high. The storm had landed special fury on the larger boats in my class: *Gauloise,* sunk with skipper Pierre Fehlman rescued by a ship; *Kriter,* broken and sunk; *Spirit of America* retired, etc.

Most tragically, *Three Cheers* and its skipper, Mike Mc-Mullin disappeared. This was a double tragedy because Mike's wife, Lizzie, had been electrocuted while working on the boat just three days before the start. Thus two people with most of their lives ahead of them were lost. By strange coincidence pieces of the yellow-hulled *Three Cheers* were dredged up off Iceland by a trawler shortly before the start of the 1980 race, or at least that is when the news came to us. It had been identified by serial numbers of the Brooks & Gatehouse instruments.

Those were relaxed times in Newport, at least at the Goat Island Marina where Peter Dunning, chief shepherd of the singlehanders, was in charge. Either there were not as many large motor yachts or Peter successfully kept them at bay, so that B Dock was largely given up to us non-paying types. We had the run of the excellent facilities, including, of course, the Pub, and there were plenty of other enticements in Newport to keep a freeloading guest tied up there. Peter's patience and diplomacy must have been tried at times. There were receptions at the Sheraton Islander with reporters in attendance. It was a fresh business, this singlehanded crossing of oceans, and aroused curiosity. What kind of strange people are these anyway? I happened to be standing near an English sailor being interviewed by a woman reporter. She kept asking probing questions about his life at sea, how could he possibly spend all that time alone, etc... Finally, I heard him say, "Yes, but what you really want to know is how often I masturbate!"

It was time for me to gather up my family, and we sailed *Mooneshine* back to her muddy berth at Cape May.

The London Observer had scheduled a prizegiving in London in early December. Nancy and I made our plans, taking in a small slice of Europe on the way, and landed in London on the appointed day. It was, of course, done up in fine style and there was happy reunion among sailors. Former Prime Minister Edward Heath, a sailor and yachtsman, improved the occasion with a small speech. And here was Lady Chichester who was to present the Gypsy Moth trophies; in the haze of my confusion I saw her as a vision in red.

Now most yachting trophies only have value while you are walking those few steps to receive it from the presenter. At home it gathers dust and reminds you of the passage of time. This Gypsy Moth emblem is not like that. It shows my crooked track across the Atlantic drawn in silver; and I had received it from the hand of Lady Chichester.

Bermuda 1977

ON JUNE 18, 1977 a strange fleet left Narragansett Bay for Bermuda. These were the singlehanders, not yachtsmen. A favorite photo in my possession, taken at Goat Island just before the start, shows an unsavory band of waterfront types; few mothers would be happy to see a daughter with one of these men. This was to be the first Bermuda One-Two Race—sailed solo Newport to Bermuda, and doublehanded on the return.

That year there was no Goat Island Yacht Club, no sponsor, no race committee. Race headquarters consisted of a post office box number in Newport. We had the St. George's Dinghy Club at the Bermuda end, and generous members of the Ida Lewis Yacht Club in Newport put their dignity on the line to provide assistance at the start. There was Peter Dunning to clear B Dock for us, and someone had prevailed on the mayor of Newport to arrange a pre-race cocktail party at the Treadway Inn. We also had the run of Goat Island's scruffy grass for cookouts, and the tailgate on Jerry Cartwright's small pickup.

The reason we were there at all was that the idea for the race had hatched in Jerry's fertile mind. He had participated in a solo transpacific race and the 1972 OSTAR, among other sailing ventures. He had been a croupier in London, a naval architect, and a writer. His most sparkling performance was yet to come—a TV ad for Nescafe, playing the lone sailor with twinkle restored to his eye by a hot mug, and actually filmed on the water.

The Bermuda One-Two Race had the serious purpose of getting more Americans on the water alone. In this it must have been successful because I count at least 15 Bermuda One-Two alumni who have now sailed the OSTAR. In other cases OSTAR sailors have joined the Bermuda One-Two. Notable among these was Michael Richey and his *Jester*, with her unmistakable springy sheerline. As mentioned, *Jester* had been an icon among single-handers since Blondie Hasler sailed her in the original Single-handed Transatlantic race of 1960. She was painted dark green, the color often seen on cellar doors. But for our inaugural race to Bermuda she lent a special authenticity by her presence.

We were there on our own recognizance, so to speak. Without the umbrella of some organizing body the awful specter of liability does not exist. In this case there were no deep pockets, or hardly any pockets at all. A few may have had hull insurance binders for the Bermuda voyage, but most singlehanders assume their own liability. I have never carried hull insurance for the longer voyages. These were innocent times, too, with alcohol liability. You could bring your own beer then for impromptu parties behind the Pub where now stands a security guard house.

Was life cheap in those days? It certainly was cheaper for participants, since equipment requirements were minimal, especially in the way of emergency items that are now mandatory and that eat away so much of our sailing budgets. Gains in safety have come at high material cost, and also at less tangible costs, such as loss of spontaneity and the sense of personal responsibility as race committees scrutinize your boat and preparation. The entry barrier has been raised for the singlehander, as in so many areas of life. Nostalgia for past times is no answer, but it has to make you ponder the true reasons we sail, and sail alone. How innocent we were, and how soon that was to end!

A successful long-distance sailing race should have a logical destination as well as point of departure. Newport has always been the (self-appointed) yachting capital of the east. It is a superb natural habitat, though lately in danger of squandering waterfront assets on trendy development. Whatever happens to the waterfront and on the boutique-laden wharfs, Newport is still a spectacular jumping off place for any voyage, or an equally appealing landfall.

The other half of this equation, Bermuda, would be hard to improve upon. If sailors had the choice they might wish to eliminate the off-lying coral reefs that extend as far as 10 miles north and west of the island. Others might argue that the reefs only add to its charm. My own feelings are mixed, since my landfalls there have been marked by acute reef anxiety followed by exquisite relief on safe arrival. You can't have one without the other. I have raced solo to Bermuda four times, and each arrival there has been memorable for scrambled nerves. How pleasant it is now to think back on circumstances I would have given anything to avoid at the time. Nature has the last word here anyway. Without the coral reefs, the soft limestone rock of the islands would long since have been worn away by the sea. There would be no Bermuda.

Progress in electronics, together with increasingly safety-conscious (liability-fearing?) race committees, has gradually eliminated restrictions on the use of Loran or satellite navigation in Bermuda races. It is the satellites, especially the Global Positioning System, that have made the biggest difference, since Loran lines-of-position usually become unreliable as you near Bermuda—just when you need them most. Anything goes now for the singlehanders, and a lot of the spice of landfall henceforth will be missing. Bermuda has also made changes by setting both Northeast Light and Kitchen Shoals Light on fixed towers, and by siting a powerful radio beacon at St. David's Light. With the new electronics, the role of the navigator with his sextant and mysterious tables is now much diminished. In the traditional, fully crewed races, navigators have dealt with this perceived lack of respect by devising ever more complex strategies for dealing with the Gulf Stream. This has occasionally been rewarding since the Stream is constantly shifting, with cold and warm eddies strewn across the route. Thanks to satellite observations we have enough information and variables to make it a great game of chess. My approach has usually been less calculated—plunge down the rhumbline on the theory that the Stream is bad news, and the best way to deal with it is to pass through as quickly as you can.

One easily falls into the welcoming arms of electronics. In later years I have gratefully made use of everything the checkbook would stand for. Recently, I served as crewman on the Bermuda Race—*the* Bermuda Race, that is, sponsored by the Cruising Club of America. Actually, I was designated navigator, in a nod to the old ways by the race committee, but there were no special duties for this navigator since it was all done by GPS. Our approach to the island was on a typical Bermudian night of black rain squalls. There was tension on board as the batteries in the handheld GPS unit were failing. Would a search through duffles produce fresh AA batteries? It did, and we were saved. Thus times change, and I am glad to have had it both ways. One does not willingly court anxiety.

THIS LOOSE MIX of boats and skippers tacked through the narrows of Narragansett Bay and out toward Brenton Tower that day in 1977. The starting line had been set up outside Goat Island; we would be tacking through the narrows in close quarters with fellow singlehanders who might be more or less out of control depending upon wind strength. It is almost always a beat here because of the typical June seabreeze. Subsequent Bermuda One-Two Races and three BOC Races have employed variants of this start. It is considered a good send-off if there are no collisions, and there have been collisions. A 60-foot BOC racer in the hands of one man invites demolition. In contrast, the Bermuda Race with its full crews traditionally starts offshore, with sea-room for all. It's a matter of style; but oddly enough, there are still crashes out here among yachting's elite.

Looking back now, it is sad to think that Brenton Tower is no more. It was demolished in 1992 to be replaced with an innocuous sea buoy after having been deemed a maintenance nightmare. Some might say that this ungainly tower never lived up to its promise or perhaps was obsolescent from the beginning. The solo sailor aiming toward the finish of a long ocean race might call it shy since the light never seemed to reach out with its published range. Nevertheless it symbolized the finish of many a race, and its somewhat strange profile will be missed by the gulls and by the singlehanders.

I was sailing in *Mooneshine,* and probably feeling over-confident after the previous summer's transatlantic outing. The only addition to my ensemble was a blue and white light-air reaching sail, delivered at the last minute. With a freshly painted bottom I thought we would sail well. The fleet was divided into three classes based on length only, with a maximum of 44 feet. The largest boat was Jack Hunt's classic Fishers Island 40, *Crystal Catfish;* the smallest was Donald Barrett's *Little Dipper,* a somewhat modified trailerable 23-footer. It was Donald's vacation—and he would trail his *Dipper* from Rochester for several subsequent races. This turned out to be a race of reaching winds. I thought *Mooneshine* was favored—in other words, no excuse to lose.

This was an America's Cup year in Newport. Sailing trials were taking place as we reached into Rhode Island Sound beyond Brenton Tower. *Mooneshine* was carrying the No. 1 genoa and beginning to stretch out a lead while I hung on at the tiller applying considerable weather helm. That helm pressure was *Mooneshine's* way of telling me she was making her best speed—and also that I was carrying too much sail. Sometimes it pays to carry on with too much sail. I found myself crossing the bow of the New York Yacht Club committee boat marking the finish line of their race. There to starboard were two 12-Meter yachts under spinnaker bearing down on me. I had to alter course to clear them, and then escaped into the spectator fleet. It was a little embarrassing, but damn it, I was in a real race. I hung on with my genoa, and to the tiller, with arms aching. Aries would not have liked this at all. Self-steering of any kind will quickly tell you when you are carrying too much sail. You don't have to listen.

Good sailing may bring you into the Nantucket-to-Ambrose shipping lanes after midnight, a perfect time and place to encounter fog. This night there were radar alarms; I passed off the stern of a quietly moving ship while *Mooneshine* sailed on at close to seven knots. I was in the Gulf Stream on the second night out with the water temperature at 84 degrees. "OSTAR was never like this!" says the log. Then I woke to the radar alarm, and looking out saw only the forward range light of a ship, and that rather elevated, while the aft range light was hidden behind the mainsail. I fell over myself in the cockpit grabbing the tiller away from the vane. Again, there was time, but I was thoroughly startled. "Close," says the log. It is true that this route to Bermuda is crossed by ships from many directions, and not a good place to take your eight hours of sleep too seriously.

There followed a day of sunny weather and faltering winds. The big reaching sail must have successfully kept us moving through this area of light air and on into livelier conditions, or such was the view from my limited perspective. When the wind returned there came another learning experience as I retrieved my new sail from the water.

On the 21st squally conditions set in with an uncomfortable sea. I began to worry about my line of approach. Because of Bermuda's encircling reefs, a prudent mariner approaches the island from the east. This wise sailor, however, is probably not a racer. With the southwest wind that prevailed, a racer would not want to find himself seriously east of Kitchen Shoals facing a hard thrash to the finish. If your approach is to the west of Kitchen Shoals you must be aware of your distance off the fringing coral. The log radiates uncertainty that day: "Wild shooting today. I have a rather large noon triangle. Most likely noon position...." And that is the last log entry. I was still 150 miles out.

From that point it was by compass and from what assurance I could get from the radio direction finder. Comfort from the latter is difficult when your small boat is being tossed. In addition, the low frequencies used are often subject to radio frequency interference from atmospheric or unnatural causes like your boat's engine. Thunderstorms are another problem. With these caveats, the battery-powered RDF is good to have, but you may find it useless when you need it most. And so I continued the rough ride down what I hoped was the best line for Kitchen Shoals.

When night fell it seemed especially dark; I knew I was rapidly approaching the island quite blind in my world of wind and rough seas. Thus began a long night of physical discomfort and growing mental disquiet. By 0200 the captain had had enough and lowered all sail; we would wait until dawn. It wasn't as if I knew what I was looking for, although in most places north of the island you are on soundings a mile or two before you are in danger, and there should be a change in sea state if you know the signs. I remember the gray damp of that early morning when the wind dropped off, and then the seas assumed the uncertain look of shallows. The depthsounder confirmed that it was time to turn left and look for buoys. The distances aren't great here; the buoy marking Northeast Breakers was soon visible, and from there it was a matter of running the compass course to Kitchen Shoals, thence to Mills, and our finish line at Spit Buoy off St. Davids.

It was visual piloting now, but hard squalls came through again, tearing at my jib hanks and leaving great scallops in the sail. I went forward to secure the yankee on deck, all the while gazing in some awe at the emerging landfall I had accomplished. We were now snugged down to staysail and double-reefed main, a tight combination that would be fine as long as it was blowing hard, but just a little foolish in the lulls. This was a Westsail kind of a day, as they used to say in the ads. And here were Brian Harrison and his wife, Judy, in their Westsail 32, out for a sail. *Mooneshine* posed for their photos near the finish line, and I gratefully accepted their guidance through Town Cut and to the dock at the St. Georges Dinghy Club. Pictures at the dock show me near drowned in my Goldberg's yellow, but grinning as if on the cover of MAD magazine. *Mooneshine* had arrived in just under four days, and that stood as the time to beat for several Bermuda One-Two Races to come.

Members of the Dinghy Club had built a new dock to

accommodate the likes of us. This was my first experience of the hospitality they continue to extend to wandering singlehanders and others, and I wish there were some way to repay them. My first reaction was the unreality of Bermuda itself, along with the surprise that I was there at all. Why is this tropical island here in the middle of the North Atlantic? Juan Bermudez had discovered it in 1505; its position was fairly well known to navigators by 1609 when Sir George Somers ran his sinking *Sea Venture* on the beach after encountering "the taile of the West Indian horocane." Even then Bermuda had acquired a reputation for wild storms. It was "the dangerous and dreaded lland of the Bermuda . . . feared and avoyded by all sea travellers alive, above any place in the world . . . this hideous and hated place . . ." Thus states the Gabriel Archer account of his "Wracke on Bermuda." Perhaps we have lost something as English spelling has been standardized. Gabriel Archer might also have produced some choice words for waterfront Hamilton today when six cruise ships are in port at once.

But when the gentler southwest wind is blowing you may catch the scents of warm earth and tropical flowers on your approach to Kitchen Shoals. These pink coral beaches, bananas, and palm trees lie only four or five days sail by small boat from cold New England rocks. No wonder it seems a fantasy to a northern sailor, and well fits its role as destination for a yacht race. There were diversions and reunions as the fleet arrived. One of our number, *Crystal Catfish,* homed in on North Rock Light while the skipper napped. There had been a mixup of radio beacons, resulting in a stressful awakening for Jack Hunt who was able to put out the necessary radio calls before stepping into his raft. He showed considerable presence of mind under trying circumstances. That afternoon a massive salvage operation was in progress. Barges were anchored off while divers worked huge flotation bags into the sunken hull. The bags were then attached to air pumps on a barge. The iron skeleton of North Rock Light looked down on all this activity in silence. Food was broken out, and I thought there was a spontaneous picnic air to the scene, especially since reef fish were already swimming through large openings in the hull as if sizing up a possible new home. These we saw from underwater photographs in the papers next day. And so the salvage effort was a failure. You could say a good time was had by all with the possible exception of Dr. Hunt. This affair gave rise to the *Crystal Catfish* trophy, now in the permanent collection of the Dinghy Club.

Everett Smith, fellow Valiant sailor in the '76 OSTAR, flew in to fill out my crew for the doublehanded trip home. It was a relatively slow event that found us waiting for wind the better part of a day somewhere in the middle of the passage, while I introduced my white skin to the wonderfully blue waters and swam with the even bluer mahi-mahi or dolphin fish. It all ended happily as we were able to keep Bill Homewood's red and white spinnaker astern in light airs the final evening out of Newport. *Mooneshine* had squeezed out another victory. This was to mark the beginning of a certain rivalry with Homewood, a transplanted Englishman, whose Britishisms have become perversely more pronounced through his stay in America. But his "old sod" and "bloody fart" were endearments usually saved for me.

Bermuda 1979

DESPITE ITS SHORTCOMINGS as a yachting event, the Bermuda One-Two was back by popular demand in 1979 and is now established as a biennial affair. The Goat Island Yacht Club came into being, with a moveable clubhouse which might be someone's basement or, occasionally, the Marina Pub. In some years the race has been dignified by an overall sponsor, bless them, to set up a tent and provide festivities before and after. With all this we have a Race Committee and inspectors to regularize proceedings, although it has not always been easy to make yachtsmen out of solo sailors.

Not counting multihull events (we don't allow them in our races because they are too fast), there are now three organized sailing races to Bermuda from the Newport area. The Cruising Club of America has held its prestigious event for 70 years or more, through peace and war and changing yacht measurement rules. Most of the famous names in eastern yachting have been associated with this race. More recently a race from Marion, Massachusetts to Bermuda was established and immediately caught on. It was for family racers—family being defined roughly as meaning no spinnakers. It was also based on the new velocity prediction programs for sailboats, now best known through the IMS rule. Like most everything else in this world the Marion-Bermuda Race has become quite a competitive business, and is bound by inspections and rules that come near obliterating the reasons you are there in the first place—to enjoy freedom and the sea. To enter this race you and your craft undergo three separate inspections. One is for suitability and structural soundness; a second covers required gear; the third is the complex measurement process for your IMS certificate. Some, like myself, are constitutionally unfit to survive this process. Luckily for us, there is the still the Bermuda One-Two.

I have forgotten now exactly why I joined the 1979 race, but I found myself back in Newport in company with other repeat offenders amid the familiar scene on B Dock. Through the years this race has seen a high rate of recidivism. We seem to prefer our own company; there has been little upward mobility, so to speak, to the Marion race or the CCA race among our group.

It was a year of light and contrary winds over much of the route to Bermuda. I had made an error in judgement, leaving the somewhat heavy Aries vane at home and relying on an electronic autopilot. No problem, I thought, for a Bermuda trip. To depend on electronics alone is an act of faith as I have learned with regret several times since. I remember the slow start into light southeasterlies that grew lighter through the night. I sat in the companionway, listening to the Boston Red Sox lose a ball game while I watched the masthead Windex. An occasional tweak on the pilot control held the apparent wind angle where I wanted and kept *Mooneshine* moving through the night. It was slow going and too much to the east; I would be crowding Nantucket Shoals. I tacked, moving south through the placid gray of early morning so typical for these waters. There was *Quicksilver*, a C & C 41, and evidently the skipper was sleeping. I would slip by silently for fear of waking him and find a better wind for myself. But two nights later we were side by side again in light winds south of the Gulf Stream. I knew I was sailing badly in the generally light headwinds. Later, I was changing jibs in a strengthening afternoon breeze and found myself on my back amid water and sail in the lee scuppers, and laughing. It's a scene I have remembered for sheer absurdity—as if waking from a foolish dream.

There was one long day yet to come. For some reason, all my Bermuda landfalls have been in obscure to grim conditions while departures were under fair skies. I have watched Bermuda sink into the sea in perfect visibility at least five times now, but have learned to expect no such luck when sailing in. The morning of the last day was sparkling blue with a north wind, and there was a multihull not far ahead. The multihulls had departed Newport just before us in their own race that year. This was spinnaker weather; I raised my big blue and white chute and thought I was doing well to keep even with this craft, which seemed to have a large crew. I noted their course was somewhat off toward the west which was worrisome—there is only one correct course for Kitchen Shoals from this point. The wind grew stronger and began to veer, gradually, as so often happens with the spinnaker up. All is well, then the wind will strengthen or the apparent wind move forward, or both, and suddenly you are on the edge, applying large doses of weather helm to keep your craft upright. Any self-steering device will have a bad time coping with this, but my autopilot began to exhibit a lunacy of its own, wildly oversteering while the spinnaker collapsed and filled repeatedly with alarming snaps and shudders. I could hand-steer, but how to work the tiller and go forward to subdue 1600 square feet of sail at the same time? The wind was now a solid 25 knots. I got no comfort from the hard reflection of bright sun off those waves. And here I was steering when I knew I should have been navigating. I was squandering an opportunity to get a sun line to establish the course, and also I didn't know how far off the island we were. Pesky multihull! Without her I probably would have been content with a jib. I never learned the identity of this craft; perhaps her destination was somewhere beyond Bermuda.

I brought the spinnaker down amid noise and some desperation; *Mooneshine* proceeded nicely with the yankee in its place. I should now have dropped everything and taken a sun sight, but didn't, probably because visibility was good at the time. One hates to lose miles, especially when that other boat is in sight. In this way I sailed the afternoon away, but with the arms growing heavy. There was a change as the wind fell off toward early evening and clouds overspread us. I realize now I didn't have a clue what to expect from the weather. In 1979 I didn't have single-sideband equipment to receive the Coast Guard weather broadcasts from

Portsmouth, Virginia that are most useful for these waters. With darkness we were doing a lot of rolling and not much sailing. Then, very quickly, wind came in from the northeast. It was a cold front, though I had no idea what was happening. The wind was building as fast as I could shorten sail, which was difficult enough without self-steering, and waves quickly built also. I watched these waves for some sign, as if I could somehow divine Bermuda's reef-induced currents. I remember putting two reefs in the main and then dropping it altogether. Poor *Mooneshine* had to make do with yankee alone as once more I was abusing her tolerance for an imbalanced sailplan. I was ashamed, but it seemed the best I could manage at the time. Winds were now a good 40 knots in near total blackness. The course was southeast at 7.5 to 8 knots. *Mooneshine* loved to fly in 40 knots, but the problem was navigation. Twice I dropped the yankee so that I could try for radio bearings (small comfort to be had from that) and there was the considerable trouble hoisting sail again in that wind. This was not enjoyable at all, if there had been time to think about it. I badly needed to find a mark, preferably Northeast, which was still a buoy that year. I did not have a depthsounder, as that had been left behind in Newport for repair. A combination of poor decisions plus mechanical failure had me in a position I would have done anything now to avoid. That's the way it goes at sea, or in my factory, too, for that matter...

Tension and fatigue were an unholy mix in arms and neck, but at this point Fortune must have stepped in. Out of oblivion there came a tiny flash to starboard—and again. It had to be a buoy, though mostly obscured by the waves. We passed at less than a mile, and I was able to identify it as Northeast. It would be hard to express the joy on *Mooneshine* at that moment. By some inscrutable luck I was exactly where I should be. I have gratefully carried the image of that faithful, bobbing light ever since.

> *Let the lower lights be burning!*
> *Send a gleam across the wave!*
> *Some poor fainting, struggling seaman*
> *You may rescue, you may save.*

But wait, this is just a singlehander out for what he calls recreation on the water. Why is it that the sea and its dangers are such recurring themes of the hymn writers? And how many of them have approached Bermuda on a thick night? Others of our numbers were out here this night, each coping in his way, but like St. Augustine in the garden, I was remarkably focused on my own salvation.

Now I was running down the last miles from Northeast to our finish line in a state of some euphoria. There was serious piloting to be done these last 12 miles, and steering. I had a chart in the cockpit jammed under a cushion so it wouldn't blow away; there was a flashlight, and glasses in my pocket I would wipe off with a wet thumb to read the chart. The course bears off slightly from Northeast to Kitchen Shoals; you know there are reefs if you stray inside this line. Beyond Kitchen the many confusing lights of St. David's show as a blur ahead. It is hard to spot the quick-flash of Mills buoy which has to be left to starboard—with more reefs. The small flash of Spit buoy marking our finish is distressingly hard to identify as you come in under the disorienting pattern of shore lights. *Mooneshine* surely appeared in loose disarray under jib alone as she crossed the line, but I had given up any pretense of proper seamanship that night. To my surprise and delight a brightly lit committee boat from the Dinghy Club was waiting at the finish to guide me in through Town Cut and on to the dock. I must have climbed the stairs to the bar, for I do remember falling asleep on my stool over drink number one.

I offer this as a cautionary tale. This is no way to make your landfall, especially on Bermuda. Unless it's a race, you may say, which sometimes takes precedence over prudent behavior.

My sailing son, Whitall, who had just turned 17, would serve as crew for the return leg to Newport. He had grown tall in the three years since the Atlantic trip in 1976. We jogged on roads near St. George, where I found it warm indeed, and especially so ascending the hill out of town and back to the Club. Youth was soon out of sight in a sobering reminder to Father of generational realities.

The voyage home was a sailor's mix of no wind, then good

sailing, too much wind, followed by far too much wind, and finally, no wind. Weather briefings by meteorologists from the U.S. Navy base in Bermuda given us just before the start were astoundingly wrong, and we found ourselves for several hours in a 45-knot northeaster as we crossed the Gulf Stream. Because there was some sun it didn't appear to be especially threatening, and *Mooneshine* loved it, taking off at eight knots with just storm jib and double-reefed main. Trouble came with the steep waves, and before I realized what was happening we watched cabin furniture disintegrating on impact in the troughs. After one crash I pulled up floorboards, almost expecting to find the keel missing. Old sea wisdom has it that in rough weather your boat can take more than you can. Like so much other old wisdom, that has to be rubbish. I have learned to take more care.

This voyage ended happily after a distressing night of no wind off Martha's Vineyard. At sundown we had watched a sail we feared, correctly, was the rival, *Quicksilver.* The night was near windless, but the electronic pilot partly redeemed itself by keeping us moving and on course through the darkness. That is a nice property of these devices—they have patience and concentration far exceeding mine in this type of situation. The morning breeze came to us first, allowing a reach to the finish line with spinnaker flying. *Mooneshine* was number one. Hooray for *Mooneshine,* we yelled. There was no one else there to cheer. The finish of the return race to Newport is very informal.

The first voyage of *Crazy Jane*. Leaving Barnegat Light, New Jersey, June 14, 1970
(photo courtesy The Philadelphia Evening Bulletin).

Happy to be here. The wet arrival in Bermuda, 1977 (photo courtesy Bernuda News Bureau).

Waterfront types. A group portrait before the start of the first Bermuda One-Two Race, 1977. The Cast: Standing, left to right: unidentified, Steve Syrotiak, Charlie Carpenter, Ralph West, Dave Sturdy, Jack Hunt, Ian Radford (with head turned), Jim Kyle, Michael Richey, Bill Maney. Front row, left to right: Peter Hegeman, Bob Lush, Jerry Cartwright, Bob Lengyel, Don Barrett, unidentified, Stokes, Mac Smith (photo courtesy J. H. Peterson).

Warm and dry again in the Marina Pub in Newport, where it all began (photo courtesy Cully Miller).

Tony Lush (r.) and the author at Goat Island before the BOC Challenge, 1982 (photo courtesy Deborah Luhrs).

Mooneshine at Goat Island the morning after. Tony Lush stands by (photo courtesy Cully Miller).

Mooneshine shows off her lines as she leaves Newport, August 28, 1982. Next stop: Cape Town (photo courtesy Christopher Cunningham).

After the start at Cape Town, the fleet struggles without wind under the Twelve Apostles.

In the Indian Ocean, *Mooneshine* runs off in following seas with storm jib sheeted flat.

Mooneshine is about to enter Sydney Heads, January 5, 1983, as passenger Tony Lush observes from the companionway (photo courtesy *Cruising World*).

Toward the finish line at Sydney. Lush wears a clean shirt (photo courtesy *Cruising World*).

The skipper at Cape Horn and in need of a bath.

Light air for the restart off Rio de Janeiro. *Mooneshine* hopes to edge past *Koden Okera*, No. 23 (photo courtesy *Cruising World*).

Yukoh Tada arrives the next morning. The winner holds a flower (photo courtesy Bergeson).

The American Challenge 1980

MOONESHINE WAS SAILING to England again, this time leaving from Annapolis on April 28. I have often wondered why our Navy located its school for future admirals on Maryland's inland sea, 120 miles from blue water whether you sail north or south. Could there have been a lingering fear of the British Navy? We elected to go north to the Chesapeake and Delaware Canal, and thence through Delaware Bay to the ocean. One reason for this route was that we knew Schaffer's Canal House offered spirits and the last good meal for a month. The Chesapeake Bay was cranky that day, according to the log: "Cloudy, some fog. Increasing headwind, also opposing current. Heavy rain and 20-knot headwind in upper bay. Strong ebb in the C&D Canal, contrary to the tide tables." Darkness fell; we motored desperately to arrive before closing time. Actually, it was I who was motoring, standing at the helm in heavy rain. My crew was warm and dry below.

I had decided to enter the OSTAR again. It couldn't have been with illusions of winning anything. I must have been racing against myself, hoping to improve on my time of the previous race. And also there was Bill Homewood, who was now sailing *Third Turtle,* having converted the year before to the multihull faith. He had sailed to Bermuda in *Turtle* the previous summer with the multihulls, arriving very nearly the same time as *Mooneshine.* In the confusion of the finish that mean night *Turtle* had damaged her rudder on coral, and luckily that was all. Wouldn't it be a fine thing if I could beat Mr. Homewood? This was to be the year of "The American Challenge" in the OSTAR, and unusual American presence among the winners, but I didn't know anything about that at the time.

Mooneshine's crew consisted of our friend, George Patton, and once again, my son, Whitall. George was a new Valiant owner, and also was there to brush up on celestial navigation. It happens that I had prepared a 45-minute short course in celestial, but to date I could not name any successful graduates. My son could not be bothered because he was involved with more useful mathematics in high school at the time. This was his senior year, when life is supposed to be serious. He would hurry back and face exams, though I don't remember many schoolbooks on board.

One of my responsibilities was communications, since I had optimistically told George we could keep in touch with his office. I had been studying Morse code with my younger son, Arthur, in preparation for a ham radio license. Near the last possible date we showed up at one of those marble-encased Federal buildings in Philadelphia for the FCC exam. Arthur passed with ease while I squeezed by to qualify for the General License. The FCC wisely requires code proficiency at 13 words per minute for this grade license, which is needed for voice communication on the amateur frequencies. For real code operators, 13 words per minute is not very fast, but if nothing else it introduces a certain needed discipline to the airways.

I installed a small Kenwood transceiver on *Mooneshine* using a whip antenna and what I hoped was a workable ground system. Science, and some art, are useful here, though it should be said that transmitters of relatively low power are successful at sea because the ocean itself is a fine ground plane to launch your signal. My small whip antenna was tuned to the 15-meter ham band, i.e. the 21 MHz. frequencies. It happened that this was a good choice for the propagation conditions prevailing that year. But something was crossed up; on the first attempt to transmit, instruments at the nav station lit up and metal parts tingled when touched. Luckily, this was at the dock in Annapolis, and the radio was sent out for quick repair. I overhauled the ground but never found what I had done wrong. The radio served me well on this trip and later around the world.

I assigned crew quarters in Annapolis. The Valiant has a nice double berth aft, or "owner's stateroom" as they say at the boat shows. As captain, I reserved that for myself, feeling just a little guilty because George is my senior, if not in years, in dignity of position. He was assigned the port settee which is a few inches wider than the starboard. Whitall, who sleeps well anywhere, drew the latter. As it turned out we were on port tack 90 percent of the voyage, and George was making the best of the uncomfortable tilt on the high side. This was a source of embarrassment to me, but he firmly resisted change.

We should have suspected from the treatment in Chesapeake Bay that this was not to be a record passage. The log of the first week is a dismal recital of headwinds, fog, rain, and more headwinds. The sailor's lot may be hard, but the recreational boater has it coming. In any case there was no one to hear our complaints.

Mooneshine was better prepared this time with a new storm jib of 135 square feet. I called this my working storm jib because it was designed to work effectively with the staysail when going to weather in heavier winds. There were now running backstays to supplement this armament. I thought I could tackle the OSTAR with confidence. I had a storm trysail ready to hoist on its own mast track. This is an awkward little sail not often seen on today's racers. But, of course, my boat was a family cruiser. I also had my autopilot to share helm duty with the Aries. This redundancy can hardly be overpraised.

Another thing in our favor was that we had three live watch-keepers on board. I set three night watches of three hours, the intent being to have good eyes on deck in the hours of darkness. Each of us would lose three hours of sleep, which would be made up easily through the day. My theory was that one or more of us would be on deck in daylight, and that was born out in practice.

As chief cook I made many references in the log to galley time and baking, especially bread baking. I was not really complaining, though, as I honor mealtimes as important rituals regardless of the weather. With George on board we also observed the custom of Happy Hour, in moderation, of course. I would like to think the arts of conversation were encouraged, since this is entirely compatible with an easy shipboard routine. In fact, days slip by easily. If it were not for logkeeping one could lose track of the days. I was scrupulous in crossing off daily tables in the Nautical Almanac because a slip-up there would confound the day's efforts with the sextant. Of course, the biggest problem with celestial navigation on the Atlantic is in seeing the sun at all. Good star sights are rare. On *Mooneshine* you might say they were non-existent though I did chase the moon occasionally.

Mooneshine was making the best of things in spite of our grumbling. May 4, a Monday, was the seventh day out of Annapolis. We were nearing 700 miles offshore. I remember light westerly winds backing south with approaching clouds. The barometer was falling as a cold front moved in. Skies were gray in the late afternoon when a white-throated sparrow came aboard from nowhere and sought refuge in the lee of the cockpit coaming. These are the small birds whose clear call so often defines early morning in the Maine woods in spring. One is always happy to offer a lift to migrating birds—after all, we're in this together—but to offer rest to a sparrow 700 miles from land lays a special responsibility on you. I was apprehensive as west-northwest winds gathered steam and we shortened sail. Water sloshed aft on the lee deck toward our passenger. It was going to be a rotten night. Then, in the gathering gloom, George suddenly appeared at the companionway. The sight of George, who is a large man, was too much for the small bird. He took off into the night just as a hard squall hit. I watched as my new friend was thrown down to leeward and to his certain watery death. The Bible tells us His eye is on the sparrow. But one has to wonder. Small birds must perish by the million out here each year, and unseen. *On mourra seul*—we die alone, said Pascal, and I believe that is so. I named my last sailboat *Sparrow*.

Mooneshine sailed on under tall clouds and lightning. Later, I took down even the storm jib as the wind gusted between 40 and 60 knots. I am not sure if running off with no sail was justified or if it was only my reaction to the noise and confusion. Aries came apart, reminiscent of this same patch of ocean four years before, but now there was only the easy business of flipping on the autopilot. That has to be progress. "Altogether, an unpleasant night" says the log.

This stretch of ocean between 39 degrees and 40 degrees north contains unsolved mysteries of the Gulf Stream. Benjamin Franklin was among the first to attempt a mapping, but I believe even he would have been amazed at the complexities revealed by satellite imaging. I would add that I seriously doubt that the satellites catch it all. Four years earlier I had received a handsome bonus from the Stream. On May 5 this year the log notes: "There is the tell-tale choppy, broken appearance of the waves, indicating current which I assume is with us." Then there is uncertainty: "Only one sun line today. The post-lunch sight simply would not work out for unknown reasons. We will forget that, use a DR plot, and get a fresh start tomorrow." What was missing was 100 miles we thought were behind us—100 miles had simply disappeared over two days, swallowed by the Gulf Stream. And that was confirmed on the following day after a series of decent sights. Somehow we had blundered into a counter-current. I might have realized that in a different way when I was suddenly pitched across the cabin from the galley into the navigator's station by an errant wave. My head hit the electric panel with a wrench of the neck wherein you hear bones crunch. The panel was unscathed, but I sported a black eye that lasted till England. I suspect this was an object of mirth to the crew since several photos were taken.

I had begun to develop contacts on the ham radio. There is an initial shyness to pick up the microphone and break into the world of amateur language—the call signs, the phonetic alphabet, the peculiar etiquettes. Once past this barrier you quickly find shoreside operators listening for "maritime mobiles," and when a schedule for contacts is arranged they are most accommodating and scrupulous in listening for you on schedule. There is an unusual dedication among these operators; just to say thanks seems inadequate. My small set with perhaps 70 watts output could cross an ocean depending upon the time of day and propagation conditions. It was my introduction to the versatility of ham radio and its multiple uses. I would listen to Bill, CN8CW, at noon daily on the Transatlantic Net. (Hams are all first-name only.) His skill, patience, and humor made a happy initiation to this electronic world. In the race back to Newport his cheery reports of sun and warmth from "Rabat, the capital city" contrasted so sharply with the cold miseries of the North Atlantic that it was perversely encouraging. A year later I met Bill in Annapolis. He had been transferred back to Washington. His had been a familiar voice; now here was the man. Somehow the two will always be separate. As you travel around the world hearing a voice, it's the voice that becomes the reality. On later trips and in times of stress the confident tones of net operators and their reliability became a prop for uncertain spirits. "The Voice of God," as one BOC sailor said. Reassuring Authority.

These airways are wide open for the world to listen in if it cares to. Even so, when you reach your party or family member it becomes your private line, so to speak. If there is a prying world it is forgotten. Most ham chatter is just that, and often boring to the point of parody. But drama in the form of family soap opera may occasionally liven it. I have dealt with marital disaster and financial crisis from mid-ocean. In 1980 it was the swimming pool being built in the backyard. Budgetary shortfall loomed, so serious it was found necessary to loot the children's small savings. There are certain arcane restrictions on conducting business over amateur radio, but since nobody really understands these it is unclear whether swimming pool finance is proscribed. Some tune in to these bands purely as entertainment. I confess I have monitored Marine Operator channels on occasion—husbands to wives, or vice versa, and assessed the state of the relationship. We racers might also listen in for vignettes of the competition that could lend perspective to our own discomfort. Sometimes I copied excerpts into my log: "It's the gen-o-a. I cawn't get it in, and I cawn't let it out!" And so on. There is also the commercial traffic. On one occasion on Chesapeake Bay I heard a tug captain calling his dispatcher. Somehow tug and barge were aground 300 yards out of the channel with the towline in danger of fouling the propeller.

This dismal situation was urgently discussed at some length. When the captain finally signed off with the operator she responded with the usual inane courtesy: "Thank you, Captain. Have a nice day." I remembered my mother misquoting Lucretius: "Pleasant it is when on dry land to gaze upon another's tribulations at sea."

The averages eventually prove themselves, even those of the pilot charts. On May 10 the wind went into the south for the first time, bringing weather we thought was plainly overdue. *Mooneshine* began to stretch out the daily runs. I see in the log for May 14 that we were indulging in the landfall game: "If this wind continues, and if we make 150 miles a day . . . etc., we will arrive in Plymouth on the 24th." As it happened, we did arrive on the 24th, though not before England put up defenses in the form of north and northeast winds. High pressure must have been anchored north of England, and this frustrated my efforts at landfall on the Scillies. We crossed Little Sole Bank, 60 miles south of the desired track. There was the marked change in appearance of the water, ocean blue giving way to a milky green, and ocean swells becoming lumps. The depthsounder found nothing despite the look of shallows.

Landfall would have to be on the Lizard. The last navigational exercise was to predict the hour (and minute) of sighting the light. I was the clear winner here, off by just five minutes as the three-second flash appeared at 2255. Perhaps even my son was impressed, though I don't recall words to that effect at the time. Coastal traffic was out in the usual confusing number as we slid by the Lizard and commenced the last quiet miles to Plymouth. Again it was a Saturday, and small boats were out for their day of sailing or fishing. I made a swing under diesel power past the Hoe and the Royal Western Yacht Club, just showing the flag, I suppose. Much to my surprise Lloyd Foster, the club sailing secretary and Ian Radford, a Bermuda One-Two alumnus, came out in a Boston Whaler and ushered us into the Millbay Inner Dock since it was high tide and the lock gates were open. We were soon tied to the familiar stone wall.

The next afternoon it was my pleasure to do the same for Bill

Homewood as he arrived solo from Annapolis on *Third Turtle.* Our race was beginning to come together.

Almost at the last minute Tony Lush arrived in his new *One Hand Clapping II,* even smaller than the original, after a harrowing 49-day passage from Florida.

BOTH PLYMOUTH AND the OSTAR had changed by 1980. If the latter had matured, Plymouth, I thought, had aged visibly in four years. How can you say that of a city that has witnessed history through its hundreds of years and shows the scars of World War II bombs? But Millbay Docks were partially filled in to enlarge the parking area for the Brittany Ferries terminal. Buildings adjacent to the dock had burned, to be replaced by a scrap iron mountain. Iron dust and grit from this heap blew over our decks. Most of us would shrug and go about our business, but not Warren Luhrs, who was there for the debut of *Tuesday's Child.* I watched with some awe as he daily scrubbed grime from his deck with powerful shoulders and hands. Would that more of us could be like him. The tide gates defending the inner dock from Plymouth's 15-foot tides were now leaking badly so that there might be a formidable drop down to our boats as the tide receded. There was no money, they said, for repairs. It couldn't have been that bad. The Pound that year was worth $2.40. I was the poor boy from America and had to keep hands in my pockets, like an aging Tiny Tim, as I looked in shop windows.

The Royal Western had changed the rules for 1980, decreeing a maximum length of 56 feet and limiting the number of entries.

One result was a fleet of boats compressed in length and obviously more competitive within classes. The monohulls were still battling for supremacy against the multihulls, a war they were bound to lose. *Mooneshine* began to look like a plough horse as I compared her with the racier yachts in the fleet.

Phil Weld had arrived with his exceptionally graceful new *Moxie,* designed by Dick Newick. She was just 50 feet long to comply with waterline length restrictions in effect for this race. Phil Steggall, then a sailmaker in Marblehead, had another fast multihull. He had crossed from Cape Cod in just 14 days. I knew that times were changing fast for *Mooneshine.*

I counted 19 American boats there, or about 25 percent of the starters. Most of all we had Phil Weld, who would show all of us the way to Newport. Phil was then 65 and was to depart this world five years later. There are very few people who cannot be replaced. A certain country wisdom prevailed at my factory: "There's always someone to take your place," we would say, and most of us knew that was so. But Phil was so generous with enthusiasm, toward his competitors, and with his time and money, that the American sailing scene, especially among the multihulls, has not been the same without him.

A movie was planned, to be based on Americans in the race, which later came to be known as *"The American Challenge."* Phil, of course, was behind this, so the screenplay featuring his victory was all of a piece. *Mooneshine* participated in this effort by accident—the ill luck, actually, of Rory Nugent from Martha's Vineyard who had built a handsome proa, *Godiva Chocolatier.* A proa is an island boat, a trimaran with one outrigger missing, which means that it always has to be sailed on the same tack. Instead of tacking, you turn end for end; the bow becomes the stern, like Dr. Doolittle's beast called the pushmi-pullyu. This is a craft for blue lagoons; as a means of crossing an ocean it is a disaster waiting to happen, and most have come to grief. It should be said that one serious purpose of this race from the beginning was to encourage better ways to cross an ocean through experimentation. Thus proas have had their honored place here, if not among faint hearts. So Rory's proa fell over backwards while sailing to Plymouth. He was rescued, but not the boat. In this way a movie camera destined for *Godiva* was installed on my boat instead. *Mooneshine* had been discovered, so to speak.

We were coached for this project by Chris Knight of the New Film Company while his team was busy installing eight-millimeter cameras in their waterproof canisters at strategic points on our boats. Mine would stare at me over the hatch. All this would probably be done now with the more versatile video cameras. When the time came for Chris to edit the art work I suspect he was lucky to work with these relatively brief film clips rather than end-less "home videos." If the film was successful, much of the credit is due to the thoroughness of Chris' preparation. As parts of the cast we had strict orders to fill a cassette daily as talking heads. Needless to say, much of this talk ended on the cutting room floor. You can be totally alone out there and still be struck dumb by the camera's eye. We were also instructed in the use of a handheld camera, which was intended for those times when hell breaks loose. Of course, that is when you need both hands for the ship, and a camera is the last thing that comes to mind. So much for *cinéma vérité* at sea. Nevertheless, Chris was able to gather bits of our performance into a creditable whole, and the film is still seen on PBS, sometimes when their stations need background for annual fund raisers. In fact, I have had reports from people in dis-tant parts of the earth who happen to tune in local TV only to see *"The American Challenge."* My younger son reported school-mates doing impressions of his father flinching from dollops in *Mooneshine*'s cockpit. Slocum would have said you could tell I wasn't a Briar Islander. "It is known that a Briar Islander, fish or no fish on his hook, never flinches from a sea." And Slocum was right; I was no Briar Island man.

The final days of preparation are a mix of private anxieties and the pleasure of being a part of this international carnival scene. Hours were spent walking to chandleries in the Barbican on the opposite side of the city. I was forcing rebellious legs on these forays; my needs were not great. I stumbled over cobbles to steps where the *Mayflower* departed, and Francis Drake. This is Devon, and it was families from Devon who settled my present hometown in Kittery Point, Maine, just 10 years after Plymoth Plantation. There was a day trip to Dartmoor with friends. We climbed tors and over ancient stone walls that serve no earthly purpose other than appeal to the artistic imagination. Some were built by unfortunates in Dartmoor prison; one can only think they built better than they knew, and for a posterity they would not have understood. In June the intense greens of the fields, moors, and hedgerows of Devon are a pleasing image to carry with you as you think about setting out on the Atlantic which may be blue, but more likely will be a cold gray. Broken clouds and showers stream overhead from the southwest as a reminder that the great wind engines of the Atlantic are there waiting. Here, on the moor in June, it can be extraordinarily cold when the west wind blows. I was cold.

This was the first time the Argos System was fitted on the OSTAR boats. We would be tracked by satellite so that race headquarters would know our whereabouts even if we did not. There are pluses on the side of safety, but with the loss of excruciating pain or pleasure of not knowing where your competitors might be. That year there was the added problem of units that failed, leaving the race committee with numerous "missing" or unreported yachts. The system has since been refined to a high degree of reliability and has saved lives in the more remote seas. Its dizzying expense has ruled out general use in more recent versions of the OSTAR, but in 1980 thanks to Argos and radio we knew how many of our competitors were faring. We were able to cheer Phil Weld as he neared Newport while some of us struggled in mid-ocean.

Deserving or not, ready or not, we were treated to champagne under a tent at the club and farewell dinner at the Guild Hall in the best Royal Western style. It is sad to me that time and champagne have dimmed the scene of that dinner when Commodore Jack Odling-Smee told lengthy stories with his inimitable speech impediment. It is also sad that he has since gone to his rest. Eric Tabarly, winner in 1976, was introduced. Always spare with words, he outdid himself that night by standing up just long enough to say, "I have nothing to say." Great applause. How many of us could learn from Eric!

Back in Millbay Dock I made the unsettling discovery that a Y-valve in my fresh water system had been slightly turned so that vile dock water could have been coming through my galley tap. Imagine 100 boats discharging into this cul-de-sac of harbor water, with floating trash and microbial horrors. I felt a nasty sore throat coming on.

Goodbyes are said, and one is sad to leave Plymouth. I walked nervously through the crowds surrounding the dock for last-minute farewells. Godiva chocolates were distributed in memory of *Chocolatier*. I gave half of mine to one sailor who had been passed by and looked about to cry. Recently I read that chocolate is the nearest thing we have to a genuine aphrodisiac—too late. There is a small reluctant finality as you cast off docklines and accept the tow, but you keep this to yourself. The start featured at least two disasters. Florence Arthaud's wine-colored *Miss Dubonnet* had been moored just ahead of me in the dock. I heard her support crew banging at something high in the rigging late into the night before. She never made it to the starting line as the whole mast came tumbling down into the harbor when she raised sail. One can imagine the tears and recriminations, but she has persevered and in later races has triumphed mightily. Another mishap sent Tom Grossman's *Kriter VII* back to the dock to repair a bow holed by collision at the starting line. Tom was a potential winner in his new 56-foot trimaran. He restarted after repairs to finish a respectable 10th place, but once again a collision at sea had ruined an entire day, and a race. Huge effort is sometimes rewarded with equally big disappointment in this business of solo racing. The pattern continues.

All three classes were to start at the same time, but the race committee had marked off a starting line a generous mile long. I found myself at the less crowded leeward end—a mile farther from Newport if I had thought about it. The on-board camera caught me grinning furiously at Dame Naomi James as she passed in her handsome 56-foot Van De Stadt ketch. She had recently returned from her solo round-the-world voyage. Then came the South African veteran, Bertie Reed, sailing in the 49-foot *Voortrekker,* which had placed second in the 1968 race. He was towing a wood cut-out of a springbok, the leaping gazelle of South Africa. Most of us are too nervously intent on the business of sailing at these starts to indulge in whimsy, but Bertie is made of tougher stuff, one of the Flying Dutchmen. As this is written he has completed his fourth solo world race.

Mooneshine quickly took her place in the plodding middle of the fleet. I watched in some awe and alarm as I was overtaken by larger monohulls coming up furiously from behind: first there was Olivier de Kersauson in *Kriter VI,* and then Kazimierz Jaworski in *Spaniel II,* with its huge fully battened mainsail like a butterfly's wing. I could only hope they saw me. These two men figured high on Phil Weld's worry list, but 1980 was to mark the beginning of dominance by the big multihulls. *Voortrekker* was to windward and moving faster, just a little; but I knew Bertie would be well showered and rested when I reached Newport—two days of rest and showers, as it turned out. To foot well in the rather light southwest wind I had to fall off to the east more than most. Eddystone Light was off to the west. Old anxieties crept in as I measured progress against others: "What am I doing wrong?" Chris Knight came by with his camera crew in a chartered powerboat. Checking on the laggards, I thought, but I appreciated the attention. He couldn't stay long if he was to keep up with the leading Americans, and the sun was low. See you in Newport, Chris!

With darkness the scattered masthead lights revealed boats I hadn't been aware of, and one was uncomfortably close. My cold was worse. I had to keep watch and set a kitchen timer for 10 minutes. What a wretched way to spend the night! I could not shake the boat to windward that I thought was a rival in my class. At dawn he had evaporated into the mists, but I could see others, and the Scilly Isles were still far to the west. I guessed correctly that Phil Weld and the other large tris were taking huge bites of the course and were now well clear of any land. The talking head appearing on film from my camera these first days shows a haggard, coughing Ancient Mariner. Time in the bunk seemed more important than the race.

Phil Weld had laid out his strategy for all to see. Extensive study of weather records shows the path of lows or gale centers generally northeastward as they move out east of Newfoundland. If you want to win in a multihull, stay far enough south to avoid those gales, Phil had said. That, I would add, might apply equally to monohulls with ample lead in the keel. His projected course would place him at 45 degrees north by the time he reached 35 degrees west, thence to the tip of the Grand Banks at 42.5 degrees north, 50 degrees west. It's so simple, in theory—avoid gales and most of the fog on the Grand Banks. And it worked beautifully for Phil and *Moxie* that year. He had also arranged with meteorologist Bob Rice for daily weather routing information to be relayed by ham radio. In his typically generous way he told us all of the schedule so that we, too, could profit. The only trouble was that he was soon half an ocean ahead, so his weather information was quite useless to the rest of us. I was too dulled by coughing during this period to pay much attention to the game of weather systems. By luck more than cunning I missed the worst of a storm that passed to the north one week out. There were gale winds that day, but no waves like those we had seen four years before. *Mooneshine* kept sailing. I didn't know it, but *Third Turtle* was not far to the north, riding to Bill Homewood's sea anchor. If I had known I would have risen from my death bed to hoist more sail.

I have never seen the Grand Banks other than deep in fog, though perhaps that is because I have been there only in the month of June. In 1980 I was approaching the banks at 46 degrees north through no grand plan but the luck of the winds. Since the cold Labrador Current sweeps down from Greenland well to the east of Newfoundland, fog settles over you before you think it should. Thus I found myself in thick soup 300 miles east of the banks proper, and *Mooneshine* enjoyed isolation in a white blanket for six days straight. Companions here were the shearwaters that would splash down next to my hull. It must have been the fog, but there seemed to be an unaccustomed bond between boat and bird. I would look at their red legs, which only made the water seem colder. I began to enjoy this muffled insulation from the world and felt (falsely) safe as if in a cocoon. I knew there were fishing vessels about and kept the radar warning device on alert. There was a cost to this because as the Argos transponder sent out its encoded signal every 50 seconds it triggered the radar alarm. Thus there was a regular 50 second pulse of the alarm to which I mentally adjusted. I would listen for untimely beeps indicating ship's radar, even in my sleep. Or so I convinced myself. There was a break on the third day when the fog lifted briefly to about one mile visibility. I was working on the foredeck when a trawler passed uncomfortable close off the stern. What do the working fishermen of the world think of carefree yachtsmen sailing in their waters? It may be as between the birds and me; we inhabit our discrete worlds.

It was a transition year in 1980 as electronic autopilots were permitted, provided battery power for same came from "all natural" sources, i.e. solar power, or wind or water generators. In light of our corruption with anything electronic now, this would seem a delicate distinction, but I had on board a small wind generator for this duty. This device had the unfortunate trait of wailing in a 20-knot wind as if there were a terrible gale. The moans grew louder if I was below. In a real gale it would spit out plastic blades and set up such a vibration that I would throttle it with a noose. All this violence was for the sake of a few watts of power. I envied those with silent photovoltaic cells. In spite of beeping alarm and groaning generator I was almost sorry to sail out of the fog, which you do immediately on leaving the banks. I felt that I had emerged once more into the real world, and in some vague way I wasn't sure that was such a great idea.

The amount of drifting ice in these fog-bound areas varies greatly from year to year. This was a light year for icebergs. Four years later record numbers of bergs and growlers were reported, which must have been sobering to skippers at the pre-race briefing that year.

The course in 1980 took me south of Sable Island, that frightening area of shifting sand shoals I have known only as a powerful radio beacon. A small depression was passing that day, bringing strong south winds and rough seas with poor visibility. *Mooneshine* proceeded with some discomfort through grim waters with storm jib and deeply reefed main. "What a rotten day for a shipwreck this would be," you think. Later, I learned that was just what was happening not far to my north as Peter Phillips' trimaran, *Livery Dole,* was breaking up. He managed to be rescued, and when I asked him about it four years later in Plymouth he shrugged it off as an everyday occurence. "I used to be a police officer," he said.

If you are lucky you will sail into open skies and even warmth in the area between the Grand Banks and Georges Bank—like opening the window to a warm, sunny day. Here I found myself in VHF radio range of *Third Turtle,* which was alternately pleasing and disturbing. I thought either Bill or *Turtle* must have been showing their age or they would have been far ahead by this time. He was vague about his position, though it wasn't clear to me if this was actually the case or a stratagem. There was a night of horrendous lightning and progressive shortening of sail, followed by the heavy fog on Georges. I thought Bill was somewhere to the north.

Now *Mooneshine* started rolling in gentle swells as the wind dropped away to nothing. I waited in vain for a promised cold front and northwesterly winds of 10 to 20 knots and rolled the night away. There are helpful notes in the log here directed to Boston weathermen, such as the suggestion that they serve some hard time, actually on the water. With nothing else to do in the morning I commenced baking bread. Here we were, perhaps 150 miles out of Newport, losing a full day of sailing. At noon the fog lifted, or simply evaporated; now I could see, but there was only the gray rolling water. In mid-afternoon a smudge on the horizon became a Coast Guard cutter with urgent business. It happened that the business was me. I watched them circle silently, at a safe distance, as if assessing my firepower. What did they make of the large race number "91" on my hull? Finally, there was an announcement over VHF that they would board to "check compliance with all U.S. laws." Oh, God! Who among us is in full compliance with all U.S. laws? And sure enough, I failed inspection. My fire extinguishers did not show the date of last inspection, and I had no bell. Never mind that you ring a ship's bell when at anchor in fog, but that there's no requirement that you carry an anchor. Also, my MSD was inoperative. MSD stands for

Marine Sanitation Device. The word "toilet" is never used at sea, while the ancient nautical term "head" is not appropriately bureaucratic. And so *Mooneshine* received demerits for having leaped off the waves and broken the porcelain feet of her MSD. I later wrote in apology to the Coast Guard Commandant and received a suspended sentence.

I should say that the boarding was a pleasant diversion on a day when I was going absolutely nowhere. The Coast Guard men were amiable and competent. I have felt badly ever since that I did not send them back to the cutter with a fresh loaf of bread.

In the late afternoon I began to detect the lightest of airs from the south. There is a pleasing phenomenon in these waters that I have often seen: The sea may remain entirely glassy while a light breeze moves above the water. I could hear ripples of bow wave as *Mooneshine* began to move. Soon we were up to five knots, though there was not a breath to be seen on the water. Hah! This was a south wind. Homewood was to the north, I thought. I would get a head start. In early morning we were still moving well with barely a ripple on the water. I got out Chris Knight's camera and photographed the clear reflection of the bow mirrored in the sea. It was one of those perfect times that helps you forget all those other times. Besides that, I was closing in on Newport.

The wind strengthened through the morning. I alternated helm duty with Aries as weather helm increased and the genoa did its work. I called Bill on VHF; didn't know where he was, he said, but he was making 11 or 12 knots. It was indeed a fine reaching breeze for *Turtle*. I was now clearing Nantucket Shoals with nothing to do but hang on. Clouds had moved over us so I took radio bearings from Block Island and Nobska Point (Wood's Hole). I wanted to get the course just right. Few things match the delight of closing in on the finish line at Newport. If it's from an Atlantic race you have run the course safely, perhaps arriving ahead of some others you have marked as special. The sea has flattened to give the impression of protected waters. Familiar gulls or even greenhead flies may look good to you now. You look forward to seeing friends, to a shower, to relaxing. All of this I felt intensely while closing in on Brenton Tower.

As it grew dark the wind went light, then lighter still. *Third Turtle* was silent. I was absorbed now in my quiet world, trying to keep the boat moving. There was a glow on the horizon from the direction of Newport, but the flash from Brenton Tower was hard to distinguish at its nominal range. (The greater the anticipation the more reluctant these things are to reveal themselves.) Another time, with depth perception gone awry, I had turned an ordinary buoy into the light on the tower and had nearly run it down. Now I did pick out the tower's five-second flash, but the problem was to reach it in the dying wind. I must have been helped finally by a flood tide, and *Mooneshine* slid quietly over the line. It was close to midnight, embarrassingly late to call in. Nobody would be up at race headquarters. Then I heard the New Zealand accents of Naomi James calling Goat Island. They answered her promptly. She was becalmed in fog behind me. So was Homewood.

I discarded my silent Eric Tabarly act gratefully. Peter Dunning and friends arrived in a launch to provide the tow in. After securing *Mooneshine* I was led to the office, where I was encouraged to wish Homewood good night as he lay out there in fog. I told him I would take his lines in the morning.

I had taken a few days off my time four years before, beaten a few competitors of choice, and learned a little more of sailing.

Mooneshine enters Sydney Heads with Tony Lush on board (photo courtesy *Cruising World*).

The BOC Challenge

SOUTHERN NEW JERSEY is extremely flat. Main Street in our town follows a ridge, the high ground. I was born on East Main Street, where my room surveyed a valley 30 feet below. This is a pretty town, with trees and side-walks, and good schools. Expectations and conventions, meaning respectability, are here in easy grasp. Why then dream of empty oceans and the desolate places of the earth? I watch my small dog, who is descended from the wolves, forever acting like a wolf pup and incapable of "growing up." I contemplate my own limits; will I ever grow up? Alas, at this late hour, it does not seem likely. If there is any constant in recorded history it is human nature. We know so much, and yet so little of substance has changed through time. Perhaps our species is too infinitely adaptable, as if we must fill every ecological and social niche with the human presence and at whatever cost to the human spirit. Now, if New Jersey were not so flat; or the streets of our town laid out in such perfect rectan-gles . . .

Thus I harbored certain anti-social impulses and was prey to dreams, while fortune was bringing people and events together to form what became known as the BOC Challenge 1982-83. I am in debt to many for this chance to sail the widest oceans. There was the persistence of David White who had sailed in a solo Pacific race and in the 1976 OSTAR in his 32-foot Westsail, *Catapha*. David was one of the early ones in Millbay Dock that year. I remember *Catapha* moored against the north wall, and David on deck radiating his American confidence. To sail westward across the Atlantic in a Westsail is a feat in itself, requiring determination and patience. The Westsail is a full-bodied throwback to earlier times that enjoyed immense popularity in the early seventies. In fact, I watched the dock at the Newport Sailboat Show one year literally sinking under the weight of people in line to board a Westsail. It was rather like the unexplained following of the original Volkswagen Beetle, an obvious dead end in automotive evolution. Westsail lines were taken from the Colin Archer designs for Norwegian lifeboats and were undeniably salty. The problem was that these boats, with long keel and heavy displacement, were designed to heave-to with contentment, not to cross oceans upwind.

David and *Catapha* arrived in Newport unruffled after a 38-day passage from Plymouth, and some at the time thought that was an exemplary way to cross an ocean. After the Bermuda One-Two races of 1977 and 1979 he was one of those asking: What Next? Since this was often asked in the ambience of the Marina Pub it was only logical that What Next meant the Southern Ocean and Cape Horn. At about the same time Jerry Cartwright was trying to establish a race from New York to San Francisco via Cape Horn—a race against the clipper ship records for relatively impecunious pockets. Individual yachts have successfuly challenged clipper ship times in recent years, and several have been lost in the attempt. Someday this may be an organized event, because it has the natural ingredients for a major challenge. In 1980 the time wasn't ripe, but David's world race was beginning to attract attention overseas.

By the summer of 1980 I had crossed the Atlantic five times, which is not nearly enough to know it, but it did encourage thinking about other oceans. I was feeling the pull again of curiosity, and the realization of unfinished business. We had all read of the unimpeded sweep of wind and water that circles the globe between the southern continents and Antarctica, and the accounts of small boats that have ventured there. Are books and pictures not enough? Do you really want to see it for yourself? I had asked myself that many times, and in fact was a fence-sitter until the last moment, even after the race became a reality.

In the end it was David's effort, plus the hard work of Jim Roos of Goat Island, that turned the race into fact. Jim was involved in the management of the Goat Island properties at that time, and he helped prepare our reception around the world by traveling to ports of call and meeting with local yachting officials. The four legs of our course were laid out; the first stopover was to be Cape Town, South Africa; thence across the Indian Ocean to Hobart, Tasmania; to Rio de Janeiro, Brazil via Cape Horn. The fourth leg would bring us home to Newport, after 27,500 miles, more or less. Half of this route is through the cold regions known collectively as the Southern Ocean. These waters used to be a highway for sailing ships carrying on the world's trade and the whaling trade, but now they are quite deserted. The Whitbread Round-the-World race for large, fully crewed yachts was the only organized event on these routes in 1982. Thus, our race for solo sailors was almost a fresh idea. Positive response to early announcements showed the concept was right and the timing good. The OSTAR was still going strong, but it was time also to move to a new venue. Why not build on the OSTAR experience and see some exciting places at the same time?

There were many meetings. I remember one at Marmaduke's noisy public house in Annapolis in the winter of 1981. It was uncharacteristically quiet as we sat by a fire that afternoon and talked over lengths and classes. Judy Lawson was there as a hopeful entrant. She sailed the 1980 OSTAR nearly to completion but had been dismasted and later picked up by an eastbound ship. She and her tiny BB 10 sloop were offloaded in Gibraltar, but in the general confusion a waterproof valise containing *"American Challenge"* footage had remained aboard while the ship proceeded to Constanţa on the Black Sea. Now she found herself wrapped in Iron Curtain intrigue in the effort to recover it from Romania. It might have been a scene from an old black-and-white movie—her purse and passport stolen by secret police as she danced in a waterfront cafe. (I preferred to imagine this cafe as "seedy," but she maintains it was opulent.) Judy and the films were eventually extricated with or in spite of State Department intervention. We met again over soft-shelled crab at White Hall Creek in the spring. The whole race had meanwhile been placed in jeopardy as David had fallen in love. Fortunately, reason prevailed and race preparations could proceed. For David, that included building a new boat, largely with his own hands, to the 56-foot upper size limit. I watched this craft grow at a boatyard in Jamestown, Rhode Island through the summer and fall of 1981. Major personal commitment of this sort was to be a feature of this race and its subsequent runnings. It has led to the personal triumphs and the devastating disappointments that have marked the event each time.

I had known Dan Byrne only as a voice on the telephone. Somehow this voice resonated with authority across the 3000 miles from Santa Monica. We have to pay attention to these chance encounters since, like pinballs, we bounce off objects in our path, and usually these objects are people. Dan must have seen *"American Challenge"* and heard me say, "You've got to do these things before you get your heart attack or your cancer," or something to that effect. It was a variation of the dismal: "It's later than you think." But Dan now bought an older Valiant 40, Hull No. 1, in fact, and sailed it in a solo Transpac. (For some reason California organizers do not blush when designating their races to Hawaii as "Transpac.") There followed correspondence with Dan over the proposed world race as Newport friends worked to bring it to fruition. Inquiries meanwhile were coming in to Goat Island.

All this could well have been meaningless. I firmly believe there are enough desperate characters on this earth that you would have no trouble selling tickets to Mars should you announce a lift-off date. I thought of Major Tilman's ad seeking crewmembers for one of his voyages to the ice: "Crew wanted for long voyage. No pay. No prospects. Not much fun." Whether for good or suspect reasons, checks were arriving at "Race Headquarters" in Newport, including Dan's. More correspondence followed, and finally I wrote to him in effect to say that if anyone as sane as he seemed to be could seriously contemplate this, then maybe, just maybe, I would join him. Thus it was that I sent off my entry fee. It was the end of December. I must have been the last to sign on.

Now, having joined this unknown cast of sailors from at least eight countries, I could relax. After all, nearly eight months remained before the start. Life was placid as I commuted often between New Jersey and the small yacht dealership I shared with my partner, Jim Cobb, in Annapolis. Meanwhile, in England, fortune was acting in her mysterious way to bring the BOC Group into the race future. BOC had been approached earlier for individual sponsorship by the young Englishman, Richard Broadhead. This, in turn, had aroused the interest of BOC's Director of Public Relations, Nigel Rowe, and led to BOC Group assuming overall sponsorship of the event. One can only marvel at the nerve—or more politely, courage and vision—of this respected international corporation. They must have known they would be shepherding an unusual crew around the world. I had thought of our group as a trial balloon, the Mickey Mouse fleet. But now we would have first-class support and a dignity of purpose that otherwise would have been impossible. When it was known as British Oxygen Corporation BOC Group had sponsored entries in early OSTARs. The ill-fated *Kriter* which sank in the 1976 OSTAR was originally *British Oxygen.* I thought of the time in Plymouth when I had paddled my dinghy under the wings of this craft.

Another asset that BOC brought to us was Robin Knox-Johnston as race committee chairman. That is Robin Knox-Johnston, C.B.E., as he is known properly, after being the first person to sail non-stop and alone around the world, a 312-day passage in his wooden ketch, *Suhaili.* Robin's presence lent further credibility to our small fleet as David White's original concept was truly being fleshed out.

Sponsorship implies commercial considerations; in deference to BOC Group's Australian subsidiary we were to be routed to Sydney instead of relatively remote Hobart in Tasmania. Jim Roos' initial overtures in Sydney had been rebuffed, but we assumed the added weight of BOC Group would change some minds there. All of this seemed far in the future and was of little concern to me at the time.

A new boat had come into my life. It was not that I looked

back less fondly at my other boats, but it happened that our Annapolis partnership had become dealers for the William Garden-designed Fast Passage, then being built by Philbrooks Shipyard in British Columbia. I had flown into Victoria by small floatplane out of Seattle to visit their yard. I was immediately taken by the graceful sheer and proud, almost clipper bow of the Fast Passage. The cockpit was small for a 39-foot boat, and well protected by its coaming. This was the summer of 1980, but I remember thinking then what a sound vessel this would be to sail around the world. Later, as the world race seemed possible, I thought again of the Fast Passage. It was a cutter like the Valiant, but slightly more compact, and there was marked tumblehome in the area of maximum beam that looked to my eye to be right at home in rough seas. My mind linked that hull with the Southern Ocean as if I had to see for myself. It may have been the existence of the Fast Passage that pushed me to think seriously of the world race; I must have been dreaming of the boat at that meeting at Marmaduke's.

By 1982 production of the Fast Passage had shifted to the Tollycraft Corporation at Kelso, Washington. They carried on the craftsmanship of the original builder and used their considerable resources in delivering a boat to me in Annapolis in mid-June. I then proceeded with the commissioning to prepare for the qualifying sail of 1000 miles, which had to be completed by the end of July. The base here was styled "Port Annapolis," a marina in Back Creek which is one of the muddy arms that make up Annapolis Harbor. Warm sunshine and the excitement of putting a new ship-of-dreams together there are happy memories. I had ordered a new Aries from Nick Franklin and asked him what spares I should have. "Better buy two," he said, but I settled for a bag of parts. That was backed up by the electric autopilot, and I felt well provided with self-steering. The Chesapeake loft of North Sails built sturdy sails, a limited inventory, but almost guaranteed not to fail. The mainsail was 9-oz. dacron with triple-stitched and taped seams; headsails were also 8- and 9-oz. cloth. I believe they would have gone twice around the world without serious wear. I went for sailing trials with John Danly of North Sails in the mild breezes off Annapolis, and we pronounced everything suitable. Of course, in later races, more exotic sail fabrics have been the rule in fierce competition. And sail budgets have ballooned to match.

Sailing instruments were simple analog boatspeed and wind-speed, but with readouts at the navigation station as well as in the cockpit. The navigation electronics consisted of a depthsounder. I would find my way by sextant, but I was asking of the depth-sounder that it pick up the warning shelf in Cape Horn waters. The truth is, I was careless of the new electronic technology and was too quick to dismiss the satellite navigation units as costly and unnecessary. Times change; I have changed. Now, with dry socks I stare at the green alpha-numeric display of the sat-nav for updated positions far more accurate than I could produce with my sextant. And all regardless of the weather. What would great-great-grandfather Whitall think?

The 1000-mile solo qualifying sail for the BOC that year was not really enough to shake down a new boat and nervous skipper. This qualifier has since been increased to 2000 miles to include an ocean crossing. For Americans this has meant a voyage to the Azores, which is barely 2000 miles from Newport, and a round trip of 4000 miles. It all adds a good chunk to what is already a major commitment of time. In 1982 my cruise went smoothly as I left the Delaware Capes vaguely in the direction of Bermuda. It's a clean tablet, you think, 500 miles out and 500 back with fine reaching winds both ways—if only you plan it right. My luck held reasonably fair except that the wind so typically died when I was in the grip of the Gulf Stream. For a while we were being carried toward the mid-Atlantic at 2.5 knots; otherwise this short voyage was so uneventful that I decided to sail directly back to Newport as if we were race-ready. The boat's name, *Mooneshine II,* was belatedly painted on at the dock in Newport. There may have been enough mental exhaustion at this point that I couldn't deal with something so simple as a new name.

So *Mooneshine* was left on a mooring in Newport while I took a bus back to New Jersey. War had broken over the Falkland Islands. I wondered if I was ready and cravenly thought it might be salutary if the start were put off one year. But our British sponsor had unquestioning faith in the Royal Marines and Royal Navy; we would go, on schedule, on August 28. The only concession to Argentina was that we were not to traverse the Strait of Le Maire, that tide-stricken possible shortcut in Argentinian waters between Tierra del Fuego and Staten Island. But that was six months and many, many thousands of miles in the future.

Most of the boats had now gathered in Newport and by mid-August we were assigned to the familiar B Dock. I was rafted outside Tony Lush's 54-foot *Lady Pepperell*. Tony's efforts to obtain sponsorship had succeeded magnificently: he not only had a new boat, but had appeared with Jane Pauley on the Today Show. Those were heady times. I watched with mild envy as people from WestPoint-Pepperell lent their excitement to Tony's enterprise, helping with food stores and small jobs on deck. It seemed that he would eat well, indeed. There was a logical connection between WestPoint and sailing since their industrial division produced a non-woven fabric used in hull lay-up by boat builders, but he carried their towels around the world, some of which bore the legend: "If there's no wind, *ROW*."

My own occupations at this time remain only as a blur. It was a time of total absorption with the needs of my boat, my project. I was shy, also, with other racers. Neville Gossen arrived a few days later in his big *Leda*, having sailed her all the way from Australia. I walked by this somewhat dishevelled boat, vaguely noting the lashed-together boom gooseneck, but I was an island to myself. There was the feeling of time pressing over all. Not once did I walk the length of the dock to look over boats I would be sailing against.

There was time to be spent in New Jersey with family details. I wasn't rewriting my will, but these practical matters tend to make you grapple certain unpleasant facts of mortal life. I visited my friendly local bank to arrange a last-minute loan. The loan officer looked at me with a banker's practiced impassivity. He handed over the money, but I detected a slight sigh. I had also initiated Coast Guard documentation for *Mooneshine* since I thought we should be sailing with the authority of an official number. I visited the same office in the Philadelphia Custom

House where I had documented *Crazy Jane* years before in a maze of archaic paperwork. Since then, the procedure has been simplified, after the manner of government, and a whole new paperwork industry has arisen. Annapolis alone now boasts several yacht documentation services. What was free now costs about $400 unless you have the patience and fortitude to see it through alone. Two months was woefully too short a time for all this, and so poor *Mooneshine* had to sail without number or papers.

In 1970 I had been threatened with fine and imprisonment, if not death, by the earnest public servant in that Coast Guard office if *Crazy Jane* were to depart for England without her official papers. Oh, those were great times in yacht documentation. But in 1982 we sailed happily, and nobody thought to question *Mooneshine*'s official status as she made her way around the world. When I returned home in May 1983, there were still no papers. I thought we had fallen into somebody's waste file, but when I called the Coast Guard a cheerful voice said, "There's no problem . . . just a few more months . . ." I told her I had sailed around the world while they were filling out some forms. Thus the world revolves, and everyone gets paid.

For reasons I have forgotten now, New Jersey entanglements seemed more pressing than my attendance at the skippers' meeting two days before the start. I know not what wisdom was offered there by Robin Knox-Johnston. A weather briefing was a part of this meeting, though it is hard to imagine what insights our Rhode Island weatherman could have offered for an eight-month voyage.

Mooneshine was bulging already with stores. I had planned vaguely, not really knowing how to provision for a two-month voyage to Cape Town—or was it three months? We would be the first racers from the East Coast to Cape Town. The route itself had to be explored. Now my sister showed up bearing the huge wheel of New York State cheese that was to become a staple for three of the four legs. It provided a race within a race—against colorful mold, and hours of amusement picking at the green pox with my knife. My other sister arrived with a small ivy growing in a Mateus bottle that later survived knockdowns and the vicious designs of tough plant quarantine officials in Australia who think that country is the last pristine spot on the globe. Quaker Oats Company pitched in with a generous supply of cereals for all. I found space for a case, and even took aboard Granola bars. These have the great advantage of being proofed against salt water in their foil wraps; I often observed them floating in my sink later on. I can recommend these bars as admirable food of last resort. And America is still number-one in packaging.

The organization of all these items could have been improved, but they were mostly out of sight. I knew that I had not installed positive latches on many lockers, but, as Dan Byrne said, there was a secret answer to incomplete preparation—it was called Cape Town, and the work list for that destination was already growing. The BOC Group helped take our minds off these nagging practical matters by throwing a huge party for all under a tent at Hammersmith Farm, a royal invitation to ghastly overindulgence, followed closely by blasting fireworks overhead.

The following morning, the 28th, we woke to the prospect of the Last Breakfast. This was a sober affair held in the Marina Pub with Robin presiding at the head of table. The Pub looked uncomfortable in this role so early in the morning. Steak and eggs were served as if we were condemned persons, while Robin announced that Tropical Storm Beryl was launched on her way west from the Cape Verde Islands. It was, after all, hurricane season. The steak and eggs were a lump in my stomach. I felt like a stranger, and didn't say much. I would be more comfortable back on the boat, at least giving the appearance of useful activity, to settle breakfast and ward off apprehension. It was time to be out on the water with the hard goodbyes behind.

It was a bland, sunny afternoon with a light southerly wind blowing through the narrows at Castle Hill. So far, so good. My propeller had been removed, and friends Chris and Erika showed up in a launch to tow *Mooneshine* away from the dock. You smile with confident ease and take in your lines while the dock is crowded with people waving, and you know most of them are happy it's you there on the boat, and not them. At this moment Al Tucker and his wife, Barbara, appeared on their Fast Passage sistership. Al was on the foredeck with his trumpet, playing something martial. I was not to sneak away quietly.

The starting line was set in the familiar waters outside Goat Island with a large number of spectator craft milling through the scene. I sought out a quiet corner on the Jamestown side and tried to identify the race committee boat marking the east end of the line while making long or short tacks as space among other boats permitted. I never did locate that committee boat. Just as the five-minute warning sounded the yacht I had assumed belonged to the race committee hauled up anchor and moved away. And so it was that I was in the back of the fleet when the final gun went off. There would be no pictures of *Mooneshine* first over the line. No matter, I had no sponsors to impress.

I set about tacking through and around spectators and some other racers. Actually, these tacks come dearly as you bend over the genoa winches, and there is relief as you pass into the wider water beyond Mackerel Cove. I thought we were ready now, with genoa in tight and flags flying. I turned the helm over to Aries while I organized lines in the cockpit and caught my breath. *Lady Pepperell* was tacking in front of me, and there was Tony fighting an errant jib sheet that had fouled on a winch. I diverted under his stern, but for an instant was treated to a vignette of singlehanded struggles other than my own. One more tack and we cleared the government marks off Brenton Reef and moved out on starboard tack toward Martha's Vineyard. And, I hoped, toward a peaceful evening.

I began to look seriously at other racers—there were 16 starters that day. David White's red-hulled *Gladiator* was a long way off ahead, but nearby and on parallel course I seemed to be holding my own against Class II boats. This is the first measure, even if you have run just the early miles of a very long race. It occurred to me that I was the oldest man in the race, sailing the next-to-smallest yacht; I had a job to do. The spectator boats had fallen away, but here were Jacques de Roux on *Skoiern III* and Yukoh Tada on *Koden Okera* in my class, and too close to ignore. I wouldn't give them the satisfaction of leaving me behind the first night if I could help it. Ahead, the horizon was now empty except for distant Class I boats. There was the brief illusion of peace as the fading pink of sky disappeared into a sea gradually turning black, but clouds were building in the west and a cold front was on the way. Martha's Vineyard was a gray shape to port, and uncomfortably close, since Nantucket Shoals lay ahead on this course. The wind was south at 18 knots and too much for my genoa. I wanted to change down, but *Koden* and *Skoiern* were an intruding presence beside me; I would hold on until dark. Nature was about to intervene, however, as the wind veered to southwest and then west, and a black rain squall enveloped us. Suddenly, I was in a private world of noise and wet confusion, heading roughly south and losing contact with other boats while I wrestled sails. Thus we sailed into the first night. The anticipated peace would wait, and contemplation of the distance to Cape Town, never mind the other legs. I lay down in foul-weather suit and boots, one of the indignities in the life of the singlehander, with the alarm set at 10 to 15 minutes, and gradually lost track of my position.

To Cape Town

A ship is worse than a gaol. There is, in a gaol, better air, better company, better conveniency of every kind; and a ship has the additional disadvantage of being in danger. When men come to like a sea-life, they are not fit to live on land.

THUS SAMUEL JOHNSON pronounced "Upon the Wretchedness of Sea-life." I would have to take full responsibility for the company, and to some extent the air on *Mooneshine*. It had been a long night in wet clothes and no warm bunk. Was I expecting some special blessing for the long trip ahead? "It doesn't seem like Sunday at all," is the sole entry in the log this day. I should have at least poled out the jib to take advantage of the strong west wind, but I was feeling worn, and queasy in the stomach if I had admitted it.

There had been a strange encounter in the night. In the darkness past midnight I saw unusual lights of a boat ahead; then a smaller craft with a powerful searchlight darted out in my direction. In my distemper I thought only of the Coast Guard on some absurd drug mission. I waited on Channel 16, ready with special imprecations, but then came the announcement from *Arco Research* that I shouldn't be tangling with their two-and-a-half-mile steel dragline. Huh? Steel draglines off Block Island? Oil? Their searchlights glanced off breaking wave crests as *Mooneshine* sailed on.

Later that day I made radio contact with a ham operator group known as the YL Net on 14.332 MHz. That is YL as in

Young Ladies, ham language for ageless, faithful operators, and their counterparts, Old Men. This net, which is on the air a large part of the day, is a most useful spot on the amateur bands to initiate maritime mobile contact. It was through the YL Net that Rob Koziomkowski, KA1SR, set up radio schedules with our little fleet and followed us around the world. This tie with ham radio operators grew informally as the race progressed and became an important part of life on the water. Marine single-sideband contacts were encouraged, but the amateur frequencies proved most useful in this race, if not in the later BOC races. I was once again reassured to know that my small Kenwood radio was heard. Never mind that we are out there demonstrating independence—we soon realize how tied we are to land and home, and look forward to daily contacts. Radio was the social link. Sailors I had met briefly or not at all in Newport became old friends, it seemed, by the time we reached Cape Town through shared frustrations and mutual dependence.

By the second morning the winds were failing me. I blamed myself. What had I done wrong? I must have gone too far south, and I worried. It reminded me that I hadn't done my homework; I was moving onto a very broad ocean and didn't know the way to Cape Town. Most of us had read *"Ocean Passages For The World,"* the Admiralty publication showing traditional sailing ship routes, traditional meaning square-rigged ships carrying on the world's business. How do you interpret these instructions for more nimble, if useless, sailing yachts carrying a crew of one? Where best to pick up the Northeast Tradewinds, and at what longitude should one enter the doldrums? The resulting course tends to be a lazy reverse S-curve, hoping to avoid the Azores high in the North Atlantic and a similar high lodged in the South Atlantic. We were laboratory creatures; if there was to be a race sequel in four years it would have to be a more formal business—and so it turned out. Among the boats in radio contact and sharing positions I could see various interpretations of route and weather at work as we dispersed on the ocean. For quite a while the language barrier shielded us from the awful truth—Philippe Jeantot had solved the navigational problem in the most direct manner and was way ahead of the fleet.

The recurring theme of the long trail to Cape Town is the search for wind, or having found it, the hope that it will hold. No wonder man turned to steam and diesel power for his ships, and how often have I envied ships as they make their apparently effortless tracks over the ocean, easily holding the desired course. I imagined spacious chart rooms, a steady bridge high over the water, and predictable progress watch upon watch. And what was I doing out here with a dying headwind and 7500 miles to go? The focus was totally on the leg in progress, and the goal, Cape Town. We were taking the world in four bites, but one at a time. It seems more manageable this way, and is one reason the format of the BOC Race is appealing. Sydney and Rio de Janeiro were out of sight and mind for now.

A ship passed on the third day. It had just made contact with Bertie Reed on *Voortrekker,* and sure enough, a couple of hours later I saw a sail on the starboard quarter. Now I would have to spend this day racing and losing to *Voortrekker.* Bertie moved ahead by mid-afternoon—but why had I been leading him earlier? Poor *Mooneshine* was always the tortoise, a pattern that was to repeat itself. We used this occasion to set up a radio schedule on the 40-meter ham band. Our little inter-boat radio net had begun to grow.

On September 2, day five, we were still working east against light winds. It was summer, and hot, but I managed a few useful tasks such as proper stowage for the Honda generator (in the vegetable bin), and oiling the steering cables. I had to demonstrate to myself that I could control some small aspects of my life out here. I had also established a warm beer taste panel to answer the question: Which of your favorite brands tastes best served at 80 degrees F.? Beer was stowed under the port settee and near the bilge, where it was one or two degrees cooler than cabin ambient. Lunch with a beer from my "cooler" became an anticipated ceremony. I have always convinced myself (and told others) that you never miss ice or refrigeration once out of sight of land.

After lunch I spied a sail four or five miles astern. There was no reply to my call, but later came the familiar voice—it was Tony Lush on *Lady Pepperell*. Two sailboats make a race, they say; I put up my spinnaker, and maybe it helped, maybe it didn't, as we moved east through a sea with lumps enough to slow progress. I stayed up most of the night trying to keep the spinnaker full in a dying breeze. In the morning we lay on a near glassy sea, but *Lady Pepperell* was about three miles ahead. After lunch the southwest breeze returned; I was soon alone once more but moving east nicely over a sparkling blue and calm sea. "OSTAR was never like this!" says the log once again, as the colder regions of the North Atlantic were still my point of reference. At night the moon was nearly full, and the cabin temperature lingered near 82 degrees in a foretaste of the tropics, though we were still at 34 degrees north.

Saturday, September 4 marked the end of week one. The log showed 861 miles run; gone were my hopes for 1000 miles, but *Mooneshine* was OK, and I was encouraged—we weren't doing badly against the others. Some boats had a chat hour on the 2- and 4-MHz. marine frequencies. I could tune in but not transmit on these channels. Desmond Hampton on *Gypsy Moth V* was using a black box to figure great-circle distances to Cape Town, some 5900 miles in the future, which was a kind of innocent amusement at this early stage of the journey. We would not be following a great-circle course in any case. I had set up a radio log to record positions but also to note weather news as traded between boats. And if the others were as small-minded as the crew of *Mooneshine,* they may have hoped for private winds while wishing lack of same for some competitors.

This was a quiet stretch of ocean in early September. Tropical Storm Beryl had maintained her steady westward course and was passing out of our world. A light swell from the southeast was all the evidence we had of her. There was a noticeable absence of bird life. A true seascape should have birds, and I looked forward to southern latitudes, home to the albatrosses and petrels that are seldom seen north of the Equator. The lure of these magnificent wanderers was one reason I was out here at all. North of Bermuda a small warbler had landed on my wrist, seemingly quite in control of his life. Bermuda is a waypoint for certain species on their incredible fall migration. These tiny birds are true lone voyagers, utterly dependent on their own resources. One notices the little things, like the two scrawny flies I met ranging out a couple of hundred miles from Bermuda. Nature puts its creatures to the ultimate test in a continuing process. Now I was being tested by the failing wind. From the log it sounded like a quiet Sunday morning with a few housekeeping tasks and some rudimentary personal grooming.

> . . . We are coming dangerously close to a halt as slick patches show on the ocean . . . barely managing three knots. Times like these, it's best not to dwell on the distance to the Cape. Two whales passed astern going even slower than *Mooneshine.*
>
> 1900. Whales to port. Otherwise it looks like Chesapeake Bay in July. A small navy ship and a cargo vessel are passing to the north. We have stopped.

At 2000 there were more whales, and closer. *Mooneshine* had gone aback and wouldn't move. Then suddenly I was aware of a sail about four miles ahead and got out binoculars. It was Jacques de Roux and *Skoiern;* he was dropping sails also. Now we had encountered three other racers out here, straining the laws of chance once more. What was Jacques doing almost on my doorstep in his much faster boat? I had logged 10 miles in the last six hours.

> A brightly lit cable ship is lying three miles to the north. The horizon is very clear with tropical cumulus spotted here and there, not moving. Above all, it's *quiet.* The whales swim very slowly—they just don't show much ambition. A one- or two-knot breeze is right out of the east. The boat will barely move so I have dropped headsails again. It's hard to imagine the wind ever blowing again. Just yesterday I thought it would blow forever.

Now I thought that by staying up all night I could nudge my boat past *Skoiern,* but it was useless. The sea was slick under the yellow moon; motionless clouds hung in the sky, as if painted. A whale spouted on the port side, very close this time, while the glow from the cable ship seemed nearer. With all the lights I couldn't tell bow from stern. I finally got my own ship turned around, gradually drifting off to the south and out of their way. It had been a magic night, for love perhaps, but not for racing. I retired for a few hours of sleep.

For no discernable reason an eight-knot breeze filled in from the northeast at dawn. It was a gift, or reprieve. *Mooneshine* again moved out toward the Cape Verdes at five and six knots, but had covered only 60 miles noon to noon that day. It was an all-time low for me, and I complained, not knowing worse days would follow. I spent time at the radio. There was news from home via son Arthur concerning certain practical matters such as repairs to my VW Rabbit. (We had a glorious fire under the hood before I left.) There was also word from Newport that David White had dropped out with structural damage to his boat and was diverting to Florida. That was sad news indeed; there would be just three Americans left in the race—a poor showing, I thought. Dan Byrne reported that his weatherfax showed nothing but high pressure with slight winds over the North Atlantic for the next 48 hours. With my natural suspicion of weather prognostication I was almost prepared to take that as good news. In later years I have learned to believe the forecasters when they predict large, immovable high pressure over the Atlantic. I heard *Gypsy Moth* reporting that only five miles separated *Gypsy Moth*, *Lady Pepperell*, and *Nike II* in great-circle distance to Cape Town.

Dan Byrne's weatherman was right. I entered laments in the log, and mused over flying fish: Are they always flying for their lives, or do they occasionally fly for the hell of it?

September 7. A day of small accomplishment, in miles achieved or anything else. I got off on the wrong foot through an error in plotting the early morning sight. This screwed up the day's work and miles evaporated. Here is the out-moded navigator spending a perfect day for sights wondering what happened. I still don't know what became of the easting I'm sure went under the keel. I listen to the 2000 chat hour for solace. Some boats have less wind than I. This big Atlantic is a basin of calm . . . What's wrong with our heat engine, Earth?

From positions offered the next day I wondered if *Lady Pepperell* had not actually gone backwards in the very patch of ocean that had frustrated me. Tony might even have watched the reverse progress via his sat-nav. I marked positions on the chart with reluctance because the day's runs were so poor.

September 10. We went into the night with a weak and uncertain north wind while I tried to resolve errors in the day's navigation. I have been having a nagging problem with early AM and late PM longitude sights. They may be 10 miles off, but not in a consistent manner. If you combine this with a later morning sight to fix position, the resulting error can be huge because of the acute angle of lines of position. It is annoying because no excuses can be laid to sighting conditions and due care was taken for accuracy. It doesn't matter out here, but there could be a time when the early or late LOP must be relied on. I intend to take more frequent sights until I find out what's going on. (Note: I am befuddled to this day.)

We wandered into or underneath some particularly black clouds in the night—here was the Black Thumb of God, again, threatening to squash my little sailboat. I felt like a butterfly with my genoa up. These things hadn't produced much wind so far, but I was fearful and took in sail. And so it was that not much happened except that the wind couldn't make up its mind which way to blow. We were being overtaken by another dark line of rolling black clouds so I retired to the bunk under shortened sail to await developments. Having done that, it was much easier to stay there, and I did until morning. Prudence, or ignoble ease? I had just finished rereading Major Tilman's book and was aware of his critical judgement. He is so very English: "This ship, the ship we serve is the moral symbol of our life." But this too, was a piece of his wry humor. Or was it?

We were now at 31 degrees north, 46 degrees west, with my next tentative waypoint at 28 degrees north, 40 degrees west. There we would plunge into the Northeast Tradewinds, or so I hoped. A good southwest wind overtook us here, lasting two days, and long enough to rebuke me for my ungrateful whining. *Lady Pepperell* reported a 215-mile day, which alarmed the crew of *Mooneshine*. It showed how the larger boats could fly away from me in steady winds. *Voortrekker* was now 160 miles ahead. I had daily radio contact with Bertie in this period before he moved beyond range of the frequency we used. We talked at length of many things, his amazing travels, and waterspouts. Just in passing, he predicted his arrival in Cape Town on October 21. Call it local knowledge. In the early mornings I aimed *Mooneshine* at my favorite star, Sirius, which hangs bright in the southeast sky. These were the dog days when Sirius, the Dog Star, rises before the sun:

Women's lust knows no bounds and men are all dried up, because the dog star parches their heads and knees . . .

(Hesiod—7th century B.C. Greece)

Our private dog days followed us into latitudes within the tantalizing dashed lines on the chart: "Northern Limit of Northeast Tradewinds." It was a time of tedium, and some magic, and occasional mild panic. On slow days there was the oppressive sense of the vast number of miles yet to be sailed. I set the spinnaker in late afternoon on September 12 as the southwest wind veered west and went lighter. We eased into a calm twilight, slipping along at six knots. I went to my bunk with hopes of a fine night, but set the alarm at 30 minutes. On one of the early checks, sure enough, menacing rolls of cloud had gathered in the northwest. One thinks these especially love to fall on you by night. I pulled the spinnaker down, stuffing it into the aft cabin. In my haste to secure things I failed to dog a couple of opening ports so an amazing amount of rainwater entered my living quarters. I did manage a rainwater shower with soap in the cockpit (not to be compared with a bucket bath at high latitude) but those first cold drops from high altitude prick at soft flesh. That was the end of sleep for this night as the wind didn't get itself organized until morning. Great junkpiles of cloud were blocking the way but finally they relented. From the deck of my small ship they seemed simply to dematerialize, but I knew they were only gathering themselves to try again later. Meanwhile, we would be on our way once more in the light southwest winds that the pilot chart assures us are non-existent here.

There followed a productive night thanks to the autopilot and a southwest wind of about five knots. *Mooneshine* sailed in peace at four or five knots. I lay in my bunk with sounds only from the slight hiss of water passing the hull, and the click of the electronic log every 60.8 feet or 1/100 of a mile. I did a little arithmetic—100 x 28,000 miles equals 2,800,000 clicks until we saw Newport again. It is best not to start counting. The sleeping was good; Sirius was brilliant in early morning. I watched the recumbent moon rise just before dawn. At sunrise pink color in the east rose nearly to the zenith before blending with blue of the west. Small distant clouds were outlined sharply in the clear atmosphere. There was swell, but no waves and barely ripples as we moved quietly at five knots. "Altogether a fine scene. What's an ex-New Jersey tomato canner doing out here?" says the log. This was the magic; I stood by the mast for some time just to watch. Unfortunately, the euphoria of early morning turned uncertain by noon and into flat, greasy calm by late afternoon. I went for my first swim, not straying far from my boat and peering with some paranoia into the depths for sea creatures.

I was kicking myself again for sailing into this particular spot. It was logical enough according to the charts, but where were the Northeast Trades? I would listen to the 2000 chat hour for solace in numbers, or perhaps to find where the wind was. The boats in radio contact were stretched in a gentle arc west-southwest to east-northeast, and it appeared none had found the trades. I was at the western end of the arc, and the sky looked vacant.

I lay with no sail all night. Stars were reflected in the water each time I rose to check conditions. With *Mooneshine* rolling and helpless, this dawn lacked the charm of the previous day. This was a time to record my first experience of tradewind sailing. I pulled my tiny inflatable from the cockpit locker and rowed off with Chris Knight's camera. There is some alarm in detaching yourself from your only home out here. *Mooneshine* seemed to ooch ahead as she rolled in the swell with limp sails. I was very aware of the toy status of my dinghy and its puny oars, especially when photographing from astern. I didn't linger; there was a sudden overwhelming need to catch up and climb aboard. Later this day I swam in the wonderfully blue and cool water. At noon the log showed eight miles run in 24 hours, although the plot by chart was 25 miles. I ascribed this to the log impeller, which was reluctant to turn at very low speed because of the tiny magnets therein. I occupied myself through the afternoon urging *Mooneshine* from one patch of slightly ruffled water to the next, like a bug hopping lily pads in a fruitless game. There was no settled direction to the wind and no progress was made.

At the 2000 radio hour *Gypsy Moth* reported light northeast winds, and shortly afterward I could feel *Mooneshine* moving, just slightly, as well. *Gypsy Moth* was about 120 miles east of my position; Desmond opined that it was the trades at last. At 2230 we were still moving at three knots with about three knots apparent wind. "Don't laugh. That is the best we have seen here in 36 hours. I have put away swim ladder and rubber boat in preparation for serious racing tomorrow."

Mooneshine was still 25 degrees north of the Equator at 36 degrees west, and positioned, finally, to plunge into the Northeast Tradewinds. Never mind that we had just experienced near zero winds for 36 hours in an area where the pilot charts show zero-percent calms. The prospect of wind, any wind, looked good now. We would be crossing the tradewind belt, meaning this stage would be all too short before dealing with the doldrums. Now I watched the early morning sun, which for the last two days had had an unhealthy white-yellow color. Nature hints at its secrets in this way, and the cause, it turned out, was a tropical disturbance at 15 degrees north, 40 degrees west on the morning of the 17th.

It would move westward and out of my future, but brought us some rough seas and 25-knot winds. Wind strength had a subjective quality, and after our recent trials by light air this seemed a near gale. I shortened sail and then worried about my race profile: was I doing my best for *Mooneshine* and the race? Rob James had said of the Whitbread Round-the-World Race that there are times you mustn't let prudent seamanship interfere with your race. But he was talking of the Southern Ocean and here I was, only in the tradewinds.

The course was a close reach, and with the wind at 20 knots or better most of the time I settled on a sail combination of working storm jib, staysail, and double-reefed main. Both *Mooneshine* and her skipper are happier with the boat on her feet, I reasoned. In retrospect, I wonder if the skipper was not acting for himself with his own comfort in mind. We were still working east to clear the eastward bulge of Brazil. *"Ocean Passages"* is dire with admonishment on this point for sailing ships that might fail to negotiate that enormous presence when caught in the Southeast Trades. All of this was fuel for baseless speculation on *Mooneshine;* I wondered if perhaps there wasn't greater fear among some skippers who were working even farther east.

It was a good period for ham radio contacts. I talked daily with Rob Koziomkowski back in Newport to relay positions. We had the morning "sunshine" net between boats. It was a cosmopolitan assemblage: Richard Broadhead on *Perseverance of Medina* used a Lebanese call sign, Bertie on *Voortrekker* had his South African temporary sign, Yukoh on *Koden Okera* had a Japanese license, Dan Byrne was a regular, and Richard McBride on his steel-hulled *City of Dunedin* would be on the air as his ailing generator permitted. There were relays from *Lady Pepperell* and *Gypsy Moth,* who used SSB frequencies. Prominently missing from this lineup was *Crédit Agricole,* and when Philippe turned up so far ahead I did not immediately pass on the news to Desmond and Tony for fear of spoiling their day. Guy Bernardin on *Ratso* was near *Gypsy Moth* at this point, but Guy, who is his own man, largely eschewed our chatter, and I respected that. Word now came via BOC that David White was making repairs in Florida and would rejoin the race on Tuesday, the 21st. Sailing east from Florida, David would be bucking tradewinds and tropical disturbances, a tough prospect, it seemed to me, as *Mooneshine* labored through our short band of the trades.

Now we were being tested for leaks:

September 18. One opening port must be leaking around its frame. It's nothing serious, but a slightly annoying chink in my armor against the outside world. The second collapsible water jug collapsed into the cockpit locker and thence into the bilge, but there is obviously more water than from a five-gallon jug. I have checked all the through-hulls and packing glands, but can't find the source.

September 19. Another day of boisterous trade wind sailing. In fact, I'm having trouble writing this as we bump along at seven knots. The seas are mostly four to six feet, occasionally eight feet, but very irregular. I never tire of watching the boat slip over them. The seas come at us at awkward intervals and angles, as if trying to catch *Mooneshine* off guard. Few manage even to send spray on deck.

For some reason, I awoke in the middle of the night and realized that the source of water coming in was the drain in the starboard cockpit locker. This drain was well-intentioned, but when the boat heels at near hull speed, it is too close to the waterline. And sure enough, when I opened this locker in the morning, water would periodically gush in. I plugged the drain with a fistful of electrician's putty and pumped out the considerable quantity of water in the locker with the portable Edson pump.

We have run 165 miles noon-to-noon today, and I don't think we can do much better in these conditions. I heard *Gypsy Moth* say she did 196 miles and LP reports 185. (I remember Francis Chichester's dash across the Atlantic in *Gypsy Moth V*. His goal was 4000 miles in 20 days—200 miles per day; and he didn't quite make it.) Using Bowditch and a calculator I figured the great-circle distance to Cape Town at 4202 miles. That was just from curiosity—we will take a longer route to the west. We are now about 400 miles west of Cape Verde Islands. The curve of West Africa intrudes on my chart. It is disconcerting to think of a huge land mass rather close to port, with all that implies.

The following morning a part of Africa lay on my deck. It was red dust from the Sahara mixing with dead flying fish in the scuppers. Some say this dust acts as fertilizer in the ocean and as far away as Florida. Nature has many ways to distribute her bounty, but one may ask if Africa can spare this good earth. There was more dirt the next day, an increasing nuisance as I tracked it into the cabin. Once again I cleared the decks of fish bodies and signs of death struggles.

Voortrekker was at 10 degrees north, two degrees farther south than I, but Bertie reported the Northeast Trades still holding. Each degree seems important because it shrinks the distance before the Southeast Trades are met. *Mooneshine* was at 30 degrees west and close to my original plan: I wanted to pass comfortably east of St. Peter and St. Paul's Rocks, which lie at 1 degree north, 29 degrees west. These tiny specks of sun-blasted rock loomed in my imagination as a snare for the sleeping singlehander and aroused the captain's usual paranoia. He held the course a little higher to gain easting.

We were racing the sun to the Equator, and losing, as the sun would have a southerly declination the next day. We should soon catch up, though, since the sun moves south about one mile an hour. *Mooneshine* could surely do better than that. These days were largely spent cooped up indoors, hiding my Celtic blemishes from the equatorial sun. Working the boat produced annoying body heat which was slow to dispel in mid-day. By design, I had opted against dorades or other vents on *Mooneshine* for this trip in preparation for colder latitudes, while flying spray of tradewind sailing often discouraged open hatches. "Better company . . . Better air?"

Lightning flashed on the southern horizon all through the

night of the 22nd, though stars were bright overhead. It was the distant early warning of change. By noon the clouds had solidified into a dark band blocking my route. I took a reef in the mainsail and pulled the yankee down with great flapping and snarling. The sheet stopper locked the halyard on the way down to prolong the mess. Then came a drenching shower and much of the African mud was washed into the ocean. The course was south now, and we said goodbye to the Northeast Trades until spring. I must have been attuned to tropic life; the 81 degrees in the cabin felt cool. We decided on hot chocolate instead of warm beer with lunch.

"It's the doldrums, but really not that different from the rest of the world." I was trusting that dumb luck would see me through, and perhaps it did. I listened for news of the others on the evening chat. Most were farther east and struggling, I hoped. My daily runs were fairly good—110 miles on the 23rd, and 90 miles the next day. It's all relative—I was pleased to hear that *Gypsy Moth* ran just 60 miles that day. I was also getting a lift from confusing equatorial currents. Little curled green arrows showing currents on the pilot chart only deepened the mystery. There was extra work for the crew, though there may have been a hint of smugness in the log: "I did everything just right last night, getting up on the half hour and generally on the job. Once, I had secured the yankee on deck and just finished pulling a reef in the main when the rainsquall struck. There was the fast downwind ride before we were left to roll around in the left-over slop."

This was typical of the area. Usually the wind decides to go around the clock before it settles in again, or worse, it doesn't come back at all. This is a rainsquall factory, a great place to study their anatomy, how they form and how they die. You can watch a band of clouds stretching southwest to northeast maybe 10 miles long; there might be rain showers at each end, and if you sail between them you could swear they are executing a pincer movement to trap you. The downwind shower will advance upwind and spread while the other moves down on you with the wind. Usually there is not a lot of wind there, but it's hard to judge, especially at night. *Mooneshine*'s crew recalled greater terror packed in more northerly rain showers, say in the Gulf Stream.

September 25 marked the end of week four. We had logged 3500 miles and were still 300 miles north of the Equator. I calculated the great-circle distance from Newport at 3295 miles. If my log had been over-reading by a small percentage, I thought our actual course must have been rather consistent. It's a small world, as that limp expression goes, but oceans are broad when traversed by a small boat. It may be that the world is properly scaled to man and his designs; or, most likely the opposite: living things are scaled to the Earth and its gravity. We should be thankful, though, that so much of it is ocean, because most of the world's foolishness occurs on land.

Weather here was always restless. The days were spent steering around and through showers, often following the wind as it shifted. Sometimes at night I was rewarded by the flash of luminous life in the water triggered by porpoises. You mark their erratic track by green globes of underwater fire in a ghostly display, and hear their high-pitched squeals. Life must be serious business for them as it is for us—but why the excess energy and playfulness? Whales, by contrast, seem never in a hurry and far more interested in their own company than in sailboats. In the absence of whalers, one thinks their life a pleasant one of relative ease and family joys. How fine is life near the top of the food chain! I was on collision course with four sperm whales and prepared to concede right of way as they were rather close, but they sheared off as if bored.

On the morning of the 26th I realized we had a steady south wind; maybe it was telling me something. I would tack and make my run to the Equator. Let the others sail on to oblivion somewhere in the east; this would be the day to unlock the doldrums. My estimated noon position was 04 degrees, 35 minutes north; 023 degrees, 20 minutes west. I squared *Mooneshine* away on port tack while feeling rather pleased with myself as I thought I had executed a bit of a shortcut. I busied myself adjusting lines to prevent chafe and tidying up in anticipation of 1200 miles of Southeast Tradewinds. The wind was about 15 knots; seas were moderate, with occasional sharp, knotty waves. I wasn't paying a lot of attention, but we lifted over one and landed hard in the trough. *Mooneshine* had done much worse. I thought little of it, but happened to look up at the port spreader. The weld on the trailing edge had opened like a dead clam. Time expands into slow frames; the brain is reluctant to accept the message from the eyes. Then it looks through its menu of excuses: This can't be me—it must be some other boat.

I ran off to drop the jib and put a second reef in the main. One running backstay had been set up on the genoa track. I moved both back to the quarter and set them up tight. Not having a plan, I put the boat back on course, moving at four knots with the staysail and reduced main. It was time for lunch. I talked to *Fantasy, Koden,* and *Voortrekker* on the 1215 schedule. I was digesting the possibilities, including alternative ports such as Salvador, Brazil, 1500 miles to the southwest, a depressing business. The race would be down the drain.

A good cup of coffee was the answer; I decided to try a repair. I would drill the spreader and insert bolts, using these bolts to draw it back in shape. My plans for the voyage had not included going aloft. Quite the opposite, in fact, as most thought had gone into obviating the need. Actually, I enjoy heights, but not the reality of climbing. I have admired and envied those I have seen climbing masts with raw muscle, but this was not my style. I began to lash lengths of line between the port lower shrouds to serve as footropes. In this way I worked my way up the shrouds, one step at a time, in slow business that took half the afternoon. On close inspection drilling and bolting seemed feasible. Hardly any weld was apparent at the break; perhaps it had been ground away for cosmetic reasons. I now brought the Honda generator into the cockpit and went aloft with the power cord tied to my belt, and with my bucket of tools. *Mooneshine* jogged along under reduced sail—I was thankful there were no squalls about—while I sat on the spreader as if on a bucking two-by-four. The drilling went slowly, taking concentration and physical effort; it was a time for reflection on my sheltered life to date. Inserting five bolts and drawing them tight with nuts and washers took until dark, but it was accomplished without mishap or the loss of so much as a washer. I put up a small jib and went below for a ration of rum while we sailed into the night with this limited sailplan. I realized that Cape Town was 4000 miles away, and most of those miles were likely to be on port tack. I would sort out my race prospects in the morning.

"THE SOUTH ATLANTIC is boring!" So declared my son, Whitall, at age 19 after a winter cruise courtesy of Webb Institute of Naval Architecture and the Moore-McCormack Lines that included South American ports as far south as Buenos Aires. He missed the fog and threat of gales in the North Atlantic. How is one to explain the subtle delights of tradewind sailing or the even more subtle pleasures of the variables to impatient Youth? Middle-age didn't have all the answers either. I was doing 60 days hard time, at the least, in my ship, my gaol.

On *Mooneshine* the routine was based on the sun. Days and nights are near equal length in tropic latitudes. Night life on board was severely limited by economies of lighting; sleep became an important part of the program. I wondered if I wasn't developing a mummified depression in my bunk. Sometimes choppy motion encouraged outrageous technicolor dreams, wild flights of fantasy seldom reached on shore. There are frequent interruptions as you tend to your ship, but often I could return to bed and resume the thread of my dream, missing hardly a sequence.

The race was the ever-present inspiration, aggravation, spice, or torment according to the day and whatever sketchy information came via radio. I watched the progress of Yukoh and Jacques especially as my immediate competition. I had a small lead coming out of the doldrums that I knew would evaporate in steady winds. On September 28 I was still one degree north of the elusive Equator. *Voortrekker* was 180 miles ahead now—I mourned the crucial miles lost on Sunday when Bertie had been just 60 miles ahead. I thought the fleet was scattering and radio contact breaking down as some boats headed east while others were taking the west route around the South Atlantic high. *Mooneshine* would follow what has become the conventional, or default route—south through the Southeast Trades and then in a gentle arc into the westerlies at the latitude of Cape Town to trace down the final easting. Cape Town lies at 34 degrees south, 18 degrees east longitude. I visualized the South Atlantic as a huge basin with high pressure dominating the center. But that was simplistic.

Abundant sunlight and gentle winds the day after my efforts aloft encouraged full sail, including the genoa. This was no real test of my repaired spreader, but confidence was returning as I worked the boat. "Just 12 minutes to make the change this morning from yankee down to genoa up and drawing (he boasts)." I watched for new bird varieties—noddy terns appeared and the dusky shearwater, and I began my Southern Hemisphere list. There was the small orange-black patterned butterfly a few days earlier who stayed with me all through a day of blustery rain squalls. Although we were 600 miles from the African coast and 450 miles from the Cape Verde Islands I never saw him alight. Perhaps they don't tire in the sense we do. There must be lessons in conservation of energy for us in this tiny life. And also motivation. I had been at sea one month and was not halfway to Cape Town.

Sometime in early morning on the 29th we passed into the Southern Hemisphere, and without ceremony except that I was arousing myself every hour to check the course and curse the wind for not being more easterly. The sun teased at breakfast by coming directly in the port side windows. With the sun's path almost over my latitude, the sun made a good compass all day—in the morning its bearing was due east and after lunch due west. I was fretting over the course, which was about 200 degrees true with *Mooneshine* hard on the wind. But South America was several hundred miles to the west. I thought *Skoiern, Ratso,* and *Nike* were awkwardly placed north of the Equator and well to the east. Was this part of a master plan, or had they blundered into frustrating winds? *Koden* was not far north and east of my position. Now the wind was stronger, and I reefed and unreefed several times with an eye on my port spreader.

If someone had asked who was leading Class II at this moment, I would have said *Mooneshine*. With about 4000 miles to go on this leg I recorded this especially for my sons, though it had little meaning at this stage.

This was the time to make distance south. We slid under the sun on the 30th. I took the meridian altitude at noon facing aft in the cockpit for the first time. The effect is almost dramatic as the sun sweeps the horizon rapidly from east to west with the mirror arm of the sextant set near 90 degrees. Dan and Tony, who were using only their satellite-aimed black boxes, would miss the excitement. The truth was, I envied them. Excitement, of course, is a relative matter when you have time on your hands.

These were sunny days of good progress. The Southeast Trades gradually back east and then to northeast. By October 5 the wind was aft of the beam—"for the first time in memory, almost," says the written log. The knotmeter log passed 5000 miles this day while sunshine and blue water made the 3000 miles yet to go seem shorter. I marked out my ideal course on the chart. It was a graceful curve, passing east of Ilhas Martin Vaz and north of Tristan da Cunha. In my imagination it skirted the unseen high pressure somewhere out there to my left. I was encouraged to believe in this track by *Crédit Agricole*'s position north of Tristan on October 3. Philippe was making incredible progress and could be in Cape Town in a week. *Skoiern* was boiling down from the northeast at an alarming rate and passed *Koden* in the night. I was chatting with Dan Byrne daily on the 20-meter ham band. *Perseverance* called in from his position at 12 degrees south, 18 degrees west; Richard was bucking right down the middle, but I wouldn't have traded his 2400 miles for my 3000. I thought Desmond and Tony would be flying out of radio range ahead of me, but they were about to fall into the variables and experience some "subtle pleasures." I watched mid-latitude cirrus clouds in the west that day while tradewind clouds lay in the east. It was advance notice that we would soon be leaving the tradewinds.

The stars in these latitudes were almost totally unfamiliar, but I was encouraged to try star sights by the clear conditions. A friend in Annapolis had thoughtfully provided me with Admiral Davies' special method of star sights for idiots—you shoot the star and the Admiral will tell what it is you shot. I turned out at evening twilight for a round of sights. Vega, Fomalhaut, and Rigel Kentaurus yielded a triangle smaller than, say, Rhode Island, but it would have held all of Brooklyn. A 10-mile error in one sight will pretty well destroy the navigator's "cocked hat." I would polish my sextant mirrors and try again. The aging navigator may have trouble with these evening sights as he juggles sextant, flashlight, spectacles, watch, and notebook. Add to this angle of heel and some seaway, and there will be plenty of excuses. A bright moon and clear horizon encouraged me to try a sight on Canopus at 0200 the following night, with reasonable result. I have to admit that navigation by stars continued to be regarded as a bit of a stunt on *Mooneshine* although I would occasionally pursue the moon and morning or evening planets.

By October 7 we were at 21 degrees south and losing the trades. A light wind from the north-northeast was barely sufficient to keep the spinnaker drawing. I went on deck early that morning to make a small course adjustment and just in time to watch the spinnaker float down like a rose petal into the sea. Damn! The halyard shackle had opened for some reason, leaving the halyard useless at the masthead. This was a small defeat for which I felt responsible; slowly it dawned that I had a messenger line and could reeve a spare halyard. We were back in racing form, but the wind continued light.

Now there came word from Andy, a ham operator on Tristan da Cunha, locating a high-pressure area 300 miles to the east. We would have light conditions for at least three days; there went my time table. We had passed Trindade and Martin Vaz, my first waypoints in this empty basin. The next mark was the point north of Tristan, 1200 miles ahead. Thus I had divided the journey into segments I could relate to in terms of days. *Skoiern* continued to gain on me and was now very close, his radio signal literally blasting into my cabin on the 1000 schedule with Desmond Hampton. I will always remember Jacques for his gentlemanly "Sank you very much" each time as he signed off. I could not join these conversations but often listened for weather clues.

Barely 100 miles were run the next day. Promise of more wind died away and instead a mighty swell moved in from the southwest. Each swell moving under the boat backwinded the sails in confusion; they filled again with a bang as the swells passed and the boat moved forward a little. I left the spinnaker up all afternoon despite fears for its safety. "And *Skoiern* is closer. The ocean this afternoon reminded me of a rolling, empty landscape, like parts of South Dakota on a gray day. It's a different medium, but the underlying architecture is the same." These were the bare hills; and from the top there was a vista of endless bare hills, and receding horizon.

Andy was right. Three more days of tiresome lament followed in the log: "There is a tendency to believe you can change matters if only you exert enough will power . . . absurd. Still, one likes to think some small degree of control is in our hands." This was not a prayer. I just wanted my way.

. . . *Skoiern* is passing me at this moment 30 miles to the east. So much for my lead in Class II . . . Only 80 miles run from noon to noon. I have been up and down with genoa and spinnaker. Every move I make to improve matters seems only to slow us. The wind moved from northeast to west twice and proceeded to die each time. At sundown the sea began to get that glassy look. There will not be much progress to Cape Town tonight.

Two slightly addled eggs, scrambled, for breakfast. This is the only style possible as white and yolk are already one. The first cup of coffee is always a high point of the day. My coffee is boiled in the pot, grounds and all. There is a ceramic filter on the fresh-water tap that removes not only particles but bacteria. The water is good but trickles from the spout with difficulty, like an old man urinating.

I just don't understand it. At 1900 *Gypsy Moth* reported southwest winds at 18 knots apparent. I'm sitting here at 2200, becalmed, sails down and rolling. She is east of us but in the same weather system. She reported the menacing black clouds that were all around me at sundown. I was doing reasonably well under spinnaker until these clouds came and snuffed out the wind. Calms and threat of calm have been the principal feature of this voyage so far. Piles of rotten looking clouds are barring the way ahead.

These were days in the South Atlantic that invoked the spirit of Donald Crowhurst. His voyage in the Golden Globe solo world race of 1968 holds a certain poignant fascination for the single-hander. He apparently cooked his logs to fake a circumnavigation while stewing for some months in the maddening winds of the South Atlantic. We can only speculate whether it was the lie, the loneliness, or simply the South Atlantic that finally led him to step off his trimaran, which was later found drifting.

On October 12 an approaching front brought threatening skies and northerly winds of 20 to 25 knots. I reacted as though this were a mini Southern Ocean and imagined angry-looking following seas. This was at 27 degrees south; I was looking at the green line on my chart labeled "Intertropical Convergence" which we would cross the next morning, as if that held some awful significance. I wondered if I would miss the tropics where sleepwear and deckwear are often one; but I had grown tired of pondering Original Sin, and like Adam, it was time to pull on clothes. That night I turned out in a cold, drizzling rain to jibe and reset the course as the front passed, but instead of lively west or southwest winds the breezes turned progressively weaker. By the next afternoon we rolled in leftover slop, unable to sail at all while I looked for encouragement in a cup of coffee and contemplated the 2000 miles lying ahead before Cape Town.

Now I was suddenly aware that the steering had become alarmingly stiff, something I thought I had taken every precaution to prevent. Self-steering systems, especially windvane steerers like

Aries, need a friction-free helm to work properly. I suspected the nylon bushing where the rudder post entered the hull. Nylon swells in water and correct allowance is presumably made for this, but here was *Mooneshine* sitting approximately in the middle of this huge South Atlantic basin with a progressively stiffer wheel. What was to be be done? In my anxiety I bent over the stern where I could look down through clear water. Skeg and rudder moved ominously side to side in a refracted image as we rose up and fell in the considerable swell. They weren't loose, of course, but I had to look. I put *Mooneshine* aback and went overboard wearing a mask to examine the skeg and bronze shoe at the rudder base. All was sound, but I noticed a number of gooseneck barnacles clinging between rudder and skeg. I hoped devoutly that was the problem, and later a vigorous spinning of the wheel from stop to stop did seem to clear away the barnacles, or cobwebs, or whatever was the trouble with the rudder.

I was drying myself in the cockpit when I noticed the Danforth steering compass reading backwards—that is, I thought we were sailing southeast, but the compass read northwest. Donald Crowhurst came immediately to mind. But the modest compass I used for a telltale at the chart table was reassuring. I now realized belatedly that all my compass cards were inclining downwards toward the south magnetic pole somewhere deep in the earth. At 30 degrees south this effect is considerable for compasses balanced for the northern hemisphere. I suppose we are provincial about this, as we are about our maps which show the North Pole as "up."

I had to feel a bit foolish after all this as we ran (at two knots) with main and poled-out jib toward Cape Town. The mainsail would back and fill under the swell, booming like a carbide cannon set to scare off crows, but the inscrutable Wandering Albatross that had been observing my strange performance was unperturbed. This is the largest and most mysterious albatross, obviously the one hung about the Ancient Mariner's neck. In weeks to come I studied the fixed expression on these birds, watching for some flicker of acknowledgement of my presence, the briefest eye contact, but received nothing. They were impassive, like painted dolls, and their world complete without me—unless I should happen to be perceived as food.

My aggravated spirit was soothed that night by a 15-knot wind from the northeast. I tried to do my part by waking every hour with the alarm and sometimes in between to check course and trim. The sky and barometer were giving no clues, as usual, but I was additionally comforted to hear that *Gypsy Moth* and *Lady Pepperell* were waiting for wind some 250 miles to the east.

Clearing skies and an unusually brilliant spread of stars the following night brought two hours of 35-knot winds from the blue. I secured the jib and retired to the bunk while the ship rolled and generally made life unpleasant. In early morning dark skies, drizzle, and gray following seas made a bleak scene to one softened in the tropics. At 31 degrees south, I dug through my clothing for the Helly-Hansen underwear, and thus warmed I made good progress through the day. The windshift came after supper. I was sitting in the head when I realized we were suddenly bumping across rather than sliding down the seas. In my hurry to get on deck I got tangled in my foul-weather pants, trying to pull them on backwards. Luckily, it wasn't blowing very hard as I clumsily put the boat on the other tack. This needs work, I thought, as drill for the Southern Ocean.

You make best use of winds when you have them here. We commenced rolling as my winds died, but what might have been a bad night was relieved by a good contact with Arthur on our Friday schedule. Perhaps the conscience is absolved temporarily upon hearing generally good things from home. The lift from this chat stayed with me through the next day. We would try again next Friday, and the following Friday . . . Cape Town?

I have thought of Tristan da Cunha as the epitome of isolation—off sea routes, and 1500 miles from South Africa. None of my dreams of escape or of island living have envisioned a life as stark as this. But where there is an island, there are ham radio operators. Andy, ZB9BV, was on the air most afternoons. The amazing Bertie Reed had stopped there for drinking water and repairs the previous March, and I was able to pass on his greetings to certain people on the island who had been especially hospitable.

Now I was 250 miles north, with the chances very good I would never pass by again. This was a dull day—sun sights were taken through rain, which made the noon position fuzzy, to say the least. There were the usual baseless anxieties when I couldn't produce a fix. Two days of thick weather seemed darker after 6000 miles of sunshine. But this day was improved by sighting the first Pintado Petrel, the Cape Pigeon. Sailors got it right this time as this small petrel with the unmistakeable piebald pattern on wings and back does resemble the city pigeon. The not-quite-serious aspect of these birds was always pleasing to my eye and spirits. They are generously distributed through waters south of 30 degrees south. Wilson's Storm Petrel and the Great Shearwater, both familiar birds of the North Atlantic summers, were moving through on their way to breeding grounds on the lonely islands deep in the South Atlantic. I watched the Yellow-nosed Albatross circle several times. As you might guess, the yellow nose is invisible unless you happen to hold it in your arms. Likewise, the White-chinned Petrel seldom shows any white at all. I have sometimes thought these names derive from small conceits of earlier ornithologists. The Ornithologists' Union meets occasionally and changes some of these names, randomly, one imagines, to keep the rest of us slightly dated. Old-time sailors were wiser and applied the name "Mollymawk" generically to the smaller albatrosses.

October 17. Sunlight through the galley hatch is moving over the table this afternoon. I have shaved and made a cup of tea to relax with. A 15-knot wind from the west is strong enough to damp much of the rolling in the large swells which seem to be a constant feature of the landscape here . . . I mention this because I sit here enjoying the easy motion and sunlight while it lasts.

I have been using the sextant eagerly today to catch up on navigation. Sadly, my guesswork of the two previous days proved optimistic and I have had to fix the noon position 20 miles short of my projection. Worse, *Koden*, 60 miles to the north, is pulling away from me, and I don't seem to be able to do anything about it. I ran all night using the autopilot, which does good work in this moderate downwind sailing and is much less affected by the swells than the Aries. The problem comes with windshifts, so I tried to wake every half hour to watch for change. I'm cautious of accidental jibe with my various guys and preventers on pole and boom. This time, the windshift came at daybreak, and I was ready. I haven't devised a better way to handle the pole when jibing, and the business seemed to take a full hour. And this was before the first cup of coffee.

So far, these weather systems have moved through here about every two days. One just left and the sky in the west hints at another on the way. This is what keeps us moving toward Cape Town and is why we took this circuitous route. *Ratso II* is fighting tradewinds on the direct route. Two days ago he was near St. Helena, and that seems a tough way to go.

The prudent mariner will leave his weather prognoses out of the log. I quickly found that there is nothing predictable in the ponderous churnings of the atmosphere at 33 degrees south. And here *Mooneshine* was again overspread by high pressure and light winds. In short, frustration: "Last night the wind was up and down, back and forth between southeast and southwest. Sometimes the speed brushed six knots, other times zero. The Alpha pilot somehow guided us through most of this while I enjoyed my typically irresponsible dreams."

This was developing into a most baffling patch of ocean. It was my first experience with a wind that rises and dies in a rhythmic sequence; and this went on for two days. Now it came from the east-southeast, precisely my desired course, and I was sailing to Antarctica. Dinner was interrupted when the log impeller suddenly stopped. This assembly is located awkwardly under the starboard settee. To clean it you extract it from its through-hull mounting, which leaves a gushing hole until a special plug is inserted. There appeared to be a slender blue filament entangled in the impeller. Both hands being occupied, I foolishly sought to dislodge it with my tongue and I felt a sharp sting, like a cut. It was the tentacle of a blue bottle, one of nature's jellyfish.

Each day there was a bout with uncertain winds. On October 20 we were on the latitude of Cape Town with 1100 miles to go. I had my list of projects to be done, with the compass high on the agenda. The lubber line on this model of Danforth compass curves over the card for easy reading. With the dip now evident in the card it would be useless in anything but easterly headings in these southern latitudes. Replacement spreaders were on their way to Cape Town. Al Tucker was concerned about my comfort and had engineered a dodger for the companionway, also to be installed in Cape Town. Helly-Hansen was sending mittens. All this had been arranged through the wonders of ham radio.

On the night of the 21st we moved into east longitude and started ticking off the 18 meridians to Cape Town. I thought I had gained a little on Yukoh, who was 55 miles ahead as of noon. There was the first contact with the South African ham net. It was Alistair Campbell in Durban who was to become the center of our communication life in the Indian Ocean. Months later, when I reentered the Atlantic after passing Cape Horn I would tune in to Alistair's net just to hear his voice once more. Gales and the threat of gales are the stuff of the weather news. I immediately looked up and saw a nasty ring around the sun, but since my shipboard weather forecasts had been such a flop to date I kept quiet.

October 22. A sail is in sight in the early morning about four miles ahead. This can only be Yukoh, but how did we gain 50 miles on him since yesterday noon? I have definitely closed on him in the last hour, but this, too, seems improbable as the wind is very light and our speed about four knots.

It's virtually cloudless this morning, and the sun feels warm on my back. With the wind from the northwest I am using the spinnaker. Long, very gentle swells from the west upset the wind and the spinnaker is not happy. At 0930 I am still overtaking the boat ahead and can see his spinnaker misbehaving.

I caused great excitement among the porpoises this morning. Schools came to me from a half mile ahead, astern, and from the south, leaping clear of the water with every breath in their hurry to see what was going on. When they found our speed was only four knots they soon lost interest. I had let them down.

Word came that *Voortrekker* arrived in Cape Town yesterday, the 21st, second boat in. Somehow he gained 1000 miles on me in the last three weeks. I remembered the day north of the Equator when Bertie told me he would arrive on the 21st.

Now I am losing to Yukoh through the afternoon in steadier wind.

Thus was ending my fourth encounter with boats in this race; and once again I was losing. I never did discover why Yukoh was, in effect, waiting for me this day. Suntori or saki perhaps? It is a very private world out there. All afternoon I watched the hare, *Koden,* move away from me and to the southeast as the wind freshened. I brought down my spinnaker at twilight, feeling guilty because I could still see Yukoh carrying on with his. Later, I changed from the genoa to the yankee. "Sail to the point of discomfort—and beyond," is the old racing boast. But not this night, I thought, and the unceasing roll made sleep difficult.

Sleep came slowly also because to my surprise and pleasure Arthur's voice came up out of the mud on the 20-meter band on our Friday schedule. Conversation was difficult, but contact is the main thing. We set the next scheduled call for Thursday. I had been counting miles not yet run, but hoped to be in port by Friday. A log entry at noon the next day: ". . . our best day's run in some time. I resist the temptation to extrapolate this over the remaining 650 miles." I was lying again; I already had.

Ham radio continued to amaze. On this day I had a call from Gough Island, a large uninhabited rock 180 miles south-southeast of Tristan da Cunha. It is commentary on the lonely life of fishermen who alone set eyes on these places. But this fisherman was a ham operator and sent word of a cold front on the way. Down there it was minus three degrees centigrade and snowing, he said. The romance of the Southern Ocean suddenly seemed much closer as I watched the albatrosses.

October 24. It has been dismal all day as the Gough Island cold front passes through, but clouds are breaking in the west at sundown and one of the most brilliant rainbows I have seen lights up the sky ahead. I can see the pots of gold at each end.

Later. It appears the cold front had more punch than I thought. The rainbow turned into a violent squall while the wind backed to the south, a cold wind. I had a lively drill getting the yankee down with the whole show of banging, flapping, hissing etc. It would be pleasant to observe this from some protected dry spot. More was on the way so I pulled down the main also. We entered the night with just the staysail. *Mooneshine* was snug enough, but cross seas made the motion tough and sometimes violent.

At 0200 I roused myself and went on deck to raise the main (double-reefed). I point out here that it takes some willpower and determination to leave warm blankets and entertaining dreams to pull on foul-weather gear and hoist more sail to gain one knot.

In this way I learned to distrust rainbows and added to my small stock of ocean weather lore. At noon the following day *Mooneshine* was on the latitude of Cape Town and 350 miles out. It was wet going through the cross seas, though we made good progress. Bertie Reed had warned me: " Approach Cape Town from 36 degrees south!" This was to allow for the north-setting Benguela Current and to be better positioned should the wind go into the southeast. But I was thinking of Yukoh and staring at my chart. I would gamble on a straight run in. *Gypsy Moth* had finished at midnight. *Lady Pepperell* was due in this afternoon. So the friends I had been tracking for nearly two months were safely in. I should be pleased to follow them in three days, I thought, but the excitement of arrival filled my head and blocked out caution.

My chances for a graceful approach to Cape Town thus slipped away, and the log for Tuesday the 26th shows my foolish shortcut falling victim to the southeast wind:

. . . I am caught 50 miles too far north for comfort and heartily regret that I didn't make more effort to move south when it would have been easier—now a southeast wind has set in. In any case, I should be third in class. *Koden* is ahead and I can't catch him. *Skoiern* should have finished today.

. . . I really worry too much. At noon there were still 225 miles to go, plenty of time for the wind to change its mind. The sky today has been a mixture of grim portent and cheerful cumulus. At sunset it looks as though the good cheer will win out.

. . . We are now hard on the wind with everything strapped in tight—typical tough going in 22 knots. I guess we'll all be glad to reach Cape Town and take a breather.

October 27. The sun is shining today and that is the only thing good I can say about this day. It was a rough night, but I continued on while being pushed north. I used the small jib alone all night, which seems a poor choice of sail, but I doubt if it made any difference to course or speed. In the morning I changed that for the storm jib and reefed main. After crashing around until I was afraid something would break, I hove to, leaving the storm jib up. Winds were Force 8 by that time. I just don't know what else to do.

This day was spent learning the lesson of the Cape southeasters. Walls of water, green in the sunshine, rolled toward me blocking off progress. *Mooneshine,* with her 5.5-foot draft, was never at her best to windward in gale conditions. Worse, I was being carried north. Wet and unreliable sun sights placed me about 100 miles from Cape Town, and locked out. Then I heard by radio that Yukoh was laying a course for Cape Town, just 24 miles out. He had Table Mountain in sight! In my present circumstances I found that hard to imagine. A more generous person could rejoice for Yukoh; I felt only envy. And now the wind was backing to the east, helping not at all. A door had been slammed in my face. I realized I had it coming.

Later I put up the storm trysail, sheeting it to a mooring cleat on the port quarter. I had practiced this procedure, but still was not at ease with this sail, which is little used. It held the bow a bit closer to the wind depending upon how the wheel was lashed, and thus we slogged along through the rest of the afternoon and into the night. I knew I was well north of Table Bay and had difficulty imagining landfall.

I thought this gale would not end. But toward midnight the wind was definitely easing. I could add sail, starting with the staysail. This immediately upset the trysail, which had to come off. I had, unnecessarily, lowered the boom to the cabintop to clear the trysail, so that had now to be raised, but at 0200 we were making a fair course to the east. The staysail caught a steep sea; at first I thought the halyard had snapped as the sail collapsed. I was relieved to find it had slipped on its winch, but now found the deck hardware for the staysail lifting, and put down another job for Cape Town. I saw the lights of trawlers ahead, just as in shelf waters in so many places the world over. There would be no sleep here, I told myself, and fixed coffee. But I lay down for just a few minutes; and when I awoke those trawlers were astern. I had left the watch to *Mooneshine* alone and will never know if we were the object of fishermen's curses. Now I amused myself over tea and cocoa to pass the last slow hours before sunrise—and landfall?

I was looking very hard for signs of land at first light, but there was nothing. Impatience made time drag; then at last the rough edge of mountains slowly materialized through the haze of early morning. Were they 20 or 50 miles off? Distance was deceptive in this light, but the depthsounder found bottom at 105 fathoms. Now the day was opening on a different world; there was an absence of swell; seawater was brownish in color and cold in the salt-water tap. A sea monster was lazing on the surface to port, and at first I didn't recognize it as a seal. Bird life had changed— now there were mostly unfamiliar shags. Wind was soft and from the south, veering southwest. The contrast to the day before was complete.

Enough landmarks were now visible to locate us just north of Dasseneiland, and about 40 miles north of Cape Town. Sailing

Directions for this area give grim warnings of underwater rocks lying in wait several miles west and south of the island, but it was hard to judge distance off. Was it the lack of features, or just the fact I was seeing real rock after two months? All this day we would be sailing down the coast under a warm sun and in smooth water. I tuned to Cape Town Radio on Channel 16. A search was in progress for a dismasted sailboat; I could hear one side of the conversation: "BIG SNAP. BIG SNAP . . . Cape Town Radio. Do you have Table Mountain in sight? Can you give me a bearing?" Pleasant it is, when on dry land. . . .

I wanted *Mooneshine* to be looking her best for the Royal Cape Yacht Club. I hung out flags, polished rust streaks off pulpits and stanchions, and did my housekeeping chores. There was plenty of time and hot water for a shave and shower as I aimed my boat straight at Table Mountain. All this day I heard the radio: "BIG SNAP . . . BIG SNAP . . ." while I continued my ministrations to *Mooneshine,* and in this way I cultivated the (false) notion that we always finished in perfect order.

We would pass inside Robbeneiland, which guards Table Bay from the north, but keeping well clear in accordance with stern warnings in the Sailing Directions. Much later I found that even the mention of Robbeneiland could stir emotions; I might be barred from international competition, I was warned. Well, International Sport wouldn't be losing much in my case; it had pleased me to think that sailing in the ocean by one's self is as removed from politics as you can get.

Now whales barred the way; I watched the rounded backs and then their barnacle-covered flukes just off the bow. We sailed through the widening circle left as they dove. A small flock of Jackass Penguins was busy off to port.

Table Bay is large, but the mountains looming over Cape Town alter perspective. I tried to distinguish the finish line long before the marks were apparent, which only made the last miles seem longer. Now we were exposed to a fresh southeast wind coming across the flats. My hands were full on the final beat to the finish as *Mooneshine* heeled sharply on port tack. I heard a gun go off on the breakwater where Royal Cape Yacht Club members had been keeping a vigil. Done! In 60 days, more or less.

Almost done. We were to moor inside the shipping docks. There was a strong breeze now, and I struggled to get my sails down and secured while a tug came up to assist, I suppose—but I watched with alarm as his workboat exterior was closing on my delicate yacht at a full eight knots. I waved him off impolitely, even with curses. After two months alone, close encounters of this kind seem somehow overwhelming. Then a sailing yacht appeared, loaded with people and all arms and legs in my eyes. Happy Hour at the club had just let out, to judge by the noise and speed, but a line was passed and I gratefully accepted the tow. *Mooneshine* was soon moored in line and next to *Crédit Agricole*. It was the first time I had set eyes on this impressive boat, even though we had both been on B Dock two months before. Philippe had been in Cape Town long enough by that time to break at least one heart.

Indian Ocean

THERE WAS AN open square beneath my hotel window in Cape Town. On some mornings I watched pedestrians bent against the southeast wind; small trees were permanently inclined to the northwest. There were fine, sunny days, but when the white "tablecloth" was hiding Table Mountain we knew the southeaster was blowing again. One afternoon we were driven 25 miles down the peninsula to the Cape of Good Hope, and climbed over the rocky promontory itself to gaze on an imaginary dividing line between Atlantic and Indian Oceans. At Simonstown, Bertie Reed's home port, the southeaster was tearing at the surface of False Bay. We shared a roadside lunch stop with baboons, as if I needed another reminder that this was not New Jersey. They squat on calloused butts and stare at you with resentment. I find these encounters with our simian cousins embarrassing, as if they understand very well they are the poor relations. On the return to Cape Town we stopped to walk over a wide beach on the Atlantic side, where the wind stripped away the tops of incoming waves. It felt cold in spite of the sun.

Our departure had been set for Sunday, November 14. There were 35-knot gusts buffeting the docks and reaching across the bay that morning as we prepared to leave. *Mooneshine* was already leaning against her docklines under weight of the wind. It was a scene to excite old gut pains, but I thought I was ready and prepared to raise a very modest sailplan. Club members took our lines and provided tows to pull us clear of the docks. Something was wrong though; Table Bay was teasing, and soon there were only occasional heavy gusts. Spectator boats had gathered like porpoises to see the action, but this was quickly becoming an embarrassment as we had difficulty proceeding toward the start area in ever lighter winds. The crowd had come to see us off, and now we could hardly leave the starting line. We waved our good-byes and waved again, but barely moved. It was a small relief when at last they left us to our private frustrations.

I worked out toward Robbineiland in company with Neville Gossen on *Leda,* thinking there might be more wind farther from the lee of Table Mountain. From this perspective I could imagine *Mooneshine* in the lead and dug out my camera to record this development. The water was slick over a gray swell, and the sky was a colorless match. I watched *Gypsy Moth* rise and disappear under rolling swells with Desmond's staysails and topsails hanging like laundry. Philippe on *Crédit Agricole* and Yukoh on *Koden* were doing inadvertent 360s. Philippe had now changed to his 150-percent mylar genoa, but it wasn't helping. Frustration and thirst took over on *Mooneshine.* I drank warm orange soda from a plastic bottle, which did nothing for the thirst or my nerves. The unpleasant taste lingered; I wondered what I was doing there any-way. Two weeks in Cape Town had softened my stomach and dented my resolve.

"The Fairest Cape in all the circumference of the world," Sir Francis Drake had called it, and we can be sure that was the truth in his eyes when he reached it in June 1580. I had time to dwell on this as we moved slowly outward and south, almost in the shadow of the mountains, but in this light the Twelve Apostles were sullen. These broken promontories that trail south from Table Mountain toward the Cape are permanently fixed in my memory as dour and judgmental. Now David White on the red *Gladiator* sailed by our little fleet on his way in to Cape Town. Thus our lives crossed once more, but all of us bent on private paths. The restart date had been set within certain imperatives—maximize the summer months in the Southern Ocean and round Cape Horn before summer gives way to fall.

My two weeks in port had been filled with activity, and

passed too quickly. Now time dragged; I should have been looking harder at my immediate preparations for sea, but my mind was in some state of lethargy, if not paralysis. I watched wisps of cloud beginning to spill over and down the mountains—wind at last. But do not ask for what you will wish you had not got. As it grew dark these wisps became streamers and the wind was quickly building. Philippe was ahead of me now. I watched him on the foredeck wrestling down his big genoa while I still felt secure with my tight sail combination. *Leda* was also ahead and off my starboard bow. Affairs were rapidly getting messy on *Mooneshine*. Neville must also have been fighting his genoa. "Dramas on the foredeck," he called them—drama spoken with the flat Australian "a" as in Alabama. I lost him in darkness. Philippe's masthead light gradually moved away, though I kept it in sight for some time.

I was now alone to deal rather ineffectively with the rising wind. The storm jib was secured in its turtle on the foredeck—my first mistake. It should have been hanked to the forestay with sheets led. Now was the time to deal with that, but I couldn't seem to muster all hands on the plunging deck. I pulled down the mainsail, secured it to the boom, and continued on with a small jib. This was to be my Rude Awakening to the nasty realities of sailing, but I was slow to wake. The spinnaker pole wasn't latched properly in its forward chock. I found it slipping aft and about to go overboard, and grabbed it while leaning from the companionway. *Mooneshine* plunged, water was everywhere, and the companionway ladder jumped out of its brackets, adding to my sense of not being in control. This episode with the pole repeated itself twice before I did what I should have done at the dock—lock it properly in its deck fitting.

The southeaster was now blowing close to 50 knots. My jib had to come off. I took the easy way, using Aries to steer downwind while I pulled down the jib and lashed it on deck. How peaceful it was under bare poles, but that was taking us north at six knots. Instead I would lie ahull and await developments. The Cape peninsula was off to port, but we would be moving farther offshore, and the Cape itself was invisible off the port bow. I was losing track of time, and lay on the starboard settee, boots and foul-weather gear on, while periodically rousing myself to watch for ships.

I may have been asleep, but there was a sudden crash and I felt the boat roll as I was showered with books, cans, bottles, and water which I thought could only have come from the bilge. The G-forces are considerable as the boat is struck by a breaking wave and lands hard in the trough. We are such creatures of gravity—it's profoundly disturbing to feel your world turning upside down. And you know something is really wrong when it is totally black and things are falling on you. I stupidly picked up a few books and cans before looking out on deck. All was secure there except my new hatch dodger was in shreds—only the frame remained to serve as a handhold. From the deck the waves did not look terribly menacing, but the wind was hard and there was no thought of raising sail.

My race preparation included the expectation of being dumped, just like this—but not yet. In the back of my mind I had known the books and canned goods stowage was not safe. I hadn't put those positive latches on the settee lockers. The light plywood retainers holding books on port shelves gave way and books from the port side landed in starboard shelves, along with canned vegetables and meat. The radios, by good luck, were just out of the line of fire, although the Kenwood transceiver received a dollop of salt water.

The wretched night was too long. I watched lights of three ships approaching from astern. This is a busy area for shipping; and with no sail I felt especially vulnerable. In my anxiety I put out calls on Channel 16, receiving no answer. I sat in the cockpit for a time watching ships and waves. It was hard to judge conditions in the darkness, but I needed no prompting to wear my safety harness. The violence of a knockdown is a frightening thing, and best experienced secured in your bunk. By morning light the cabin was in pretty good order. You may fool yourself that you are in control of larger forces by restoring calm to your immediate surroundings. My small world had been scrambled in less than a second. Bottles of wine, a gift from a generous Cape

Town resident, escaped from their table stowage to shelves behind the radios; butter from the ice box was in the waste basket; a heavy fishing sinker had flown from a galley drawer to the shelf at the navigation station; my big green cheese had jumped from the ice box and onto the nav table; binoculars from the shelf over my bunk in the aft cabin had also landed on the nav table, and so on. It was an impressive show of flying objects. I had to be thankful for all that I had stowed safely.

The wind was still fierce in the morning. I knew I was doing very badly compared to others because I had not carried on with sail. The wind was southeast; our course was to have been roughly south passing the Cape but continuing south to clear the Agulhas Bank and in hopes of sailing into those westerlies. *Mooneshine* was never at her best beating in conditions like this. I hanked on the storm jib and rigged the storm trysail, though the net course was about southwest at 3.5 knots. Later that day the wind blew harder and I made the mistake of lowering the trysail. With storm jib alone the effect is about the same as lying ahull, i.e. we made slow forward progress but lay nearly beam-on to the seas. I thought we were safe with this rig as night fell and slept in my comfortable aft cabin with the bunk board in place.

Sometime in the night, I have no idea when, there was a crash, and my head hit the door jamb as I flew out of my cabin. I was on the floor in the passageway, badly shaken. There was the same mess in the cabin. Two ponderous volumes of Gibbon's *"Decline and Fall of the Roman Empire"* again had flown from port to starboard; dirty pots from the sink were on the chart table. This time we didn't go as far over, but it was more violent, like being in an auto accident. My ribs on the left side were very sore.

Once more the waters off the cape proved strangely savage to small boats. I thought of *Big Snap*, which had been towed to a dock at the club looking disheveled and diminished without her mast. Then Dan Byrne on *Fantasy* called in to Cape Town radio. He was returning for repairs after losing a sail, watching his water tank pull his port settee and lockers apart, and experiencing a fire in his ignition switch, which also damaged the engine starter. *Koden* and *Spirit of Pentax* had been flattened by waves. I was worried about my radio, which didn't seem right when I called Alistair Campbell on the morning net; then it quit altogether. I found water in the fuse holder and finally cut it from the power leads. Despite salt water this little Kenwood continued to serve, with only occasional hesitations, and still serves after more recent journeys. I did resolve to cover it with plastic and padding in future bad weather. We were under severe notice by Race Committee to maintain our radio contacts. I also successfully glued my battery-powered RDF radio together after its flight across the cabin.

I was putting my life back in order. Except for those who had to restart, *Mooneshine* must have been the race laggard.

Sure enough, I was disgusted to hear Cape Town radio coming in clearly on Channel 16. This was almost two days into the race and I was still in VHF range of Cape Town. The wind was easing through this morning, but I was slow to raise sail from soreness and lethargy. Seas had calmed remarkably by afternoon, though the wind remained from the southeast. My position is recorded as "noon guess" at 37 degrees, 15 minutes south, 014 degrees, 48 minutes east. Since Cape Town is at 18 degrees east longitude *Mooneshine* was approximately 120 miles west of her starting point, and certainly off to a dismal beginning of a journey 6500 miles east. A journey of a thousand miles begins with a single step. But backwards?

The next day, Wednesday, November 17, found me still about 100 miles west of Cape Town, but there was peace and warmth. I even enjoyed calms in the night and early morning. I compared progress with Richard McBride on *City of Dunedin*. Richard was ahead of me in his 41-foot schooner because he had stood up to the challenge of the first two nights better than I. And this was after his brief three days in Cape Town. We had chatted on the ham bands on that first leg until Richard's small Clinton generator failed him. Our last conversations back then had been my less-than-helpful advice on soldering the disappearing, broken leads on his generator diodes. He badly needed a Honda, I thought. A steel staysail schooner in the South Atlantic high will try your patience, especially with enforced radio silence. I remember eating breakfast with Richard at the Royal Cape Yacht Club when he arrived after 70 days at sea. His conversation was like the tumbling of released flood waters. We maintained a lively contact all across the Indian Ocean, comparing bird identifications, but also engaging in our private race as our boats were rather closely matched for the Southern Ocean.

The routines of sea life had gotten off to a shaky start on *Mooneshine*. Curiosity about this ocean had led me this far, and anxiety of the unknown. I had sailed a lot of miles, but now felt as if I was beginning again. The two weeks in Cape Town had been crowded with preparations to the boat and with the amazing hospitality offered by the people there. There was the over-eating: I remembered incredible luncheon delights at the Lanzarote Inn at Stellenbosch—and what a pity it was not to be able to repeat this extravagance, after the manner of ancient Romans. This was a magnificent Dutch Colonial setting wherein I imagined parking my Mercedes in their brick-paved drive. This indulgence was repeated at other locales. I could feel my seagoing pose melting away and thought I had gained 10 pounds.

Meanwhile, the BOC Group and its subsidiary Afrox had been alarmed by the emaciated appearance of some, and provided a bus to haul skippers to a grocery store. Food on the next leg would be courtesy of the BOC Group. Naturally, being singlehanders, we took full advantage of this. It may have been Paul Rodgers on *Spirit of Pentax* who was the proximate cause of this. He had arrived off Cape Town semi-starved in the tradition of early seafarers; then had been blown out to sea again by the southeaster for another frustrating 36 hours before finally crossing the finish line and receiving food offerings from waiting craft.

The short two weeks in Cape Town tweaked a latent obsession with what I consider the civilized necessities of larder and cellar. It must be the Dutch influence, I assumed, since my English Quaker ancestry was comparatively primitive in these matters. *Mooneshine* left Cape Town stocked with a variety of whole grain flours, Dutch coffees, and local wines. Lone sailors may cover the whole spectrum of cooking and eating habits from the near-savage to the cultured. I can admire those who exist simply on brown rice, but that was not my style. Some of my lasting memories of Cape Town are of food, and generosity toward our diverse band.

The Argos transmitters that would relay our positions to race headquarters via satellite and computer were another benefit provided us by the BOC Group while in Cape Town. These were similar to the units we had carried in the 1980 OSTAR, minus the occasional failures that marked that event, we assumed. Anticipated battery life would shepherd us across the Indian and Pacific Oceans. In practice, they carried us back to Newport and were still beeping their coded signals when stowed away there in Peter Dunning's trailer. It is safe to say we were grateful for this addition to our sense of security; and the system was to prove its worth later on. Living in this age of space has its civilizing advantages, providing we can live up to them. The other consequence of having Argos in a race is that you can often follow your competitors' daily progress as relayed by ham radio. You know that every day is a new race, and are more likely to rise from the warm bunk to shake out a reef.

The days in Cape Town were full, the time too short. I was busy on boat matters while others took time to make the climb up 3000-foot Table Mountain. I would save that for my next trip. We took advantage of the marine railway facility next to the club for a haulout. Slow days in the South Atlantic had left the amazing gooseneck barnacles around my rudder apparently thriving on bottom paint so poisonous that it has now been banned in the U.S. Tony Lush was certain these creatures were ingesting gelcoat on *Lady Pepperell* since they had turned a systemic resin-blue. I now installed the new and heavier spreaders sent by my sparmaker in response to my cries over ham radio. The inner forestay was reinforced by an aluminum weldment fitted under the deck. And, finally, I added plexiglass shields to my larger opening ports which would serve as storm shutters. These were to prove their worth a number of times.

In spite of excesses of food and drink the time in Cape Town was well spent. Many kindnesses are remembered. Will I ever return? Alas, probably not on my own boat.

NOON ON NOVEMBER 18 found *Mooneshine* at 39 degrees south, 20 degrees east, which is just east of Cape Agulhas, the southernmost point of Africa. The first of the "Great Capes" had been passed. One thinks this concept of the five Great Capes of the Southern Ocean may be just a fancy of the singlehanders, some of the "greats" being more geographical generality than noble promontory. Technically speaking, *Mooneshine* would short-circuit the system by aiming for the Bass Strait rather than sailing south of Tasmania, and thence north to Sydney. I doubt if I was thinking that far ahead on this day, or very realistically about the 130 degrees of longitude stretching between me and Sydney. It's easy to become parochial about oceans and forget that our Atlantic is about half the width of the Indian Ocean. David White's dictum on the OSTAR, "It's just a sprint," has a measure of truth. Here I was, timidly stepping into the Indian Ocean and not yet quite into the Roaring Forties. The rib cage was sore, and the No.1 yankee jib still in its bag below. But on this day I received a gift from the sea in the form of free miles from a beneficent current. We had covered 180 miles in the last 24 hours without corresponding effort on my part. The following day we seemed to have done even better, though clouds wiped off the noon sight. Argos position reports later showed *Mooneshine* covering more longitude than any other boat that day. If Argos reports this it must be so, I told *Mooneshine*. Perhaps the sea was feeling kindly in place of earlier rudeness. But we know the sea is as indifferent as the stars. This was the Southern Ocean at last, or the edge of it, and the westerlies. Late spring in our part of the Indian Ocean brought a steady march of depressions, the windshift northwesterly to west or southwest with frontal passage, and always the lingering squalls. Often signs of the next weather system would rise in the west before the last cluster of squalls had passed through to the east. Alistair Campbell's faithful net reached out to us well beyond the purview of his weather sources. You piece together a mental weather map from vague advisories in a vain exercise. Satellite imaging has improved greatly in recent years, but then I thought of weather forecasters as being like early cartographers who conceived "Terra Incognita" and proceded to bless it with reality on their maps. They were, of course, artists. Likewise, our weather prophets can be carried away by the logical curve and symmetry of isobars and fronts, thus bringing order to chaos, on paper. If this license is perpetrated on the middle of the Indian Ocean, who is there to care? The sailor knows this, but still bends over his radio straining for any scrap of weather news. Race strategy is the ostensible reason; anxiety may be a part. I will speak for myself here. Perhaps other sailors did not look over their shoulder for incoming cirrus clouds or that ominous halo on sun or moon as I did. I do know that more than one of our group was still somewhat awed by events of those first nights out of Cape Town. I overheard a radio conversation between Desmond Hampton and Tony Lush in this early period. Desmond said his tendency is to carry all the sail he can until something breaks; Tony said he holds back because he is afraid something will break. That described our position, I think, with thousands of miles lying ahead, and certain struggle to regain South Africa should that be necessary.

November 20. The weather uncertainties yesterday finally turned into a gale last night, a small one. I made a lot of extra work for myself by vacillating on the choice of sails and by poling out the small jib late yesterday. The result was I was up and mucking about on deck almost continuously until 0300 Cape Town time. Rigging the pole means stringing and restringing lines and handling the clumsy pole on a pitching deck. It will take a lot of persuasion for me to repeat that exercise soon again. Besides, the results weren't much better.

The barometer dropped fast in the early evening with more frequent patches of black squall with lightning. I should have put up the storm jib and retired, and next time I will. After stowing the pole I tried the small yankee alone. We seemed overpressed so I tried bare poles for about an hour. The rolling was just awful. Then it was back to the storm jib, sheeted flat, and the Aries to follow windshifts. After that I got some sleep, though wakened in one squall that must have driven the rail under. Next time I will follow the simpler routine for more sleep and probably more miles. I am still feeling my way into this ocean and am very conscious of not breaking anything. Radio this morning brings word that *Gladiator* and *Pentax* are returning to Cape Town with self-steering problems. That is a position I don't want to be in, and in fact I'm not sure I could sail back against wind and current.

Fantasy restarted yesterday from Cape Town and right into a gale. Weather broadcasts here are very sketchy. This particular cold front and gale were omitted from forecasts yesterday. Sunshine and clouds are mixed this afternoon but the appearance is generally cheerful. The wind is slow to abate and is still a good Force 7. We hold an easterly course with most waves sliding under the starboard quarter. Occasionally a breaking crest slams the hull and spray bursts over all.

November 21. It must be the periods of sun, but I am enjoying myself here today. I also brought out the new Atlantis foul-weather suit and feel well dressed. The wind continues at 25 to 35 knots with hard squalls, some of 50 knots and the water turns white; you sense the wind as something solid. Conscience kept waking me last night because I had only the storm jib up. Each time I woke, whining in the rigging told me I needn't go on deck. So, it was a good night.

After all this time and miles I am still fascinated by

the waves rolling up and sliding under the stern. Sometimes the crest will break just as we are on top. I have seen water spill into the cockpit from the side but not as yet over the stern. You would think that mass of water would destroy the Aries gear, but that seems as much at home here as the sea birds.

November 22. The rolling was bad last night. I slept in the aft cabin and three times was awakened by an alarming roar of seas breaking at the stern. Normally, it's quiet in my bunk, even cut off from the elements. I thought I must be doing something wrong—too little sail or wrong angle to the wind—you just can't tell in the dark. By daylight it seems the sea is especially irregular with waves coming from southwest and west, or northwest at the same time. But the barometer is rising and the wind definitely lighter as morning progresses. I now have the staysail up and am wondering what to do next.

It has turned into a quiet gray afternoon. The sea has subsided so that the motion is easy and we are running with three sails up. Prions, or ice birds, have gathered around us by the hundreds now as if we were a fishing boat or a garbage truck. These are small petrels delicately marked in blue-gray with an inverted W in white on their wings. I try to grasp their feeding habits as they do not alight on the water.

Mooneshine finally made it officially into the Roaring Forties some time in the following night. I remember it as a night of distressing lack of wind and horrible noises from sails and hardware as we backed and filled in the swell. I managed to tune it out and sleep. The radio was reporting general complaints among the fleet of a lack of wind, but *Gypsy Moth* and *Crédit Agricole* were already 10 degrees east of me and making a real race of it. Of course, we on *Mooneshine* were cheering on old *Gypsy Moth*. Desmond would be snapping at Philippe's heels right into Bass Strait. *Mooneshine* managed to hold second place in Class II with *Skoiern* well ahead and uncatchable. Meanwhile, *Nike II*, which had started a day late from Cape Town, was coming up fast. We were receiving position reports on most yachts via Argos and Alistair's transmission from Durban. I had daily conversation with Dick McBride, whose heavy boat must have been quite at home in this ocean. We started comparing bird notes with the help of my borrowed copy of W. B. Alexander's *"Birds of the Oceans."* I had been a seabird watcher from my early years, but it never was like this. Albatrosses, shearwaters, and petrels—they are your world, the same as the sea, the clouds, the sky. All one, it seems. And not a bad life for these birds, who must understand solitude, but report home once a year for family duties.

November 25. Low clouds and fog in the early morning made a gray Thanksgiving day, reminding me of many similar gray November days at home. I thought of the family gathered, hoping all is harmonious and their travels safe. The Thanksgiving holiday is a good concept. I salute the day and send greetings to all at home.

But progress is slow. No wind last night was followed by light headwinds today. I slept too well. Instead of following every little wind shift I dreamed I was a young man and preparing for a job interview at Sears-Roebuck. Where does all this crap come from?

The ocean is rather placid with a light but irregular swell. Weather information we get via ham radio is the best there is but is still very imprecise. A weather eye and the barometer are the best guides. The weather eye today sees only fog however. The wind has done a 360 in the last 12 hours.

November 26. There was fog all night but good progress with a moderate north wind. I reefed in the night to keep things in balance. By early morning light (0200 by Greenwich time, to which my clocks are set) the sea was unusually quiet and the boat's motion as smooth, say, as driving the New Jersey Turnpike. All this was a short-lived phenomenon as the wind was increasing and the barometer falling. Wind from the north meant a beam reach, certainly better than on the nose, but hard going when it reached 30 knots. I am still feeling my way in the business of matching sails to conditions and trying to understand the waves and how the boat handles them and vice versa.

Storm jib and storm trysail were driving too hard for the increasingly rough seas. I had to stow the trysail, getting wet in clumsy exertions. Beam seas to port made me nervous as the wind grew stronger through the afternoon. Then, for some reason the wind veered northeast before finally moving back to northwest and easing after dark to my great relief, if not joy. Tension builds in a gale from the noise and motion, and the uncertainty whether you are in charge. I was securing everything below for a rough night, including washing the pots because I wanted everything out of sight, when I felt the change. I am too old to dance but may have hopped a step or two right there in the galley.

Cheer returns with sunshine after a gale. It was glorious and typical, if there is such a thing, for the Roaring Forties. I looked to my comfort and had the cabin heater going. An occasional hard squall hit, lifting spray from the water and turning the sea white. I would take over the helm from Aries in the worst of these. The seas were large, but I was gaining confidence. *Mooneshine* and I were OK.

We were two weeks and 1750 miles out of Cape Town. My daily runs now were fairly good, though I wondered if I could have pressed harder. *Nike II* was ahead of me now; *Skoiern* was well in front and moving away. There was a common complaint among the fleet of self-steering woes, but my Aries and electronic pilot were healthy and performing well. I also thanked William Garden's big rudder. We sailed easily, often catching the big wave for a sweeping ride. There was always the odd wave to slap you around, slew the boat sideways, or put the rail under.

Isolation would have been complete if it weren't for radio. On the morning of November 28, I tuned to Alistair's net at 0630 as usual. Tony Lush was heard with a very poor contact. This was unusual because his SSB radio was not easily tuned to the 14-MHz ham frequency. In addition he had not been transmitting on the 2056 or 4143.6 KHz channels, where he had been a regular.

There was keel trouble on *Lady Pepperell;* he would turn back, perhaps to Durban. "No immediate danger," were among the few words Alistair could distinguish. There was also news from David White that he would not be restarting from Cape Town. The reason given was that the new autopilot shipped to him there was not working. Of the Americans, now only *Fantasy* and *Mooneshine* were still making a race of it. Paul Rodgers had already put back to Cape Town. *Cherchez la femme?* (Paul had spent time in Cape Town previously.)

The log entries for November 29 are brief:

0700. Lying ahull, trying to effect a rendezvous with *Lady Pepperell.*

1930. Raised staysail and reefed main and resumed course for Sydney. Tony has brought a bottle of Scotch with him.

I had tuned to the 0630 net that morning. This time Tony's transmission had been loud and clear on *Mooneshine.* It was the first time I was able to contact him directly since Cape Town. "How are you, Francis?" was his greeting, which I thought oddly generous under the circumstances, with his own prospects in jeopardy. I must have assured him I was well; it also appeared that *Mooneshine* was the closest to him among the BOC fleet. From positions given I thought I was about 50 miles downwind from *Lady Pepperell.* Tony's news that his keel was swinging through a 20-degree arc seemed to make his situation precarious. I told him I would lie ahull trying to hold my position while he thought over his options. In fact, I didn't think he had any option but to get off *Lady Pepperell,* and rather quickly he was back on the air. We would rendezvous.

Several things worked in our favor. Most important was radio contact. It was a tenuous link but worked for us that day. I believe that our proximity allowed ground wave propagation between us on 14 MHz. This frequency is used mainly for long-distance communication and depends on reflection from the ionized layers above. Tony's radio had not been working properly since Cape Town; we thought later that his radio ground system may have fallen victim to vigorous last-minute housecleaning there. We arranged a regular schedule and set about some serious navigation.

The second piece of luck was the weather, which continued to moderate and provided sun for my sextant. My part was to hold my position and relay it, with accuracy, I hoped, to Tony. It placed the larger burden on him of navigating his way down to me. He would be easing *Lady Pepperell* downwind, which he thought was feasible. Thus began a long day. Tension on *Mooneshine* was centered on the navigation; I had to be sure of my position. The navigation log shows sun lines following the sun in its arc through that day. Surprisingly to me, the intersection of these lines indicated *Mooneshine* holding close to her early morning position. What happened to drift from wind and current as I lay ahull? I never found out.

We also had the backup from the ham network—Rhode Island to Durban to David White on *Gladiator,* now in Cape Town—and we would be given updated Argos positions as they were received. This was a sporadic thing as the satellite made its pass, the signals processed, and then transmitted to Race Headquarters in Newport. In the afternoon new Argos positions came through from David. *Lady Pepperell*'s coordinates were reassuring. I thought *Mooneshine*'s Argos finding was 30 miles off, and chose to assume it was an earlier position that had not been updated. Still, it added to my disquiet. If I was nervous, how was Tony faring on his leaking vessel? On the radio he sounded cheerful and collected. Later, he admitted to barfing.

Lady Pepperell had taken an unladylike somersault-roll in the gale of two nights previous. Acceleration forces had done the damage to the keel support structure so that she was taking water, with the keel tenuously held in place only by the fiberglass skin. A side effect was damage to his sat-nav antenna, and he was not getting fixes by satellite. Fortunately, on this day he was able to make repairs and receive at least one fix. He had dug out his sextant, but to enter tables and do the plotting under the circumstances, and after a considerable period of neglect, would take a large measure of coolness. I'm sure Tony would have risen to the occasion—I'm not as certain I could.

The sun gradually disappeared into clouds in the west; there would be no sights beyond mid-afternoon. I went over my figures and periodically climbed the ratlines still tied into the port lower shrouds to scan the northwest horizon. I felt a terrible impatience, as the light would soon fade. Then I saw masts, nearly three miles off, and a little west of my anticipated point. I hurried to the radio—still the ham band because for unknown reason we were not making contact on VHF radio—and fired flares to help guide Tony in, or perhaps by way of celebration.

The lone sailor must be at his best when just that—alone. The sight of another boat can upset orderly process. In this case the captain of *Mooneshine* sat mesmerized watching the stately twin masts of *Lady Pepperell* gliding downwind and silhouetted against the gray western sky. Tony had just one sail partially rolled out from his foremast. The sea was a lifeless green with eight- to ten-foot swells, which were quite forgotten until the relative motion between our boats became all too obvious. Without VHF radio we hadn't planned the awkward business of relocating Tony. My thoughts had been totally absorbed with navigation and successful rendezvous; now euphoria was turning to stupor of inaction. The boats had to be kept apart because of danger to my rigging from Tony's masts. We would fix a long tether between us, and I dug into the cockpit locker for a light line which we managed to pass. Then I watched in horror and some fascination as *Lady Pepperell* swung nearly at a right angle and, like a dumb elephant, was about to back her rear into me. Now her outboard rudder crunched into my starboard quarter with a splintering of fiberglass (mostly hers). Had it been a few feet farther aft it would have nicely removed my Aries steering vane. Tony now improved matters by adjusting his steering and tying it off. A second line was passed, and I hauled over a mysterious bag of selected items. Almost before I realized what was happening, Tony was in the water between the boats with a line around his waist. I don't know how much help I was to him on his short journey because late in these proceedings I realized the boarding ladder had not been deployed. I was rummaging for it in the locker with one hand while the other was on Tony's tether. Now he was squeezing through my lifelines. I couldn't find my knife to cut away the remaining line to *Lady Pepperell,* then had trouble clearing and hoisting a headsail to get free. All told, a clumsy business.

But never mind, Tony was aboard, wet and just a little untidy. *Mooneshine* was ready, and we had plenty of stores to take us to Sydney. It was close to dark. I asked Tony if he wanted to watch over *Lady Pepperell* any longer, and he declined. I raised more sail, then retired to the cabin, where we opened the J & B. Half a bottle later we decided to hold the rest till Christmas eve. Celebrating Christmas in the Indian Ocean seemed like a good idea anyway, far from shopping malls.

> *December 1.* The barometer is high and unmoving. Six hours without wind and then very light, gradually backing northwest. A fairly good drying day and warm in the sun. I would say not much accomplished this day. We had a fine meal of rice, beans, ham, etc., plus wine. Tony tells me he never learned to swim.

Here the log for the voyage to Sydney ends. I was adjusting to a new life of civilized company. I had looked forward to a wide ocean of solitude, and Tony was sensitive to that, but to sail 4500 miles of a 27,000-mile race with a companion was rewarding also.

I first assumed that my race, at least for this leg, was over. I was no longer a solo sailor, but gradually it seemed reasonable that if I worked the boat as before with no assistance from my guest I might still qualify as a singlehander, and that is the way we proceeded, with the exception of some household matters. After only two of my meals Tony almost wordlessly took over in the galley at the dinner hour. Quality of life on *Mooneshine* improved perceptibly. I had the luxury of being the only singlehander who could look forward to be called in to dinner; gentle conversation was fostered. Wine was served. I conveyed some of this to the Race Committee in Sydney on arrival: "Having someone aboard with you changes the character of your race in that there is someone to share the anxieties and frustrations. You gain in companionship but lose the pleasure of solitude. I believe the net result is to detract slightly from the racing effort."

Tony had thrown remnants of life on board *Lady Pepperell* into the sailbag we had hauled between boats, revealing interesting priorities. There was his Argos transmitter—we had been instructed to guard these under pain of death—and *Mooneshine* henceforth would give off two beeps in a demanding test of system accuracy. Could it distinguish between foredeck and cockpit locker? There may have been a change of Helly-Hansen underwear, but he had no shoes. There were four books—three copies of Slocum's *"Sailing Alone Around the World,"* and Garrison Keillor's *"Happy To Be Here."* It was more notable for what didn't come: the mouth-watering electronics like sat-nav, weather fax, and the radios all went to the bottom. The life-size inflatable woman supplied to the expedition by the folks at WestPoint-Pepperell (whimsy, we suppose) was abandoned also. One thinks she might at least have been released into the environment where, with luck, she might have pleased some lonely fisherman.

Looking back over this affair, I have often wondered how it might have been accomplished in more seamanlike fashion, since there is seldom a chance to rehearse this sort of thing. Working VHF radio contact is certainly desirable, so you know each other's intentions. Each case has its unique circumstances and there can be few rules. Would it have been better for Tony to have deployed his emergency raft, which I then could have brought alongside *Mooneshine*? In rougher water the answer is definitely yes, but the transfer first into and then from the raft presents its own dangers. In our case the hazard was to have Tony in the water between two boats wallowing in swells and not under control. There are always tradeoffs. I am left with this reminder to myself: have those heaving lines ready, and the boarding ladder, also.

MOONESHINE was now 42 degrees south, 54 degrees, 30 minutes east. Sydney was still a very large ocean away, about 4500 miles. Tony was my guest, but this was no cruise ship, and the weather was inclement on most days. There were days at a time when he never ventured on deck—*Mooneshine* as gaol. He was a voracious reader and was going through my library at an alarming rate, several books a day. They would never hold out until Sydney this way. Luckily, there were the two thick volumes of Gibbon; I sensed him bogging down, finally, in the second volume. I was afraid the days would pass slowly for him—and there were to be 35 of them until Sydney.

Our entertainment center consisted of one Yaesue shortwave receiver, bulky and hard to tune, but reliable for the BBC and Radio Moscow, and sometimes our Armed Forces Radio Network, which at that time seemed to be somebody's unloved stepchild. The BBC was often excellent while Radio Moscow in those days would alternate the best in classical music with fearful missile rattling. On those occasions one was happy to be lost somewhere deep in the Indian Ocean. Later, as we approached Australia, famous cricket matches were on the air. Tony actually understands this game and labored for some hours to explain it to his dull-witted captain with limited success. I was becoming a vicarious world traveler through the shortwave AM broadcasts, creating images of nations from the air. I recall Australia as a land for the unashamed enjoyment of popular old favorites in music. They could only get away with that deep in the Southern Hemisphere, I thought. I can be an unsophisticate myself, and much later I became attached to an early morning show from Brazil, to catch the infectious high spirits of the announcer—not understanding a word—and the music. I kept that happy reminder of Brazil long after signals faded as *Mooneshine* moved into the North Atlantic.

Most small boats have at least a tape player and supply of favorite tapes. I had decided against this, calling it my experiment in sensory deprivation. The result was that more hours were spent at the shortwave dial, and the occasional success in searching out especially treasured music would become an event. I was content to leave it this way. The death of Arthur Rubinstein was marked while we were in the Indian Ocean with special broadcasts. It was an occasion for me also as this man had been a presence in my life for so many years. I remembered what he had said on his 85th birthday: "We lead short, horrible lives. No god, no religion ever told us what it's all about. All we know is what our senses tell us . . . Schumann . . . Brahms . . ." But he lived a long, extraordinary life and died at 95.

Except for special treatment at the dinner hour my daily routines were unchanged. There was the navigation, radio schedules, and the sailing, even racing. The radio log shows we were receiving Argos position reports most days, which were cause for celebration or the reverse depending on who was gaining or losing. My most immediate competitor through this period was Dick McBride. *City of Dunedin* was even with us but about 100 miles south. *Skoiern* was reported to have steering problems and considering diverting to Reunion, but Jacques decided to carry on, which he did with success, and much hand-steering, I assume. *Nike* was ahead but had disappeared from reports amid strange rumors of Cold War intrigue since Richard had absconded on *Nike* from behind the Iron Curtain to join this race. The truth was simpler: he was hand-steering his way to Fremantle—a long, long way—after losing use of his Volvo engine in a knockdown. *Nike* had only an electrically powered hydraulic autopilot, which then became useless.

Tony and I followed *Gypsy Moth* in her wild chase after

Crédit Agricole, cheering for Desmond, of course. They were one, then two time zones ahead of us. Neville Gossen on *Leda Pier One* was struggling with a broken headstay, again, and had worked as far south as 50 degrees in the vicinity of the Kerguelen Islands, which I imagined as perpetually bound in icy fog. That is close to the truth since isotherms are closely spaced here at this time of year. Neville, purposely or not, was near the track that would be followed by most boats in later BOC races. You now risk ice, fog, and headwinds in following a shorter, modified great-circle route to stay with the competition. That would not be in my future; I was not looking beyond the next gale, and these were coming with regularity. I recall six or seven in this ocean crossing, with no two alike. I never got used to them, but I did have my routines and confidence in my boat.

Now when I think of the Indian Ocean I think of ravines, for that is the lasting image I have of the waves. They would build quickly as the wind approached gale strength, and typically they were closely spaced and steep. Oceanographers speak of "fully developed" waves, assuming that time and fetch allow a mathematical spacing commensurate with wave height. In my experience, that happy state is rarely achieved in this ocean, which more often resembled the mathematics of chaos. There are good reasons for this. The most obvious one is that depressions tended, at least at that time of year, to move quickly. Backing winds as fronts pass leave conflicting wave trains, and seas that build quickly are known to be steep and more likely to break. Underlying swell is rarely absent; I suspect this is one reason wave size may increase more quickly than is typical for the North Atlantic as wind and sea surface interact. There is also the sweep of current and the complexities arising from it.

Artists would dispute me, but I say it is rare for the artist's eye to catch this chaos on canvas. A painter may capture the subtlest expression of the human face; the sea must be more complex. I never tired of watching this play of form, light, and color from my cockpit. The tumbling portion of a breaking wave will lunge forward at perhaps twice the speed of the wave itself. You sense the added destructive power when strong winds drive that breaking top. It can be pleasing to watch these waves break to port and starboard, sometimes with acres of white water. Your good luck is tested, as timing and position are all. Countless waves rise astern and pass under you with roller coaster effect. But you don't win every time. I tried to keep the stern square to potential breaking waves because a wave catching you under the quarter can easily toss your boat sideways into the trough with unpleasant consequence. At night and with waves coming from more than one direction you watch the masthead fly . . . and sleep. These were days when Aries was at risk. I could be in the cabin and hear the solid "k-chunk!" when tumbling water snapped the breakaway coupling to the servo oar. On several occasions this coupling and the plywood windvane itself were broken by the same wave. I would switch to the electronic pilot until repairs could be made to poor Aries. By the time we reached Sydney it was ready for professional help.

I'm sure we were spared the worst. Dick McBride, 100 miles south, must have been nearer the center of our most severe gale and was tumbled in white water. Guy Bernardin on *Ratso* was behind us and having trouble controlling his 38-foot boat, smallest in the fleet. "Piece of soap," he called it. He was in the cockpit when his boat went all the way over. He only saved himself by grabbing a running backstay. I heard Guy on the radio the next day—Guy who normally kept to himself when it came to radio. He said he would be sorry to get to Newport "because the big adventure will be over." And he meant it. But that was Guy, and he has gone on to bigger adventures since.

Now I discovered the source of water that soaked my radio the first night out. It was one of *Mooneshine*'s less successful reactions to a breaking wave. Tony and I were in the cabin as we were slammed into a trough on our port side. I watched sea water squirt through a dogged port light in spite of its protective shutter. At the same moment I was hit on the back of the head by my wretched radio direction finder as it flew from its bracket. This radio, now beyond repair, is not to be confused with the Japanese RDF previously mentioned.

Other more mysterious leaks, plus seawater forcing its way in the companionway hatch, were now impinging on quality of life on board, but the dinner hour was still observed. The aftermath of gale events was often glorious days of sunlit green and white water, large but more benign waves, some squalls, and always the marvelous birds. I was adding to my list of new birds. Typical daily runs of 160 or 170 miles under these conditions were good but not spectacular. *Mooneshine* was capable of impressive surfing down a wave face, but never made a record run through large seas.

When I read the accounts from other skippers I realized how the same weather system may have treated us to greater or less extremity depending on our location. Experience says if you go farther south you are likely to be treated with harder conditions. You are also likely to encounter headwinds as a depression passes to your north. Once at 50 degrees south, Neville Gossen was forced even farther, to 55 degrees south, and all the while nursing his broken headstay. His frustrations were on a biblical scale. And still he finished a creditable fourth, just nosing out Jacques de Roux at Sydney. After reading the stories of others I felt that luck had been with the crew of *Mooneshine*.

On December 19 we were still 1700 miles from Sydney. Then came the astounding word that *Gypsy Moth* was on the rocks of Gabo Island. Philippe heard this news as he crossed the finish line that morning. Desmond had just 250 miles to go after a magnificent chase for 6500 miles, but had been victim of a windshift as he lay down for a short nap after negotiating Bass Strait and the area of offshore oil rigs that follow. This rocky islet marks the southeast corner of Australia; *Gypsy Moth* was at rest almost at the base of the lighthouse there. Was this a tragic or a fitting end to Francis Chichester's last boat? In any case Desmond acquitted himself well under the most trying of circumstances. He is recorded on film at the site: "You take responsibility. It's the essence of singlehanding." I would not attempt to improve on that.

Holiday season was now approaching. Christmas in the Indian Ocean had been one of my fancies from the beginning. More accurately, we were in the Great Australian Bight and headed for Bass Strait. Our celebration took place on Christmas Eve and involved the bottle of J & B. There may have been some things of note discussed over the remains of that green container, but I don't recall them. What I do remember is a Christmas Day of perverse headwinds where the pilot chart shows zero possibility of east wind, and a hangover of considerable dimension. I have not looked kindly on this brand of Scotch since that day.

I struggled to make eastward progress all day against an unrelenting chop, trying different sail combinations and sheeting angles, to little avail. All this time we knew that boats to our west were gaining in fair winds. Philippe had been in Sydney for six days; we had 1000 miles to go. But sometimes a distance of 1000 miles by sailboat seems shorter than the same journey on land. It's a function of time, which at sea is measured in days rather than hours and minutes.

There is a note in the radio log for December 30 from Tony Lush to Don Downes of WestPoint-Pepperell: "Off Cape Otway; short of clothes; need shoes." We were about to enter Bass Strait and had begun to think of civilized custom. I remember a golden afternoon and sunlight on distant white buildings. King Island was well off to starboard and the southwest wind was going light. The sea was slight, as if we were on some inland body of water. The mountains of Tasmania were visible in the far distant south. I was frustrated by a light fog and almost imperceptible headwinds as night fell. We drifted north toward Port Phillip while I felt myself giving way to sleep; there are times when nothing else matters. Tony was sleeping, as usual. It was a night of fog and oblivion, a break in our race, almost a time out, although Yukoh and Guy were coming up fast.

I tacked in the early morning and worked slowly south while vague about our position, though it gradually cleared enough to get a noon sight. We were still south of Melbourne and making little easterly progress as fog settled in again with darkness. My immediate goal was Redondo Island, which guards the eastern exit of the strait. About midnight it cleared briefly, so that I was able to get a bearing on the light there and set a course. We moved silently east through quiet water, and Tony slept. At first light the dark mound of Redondo was a vague shape on the port bow; fog was lifting off the water to reveal a magical slice of this rock through purple light. I awakened Tony to behold this wonder.

Back at the Royal Cape Yacht Club we had held a sometimes heated discussion of whether the race should be routed south of Tasmania for safety reasons. I had voted for Bass Strait, and now we were to be rewarded as the many islands of the Kent and Furneaux Groups came in view. Our position for noon of January 1 was by visual bearings—a pleasing thing in itself. We had made only 100 miles since the previous noon, but now were moving easily and absorbing the sight of scattered islands, rounded humps of bare rock in a blue sea. In foul weather it could be a threatening sight, and one credits captains driving their unwieldy ships through here in the last century with no electronic aids. Four years later, the next generation of BOC sailors encountered some of their worst weather here. Speaking of unwieldy craft, Slocum had passed here in the *Spray* in December 1896 and had gammed with the keeper of the light on Wilson's Promontory, which we had just passed. One hazard he did not have to contend with was the oil rigs that now dot the shelf waters south of Victoria.

We had lost a day to light winds in the strait, but that was quickly forgotten as we left one ocean behind and broke into the Tasman Sea on a day that was turning blue and the sailing easy. We had left Dick McBride to the mercies of the Indian Ocean as he had elected to pass south of Tasmania, not a great idea as it turned out, when he encountered persistent light air. My job was to keep ahead of Guy, who had gained on us while we slept in the strait. It was now 200 miles to the turning point at Cape Howe, and thence 250 miles to Sydney, but the end of this leg seemed almost at hand.

It was a good run, oil rigs and all, to Cape Howe. Gabo Island Lighthouse was off in darkness to port as we sailed by at nearly eight knots the next evening. The sea was mildly rough with a southeast wind; lights of commercial vessels farther offshore would be keeping me awake while Gabo and the bones of *Gypsy Moth* were quickly left behind. I lacked local knowledge of currents off this coast, and was unsure whether to hug the shore or keep well off. My information came from Admiralty Sailing Directions wherein were dire weather advisories on "black north-easters" and "southerly busters," usually accompanied with upside-down warning signs such as rising barometer. But it was summer now, and so warm that Tony was a layabout in the cockpit, absorbing sun as if this were a Caribbean charter. We were close enough to examine details of headlands as they came up in turn. The oddly named Cook's Pigeon House is a prominent mountain here, actually a suggestive mound, with a knob on top. Could I have experienced a long-forgotten tingle as I explored this through binoculars? But now the wind was going light and threatening to come in on the nose. There were still 200 miles to go and work to be done.

The next day was spent on long and short tacks, some of them fruitless, it seemed. I blamed it on bad current; more likely it was poor sailing after several thousand miles of the Roaring Forties at my back. That night I made a long tack offshore, increasingly frustrated and unsure if we were making progress at all. I was in the cockpit all night, fretting and uncomfortable. Another tack westward in the early morning brought us close to shore in a dying wind. I was now on the air with Sydney Radio as we were to call certain numbers in Sydney with estimated time of arrival. It wasn't far now, but there was little wind and even that seemed to be leaving us. We were off Botany Bay, which despite its historic ring, is something of a disappointment. Captain Cook had explored this coast and somehow missed the infinitely more significant Sydney Heads and harbor complex 12 miles north. With almost no wind I despaired of reaching the Heads that afternoon. There was one more tack to the east; but what was that meandering gray line out there? It may have been only an illusion, but I thought *Mooneshine* was awfully reluctant to move through this unpleasant matter. Next time I will be quicker to recognize undertreated sewage. We were indeed close to civilization.

At this moment, out of blue sky and sun, came a "southerly buster." Buster would be exaggeration, but the 20 to 25 knots of south wind was a welcome gift. I called Sydney with the news and set an ETA. We were running easily but would harden up to enter the Heads; from there it was a beat to the finish line. A helicopter circled overhead now. I sought to make things easy for myself and pulled down the big genoa—we would do well with the reefed main and staysail. Tony was putting on a clean shirt as the red tile roofs of Sydney environs slid by. Small boats were emerging from the Heads and cut the water around us with their wakes. It was much ado about very little, but the happy crew of *Mooneshine* were not there to argue. After 6900 miles we were at the welcoming entrance to Sydney Harbour and would soon be amid shore-side pleasures of friends and food and drink. Now, with my shortened sail, it was easy to tack smartly to the finish in the fresh wind. We proceeded to the designated area where customs and immigration, and then quarantine officials came aboard in turn. I was greatly assisted here by Tony, who dealt with these gentlemen in the cabin while I managed the deck, jilling about on short tacks in lieu of anchoring, which is their normal procedure. Actually bringing anchor and rode on deck loomed as an impossible task for the captain just then. Officialdom was discharged, and our little parade proceeded the few miles up the harbor. It was a fine thing now to be secured alongside a police launch for a hands-off ride through the sights of Sydney Harbour, past the opera house, and under the famous bridge. We were going to Pier 1, just beyond the bridge, and many hands were there to help moor us bow-to at the dock and next to *Skoiern*. Nigel Rowe, in a burst of pent-up energy, had hired a band as part of the welcome, and we partook of champagne. All this production was for the second-place finisher in Class II, and sixth overall on this leg. But *Mooneshine* had been the first to finish by daylight, in business hours, which must have been the reason. *Mooneshine* was secured, Tony, my prisoner for 35 days was now released, and I was hugely pleased to be there.

Sydney

MOONESHINE WOULD HAVE 10 days of rest in Sydney. The restart had been set for January 16, as we were again to be hurried on our way. "Work expands to fill the time available for its completion," said Parkinson. But I would be hard pressed to accomplish my chores within the constraints of time allotted, and especially so as the Australians were then in the midst of their year-end holiday. I wish them luck with this charming and fun-loving custom in an increasingly competitive world. Life became a scramble as I tried to arrange boat projects and reached only telephone-answering services. Luckily, Arthur was on Christmas holiday and flew in to help. We stayed at the Kingsgate Hyatt through the great generosity of Tony's friends at WestPoint-Pepperell. I slipped into this life of comforts (especially the air-conditioning) all too readily. Arthur had brought his trumpet to keep abreast of lessons. We never heard what other guests may have thought of variations on "Carnival in Venice" filtering over the 12th floor. The hotel was our oasis and resting place between early-morning taxi rides to Pier 1 and the usually harried searches for material or services. These were exhilarating days, but we knew the Pacific Ocean and Cape Horn were waiting, and this lent an urgency to our labors.

Because of the politics of Australian yachting (about which I was happy to remain ignorant) our eccentric band was not welcome at any respectable yacht club in Sydney. The Australian Yachting Federation was frowning on the singlehanders at that time. Was it too dangerous, or the practitioners viewed as flawed persons? I never found out. It was through Neville Gossen that we were accommodated at Pier 1, a former ferry terminal now converted to restaurants and shops. All of this was fine with me. It was a lively place, and colorful; on some afternoons a folk singer was on the deck above: "Here's to you my rambling boy / May all your rambling bring you joy." I carried the sound into the Pacific with pleasure.

The ramblers in Class II were arriving—Guy, Yukoh, Dick McBride, and Dan Byrne, who had plowed steadily on after his restart from Cape Town. Somehow, I was always there to help Dan's wife, Pat, clear decks and stow sails on *Fantasy* upon Dan's arrivals—Pat wearing her signature high heels. Boating shoes were not for her.

Richard Konkolski was still making his way to Sydney after some fast remediation in Fremantle. He had installed a small generator that would provide power to his autopilot (and was to be nearly the death of him later on). He would face the unpleasant prospect of arriving at Sydney shortly after the rest of us had departed for Rio. I'm not sure I have seen a mop of red hair and overgrown bush of matching beard the equal of McBride's when he arrived. Dan Byrne now had the old salt's white beard, while I continued to scrape off my own growth once a week or so for the duration. Those occasions became little morale boosters.

As usual, time was short to complete work lists. Tony's sponsors donated a fine Sestrel steering compass to *Mooneshine,* with a card properly balanced for southern latitudes. It pleased me to add a touch of English class to my cockpit. I also had my salt-pocked sextant mirrors resilvered at the estimable Edwin Bowers & Son. If not for their efforts I might not have found Cape Horn. Similar work had been done back in Annapolis and had not lasted. Since this is the home of the U.S. Naval Academy it could be cause for alarm if the Navy was still serious about sextants.

All the way across the Indian Ocean I had dreamed of a sat-nav. Now my boosters in Annapolis prevailed on a West Coast manufacturer to lend one for the next two legs. Arthur helped with the installation, while I entertained visions of navigation from my bunk.

I was particularly grateful to Don McIntyre, the Australian

representative for Aries at that time, for his timely and economical labors on my damaged vane steerer. The oar shaft was straightened, new bearings installed, a renewed stock of wood windvanes procured—not an easy job in Sydney. On some of these he had painted in target bullseyes for the amusement of Argentine gunners should the Falklands war flare up again. Don's own target was a future BOC Race, and I was pleased to see him show up in Newport for the race in 1990. I also prevailed on a professional rigger to supplement my own inspections aloft and lead new messenger lines for spare halyards. My goal was always that elusive peace of mind at this halfway point of our journey.

Other vignettes of our stop in Sydney remain. I watched a technician bring a new sat-nav to Jacques' boat, which lay next to mine. From time to time waves would roll toward us from ferries plying the harbor. Now this man carefully balanced his expensive machine on Jacques' bow pulpit as he prepared to climb aboard, but at this moment waves arrived, there was a splash, and $4000 disappeared into the harbor. I watched the little saucer-shaped antenna float away. There is more than one way to ruin your day.

I searched out a doctor on arrival because I had developed salt-water pustules on my left hand, most likely a staph infection. This competent man proposed a cure by treating the whole body— I was given antibiotic cream for the hand and some bright red capsules for whatever. It must have been these pills that wiped out intestinal flora and brought on a violent bout of itching hemorrhoids. Here was the singlehander with one hand grabbing at his butt as he walked around Sydney. I tossed out the rest of the pills.

Arthur and I could have used a guide to culinary high spots in Sydney, for if there were any we never found them. As a general rule we avoided the establishments with elaborately folded napkins since this had an inverse effect on the food—one of life's lessons that I try to follow today. In defense of my shallow pockets we ate most often at McDonald's, but BOC came through handsomely with food stores. On the last day great supplies of excellent produce—cabbages, onions, carrots, tomatoes—were delivered to the dock. I had more than I could properly stow, as I found later.

Many displaced Poles were scattered around the globe at that time. Here was Zbigniew Pulchowski, whom I had last seen in Millbay Docks in 1976. I have a photo of his slender *Miranda* rafted there beside the callipygous *Mooneshine*. Richard Konkolski's *Nike I*—this *Nike* was barely 24 feet long, and Richard was to take her around the world later—was next to us also. There were parties and song on *Miranda* that year late into the night. The French had their women, the Poles their parties. And the English? Ziggy had business aloft there on several occasions. I would watch him don white boots and pull himself up unassisted. After the OSTAR he had wandered in *Miranda* across the Pacific and eventually to Sydney, a man without a country. Now he was making a life here with a new woman and a new language. He had a car, and I was looking for rubber strips, the better to weatherproof my hatch. We drove around the city, each more lost than the other, but finally landing in the right place through sheer willpower. It was a good afternoon.

The last afternoon at the dock I was aboard and busy with final details of my new compass installation. Philippe and a friend on *Crédit Agricole* were donning wet suits. Now I realized they were in the water alongside and offering to scrub the bottom of my boat among others. I have always thought of that as the spirit of this race. Philippe showed us the way around the world and also displayed a generosity extending down to this also-ran in Class II. Where else in the world of sailboat racing will one competitor go in the water to clean another's boat?

And now Yukoh gave one of his dock parties with seaweed specialties, some saki, an art show, and music . . .

Cape Horn

Sunday, January 16. Race start 1400 hours local. No problems.

A ND THAT COMPRISED the log this day. I believe I meant there were no dismastings or sinkings among our little group of 10 starters, actually nine because Guy was back at Pier 1 restringing his steering cables. (It is surprisingly easy to mislead new wire cables to your wheel and find the boat turning left when you meant to go right, etc.) My most vivid memory of this start was thinking I could move a great slab-sided sightseeing ferry out of my way by wild, perhaps uncouth gestures. I thought, incorrectly, that *Mooneshine* owned the Heads at that moment as I followed *Skoiern* out into the Tasman Sea. You tend to have a narrow view of the importance of your own affairs at the start of a race. That Sunday was something of a festival for Sydney with the annual ferry races and a multitude of sailboat races of their own in progress. Besides it was simply a great day to be out there, with sun on blue water and a good northeast breeze.

It had been festive at Pier 1 also, with decks on both upper levels crowded with spectators, flowers, and balloons. There was a band of kilted pipers on our floating dock while I was below trying to write last-minute postcards, and the whine of bagpipes gnawed at my stomach. Robin came by to offer farewells in turn.

Time hangs a little heavy; it is a relief finally to cast off. We would be towed the few miles through the harbor to the start area and had the help of deputized customs agents, actually local yachtsmen dressed in orange jumpsuits for the occasion. I was soothed to have their assistance with the line handling. These men had an official role, though I never figured out what that was; they had to be certain all these singlehanders truly sailed away.

I remembered all this when I passed through Sydney four years later, by air this time. It was May 1987, and going into the Australian winter. From curiosity I walked down to Pier 1. Where were all the people? Many shops inside had closed. It had the air of twilight and sadness; the crowded decks I remembered were now empty. I had the strong sense of the passing of time. Later BOC races have moved to more stylish venues in the harbor. On this trip I took a harbor ferry to Manly and walked the bluffs of North Head facing the Tasman Sea, but the Tasman was a quiet blue that day, giving away no secrets. The phone book gave away no secrets either, and I was unable to find Neville Gossen— Neville, who had sailed one and a half times around the world and endured much to complete our race.

Now we were safely in the Tasman Sea, *Skoiern* ahead, as usual. I had to look for a trial horse nearer my speed, and there was Dan Byrne conveniently to leeward. We were closely matched in the reaching breeze, which was of particular interest for me as a former Valiant owner. Later I reefed because *Mooneshine* didn't like too much angle of heel. Still, I couldn't shake Dan, and we went into the night all even. I would stay up all night if need be to settle this, but by midnight the wind had dropped to four knots, and I wasn't doing much better than two knots. By morning light Dan was gone, but where? The wind had shifted to southeast and freshened. It was a beat, and now Yukoh was two miles to windward. I spent most of this gray day watching *Koden* pointing higher and going faster than *Mooneshine*. It was a sign; I didn't know it then, but Yukoh had a plan. By nightfall he had escaped me, which was to be the story of this leg. I had gained a little time on him in the Indian Ocean after the first nights off the Cape of Good Hope when *Koden,* and Yukoh, too, had sustained some damage. In Sydney he had strengthened his "bergsprit"—to fend off bergs, he said, though we were never quite sure.

I think of the following day as a Tasman day, a gray Force 7 with Tasman waves—that is, steep lumps. Dan later said *Fantasy* sometimes preferred going through instead of over the lumps which is not usual behavior for the buoyant Valiant 40. I also recall this day with some pain for the paranoia experienced when I spied what I thought was a transverse crack in the mast just above the spreaders. I examined it with binoculars; nothing would do but that I haul myself up there to look. It turned out to be a streak of silicone. I was jumpy after talking with *Perseverance*: Richard Broadhead had found a misplaced clevis pin on his head-stay and asked about possible havens for repair in New Zealand. My chart revealed only a long, rugged lee shore in the event of westerly gales. Why the Tasman mystique? It's 1200 miles wide in reasonable latitudes. Maybe I had read too much of Chichester in *Gypsy Moth IV* and Robin Knox-Johnston's passage of the Foveaux Strait in *Suhaili*. But New Zealand's South Island extends its broken coastline southwest toward our route into the Pacific. I was anxious to move south and clear of land.

It was here that I received with great joy a few fixes from my newly installed sat-nav. If I got two in one day I felt wonderfully blessed. This mysterious box would lock on to satellites one after the other in order, and could tell me courses and distances on command, but had a menu of excuses why it couldn't produce a fix from a particular satellite's orbit. I tried various little improvements with the antenna arrangement without much result.

The two small island groups south of New Zealand have the unfortunate names of The Snares and The Traps. I proposed to keep clear of these and set my turning point at 48 degrees, 30 minutes south. On the 22nd a satellite fix showed 324 miles to go. Progress had been slow through irregular seas and 40-knot squalls. I heard New Zealanders on the radio apologizing for their summer weather—"Most unusual," they said, which I found hard to believe. We were receiving weather information from the tireless New Zealand ham operator, Matthew Johnson. "But what did he say?" we sometimes found ourselves asking after a long recitation. I have occasionally asked the same after listening to our very own NOAA weather. These prognostications extended well into the Pacific before mercifully fading away. Later, Race Headquarters back in Newport was able to tap into secretive U.S. government weather sources in the course of the Jacques de Roux rescue, but this was not ordinarily available to wandering yachtsmen. In later races the French, especially, have provided such enhanced weather routing for their yachts that it is now proposed to place restrictions on private weather sources.

When I reached the magic turning point south of Snares, where I would truly break into the Pacific, I was met only by the lightest of east winds. My depthsounder picked up the tip of banks there at 160 meters; boatspeed was zero, and I was surrounded by porpoises. It was at this very spot 15 years earlier that Bernard Moitessier's porpoises had led him from danger and pointed out his proper course. This was during the Golden Globe Race of 1968, wherein Robin Knox-Johnston had distinguished himself and Donald Crowhurst met his lonely end. Moitessier, of course, was famous for sailing on, and on, to Tahiti and a new love instead of to England where Françoise waited. His porpoises communicated; mine were simply bored. They knew I was a clod who no doubt would turn left at Cape Horn and sail home. I did not neglect to thank them when a breeze filled in from the south a few hours later. I was also enjoying the greenhouse effect of the sun through my main hatch.

This was deep in the Roaring Forties, but there followed six days of generally light winds from the westerly quadrants with a high barometer. This was summer, after all, but I was sure I had less wind than anybody else and daily runs were a disappointment. I passed between Bounty and Antipodes Islands about midnight January 28 as I slept. I had been navigating with special care that day as I thought of this as threading a needle. Actually, they are 100 miles apart, which shows how small dots of islands on an otherwise empty chart loom as unreasonable obstacles. There was now absolutely nothing between *Mooneshine* and Cape Horn. You sail without lights on the reasonable assumption there are no ships. This is not strictly true, but close enough. In the Indian

Ocean I had heard Yukoh on the air with Japanese tuna boats—not understanding a word, of course. But the following night I saw the hint of distant lights, and in early morning looked out to find a Japanese trawler crossing my bow less than a quarter-mile off. This was a rough, windswept waste, 2000 miles from the nearest land. What do we know about these men's lives? Perhaps we are incapable of caring, and invent gods to do this for us.

The next day we were in west longitude. I had crossed the International Date Line and had gained a day, or had I lost one? I read and reread Bowditch. It would have been simpler to leave the problem to my satellite navigator, but this device was keeping its own council just then. I wasn't the only one confused—two days later I overheard Guy on the radio: "What day is this?" True to his independent nature, Guy had rounded the North Cape of New Zealand to take his chances with anticipated lighter winds on a slightly more northerly route. In Sydney he had added 500 pounds of internal ballast to *Ratso* in the form of sandbags to improve stability. I also watched him add considerable ballast in the form of food, and I credited him with the finest appetite in the fleet.

At this time Yukoh was plunging south. I didn't realize his goal was 60 degrees south or even higher, and wouldn't have had the stomach to follow him. At 60 degrees latitude a degree of longitude is only 30 miles. He would be chewing into longitude but sailing into potential headwinds, cold, fog, and the threat of ice. *Mooneshine*'s track by contrast would have shown as nearly a straight line on a Mercator chart from the Snares to Cape Horn.

Mid-summer in the Southern Ocean—high pressure drifted slowly, slowly over me, the barometer falling only five millibars a day over four days. On the 31st I watched impressive frontal clouds pile up in the west and went to bed with my boots on; nothing happened. But easterly winds from 18 to 20 knots developed by mid-day as a trough settled in—for good, I thought, when the barometer was stuck on 995 millibars for two days with wretched progress. By February 3 the wind was veering toward southwest and increasing to 30 knots. Daily runs were stretching out to the 160 and 170 miles that I thought we deserved. Squalls were frequent, limiting sail. Most often I sailed with storm jib and double-reefed mainsail. New Zealand weather broadcasts had faded away; nothing was learned from the sat-nav. I tried my best to come up with a daily noon fix, though it was a game between clouds and sun. I tried to measure each day by miles run noon-to-noon so that it became a point of honor to be able to prick a noon position on my chart. I had one chart for this ocean, and it was basically a blank sheet between New Zealand and Chile, marked only by the meridians and parallels. With Moitessier in mind, I had brought a chart of French Polynesia, but put it aside this time. Four years later all my world charts went to the bottom with Dick Cross' *Air Force* on his short-lived venture in the second BOC Race.

By February 5 the barometer had been virtually stuck on 994 millibars for four days. Rain squalls with winds to 35 knots alternating with spectacular lighting effects through cloud breaks east and west made rough sailing, but it was seven-knot weather for *Mooneshine*. I was sorry to see the wind ease as it gradually moved to northwest the following day. But I could see heavy clouds rising in the west from a new front on the way. Late in the day a northwest wind built quickly to 25, then 40 knots. I was amazed to watch as gale waves formed almost as quickly. The barometer, which tells you what is happening, as if you didn't already know, had dropped five millibars. I ran off under storm jib with the windspeed hitting 50 knots. I should have adjusted Aries to steer us more directly downwind, that is, southeast, but I think I was suffering from some unreasonable perception that I wasn't ready to sail in the 50s, or was too bent on preserving my straight line to the Horn. About 0200 a wave hit us under that vulnerable port quarter, throwing *Mooneshine* hard into the trough on her starboard side. Sydney vegetables, and the carton of now overripe tomatoes, were spread through the cabin. There was a perfect arch of tomato pulp across my living room ceiling. The Aries vane had been broken and the dodger frame bent. With the dodger itself long since gone, I never found how the fixed frame was twisted.

Part of the morning was spent on the cleaning and sorting. Later I was in the cockpit watching ocean and birds when a wave came from behind and dropped into the cockpit, filling my boots. It seemed a sneak attack, considering the moderate wind and sunshine. I thought it odd that *Fantasy* and *City of Dunedin,* 200 miles behind me, had experienced none of this. It's no wonder our land-based forecasters were limited to generalities. I did not know that my quick gale was a developing storm that would engulf *Skoiern* and *Leda* that night, February 8.

It was disturbing to hear via New Zealand on the morning of the 9th that Jacques was in trouble. All we knew was that he had set off his Argos alarm that morning. Neville had not been heard from, though Argos showed him closest to Jacques and roughly 400 miles southeast of my position. I was uncertain and worried whether I should change course. For some reason my radio contacts were poor through this period, and I could not copy most of the ham radio schedules which were then set up. Matthew Johnson was on almost hourly, but I missed most of this. With *Leda* off the air, contact was established with *Perseverance,* which in itself was lucky because a variety of radio and electrical troubles had kept Richard silent for much of the two previous legs. In this way chance intervenes better than we know. Richard would turn his big boat around and sail the 300 miles southwest to *Skoiern,* though it was not known if Jacques was already in his raft. It was a 60-hour period of great stress for those directly involved. By contrast, on *Mooneshine* this was a day of high barometer and a breeze of 12 to 15 knots from the northwest. I did not know that Jacques was bailing for his life while I was secure, even comfortable in my floating home: "It's nearly cloudless and quite beautiful in the Southern Ocean today," I wrote in the log. No man is an island, entire of itself, said John Donne, but I was a (floating) island those days, minding my own ship.

My radio log for this period is a string of barely intelligible scrawlings, but on the morning of the 11th there are two lines:

1927 Z. *Skoiern* sighted. Dismasted and sinking.

2025 Z. Jacques is OK and on *Medina.*

Thus ended this remarkable rescue sequence in which I was a useless member of the radio audience. These were "real time" transmissions from *Perseverance* and were fine business, as the hams say, when received in my damp cabin. *Skoiern's* last positon was given as 55 degrees, 24 minutes south, 125 degrees, 20 minutes west. At noon that day *Mooneshine* was at 52 south, 129 west, about 250 miles to the northwest. *Leda* had been violently rolled in this storm, throwing Neville across his wide cabin and injuring his back. Later, in Rio, he showed me joinery broken by his head. His radio was out and the starboard chainplates had lifted, leaving a widening crack in the hull. He would attempt to sail *Leda* to Rio largely on port tack. With 4000 miles to go that would seem a daunting job for one man incommunicado, but Neville was in Rio when I got there.

With Jacques safely on board *Perseverance,* life resumed its disorderly routines on *Mooneshine.* I managed only one radio contact with Richard in the days that followed, but I hope I conveyed admiration for the job he did. I was attached to Richard for his shy ways. In Rio he told me of his visit to the yacht club nurse for aid with constipation. Since he was new to Rio and its water she naturally assumed his problem was the opposite and provided the usual tourista remedies. He was too shy to protest.

Thanks to a log format prescribed by Robin and supplied to us by the BOC, I have a rather thorough record of wind conditions, barometer, and my course and boatspeeds for this leg. This is just one account of a six-week period in mid-summer Pacific at 50 degrees south. A surprising thing to me as I look this over is that barometric pressure was often steady for days at a time. Pressure changes were typically gradual. I see double exclamation marks next to a set of entries showing a rise of one millibar in one or two hours. This is not to say that a lot of wind might not come with little discernible change in the barometer. Stable is the wrong word to describe it, but there had been only one gale so far, not counting those fragments of gale in the Tasman. You know the potential is there, though, and watch the barometer. I kept an eye on the western sky and looked at Cape Horn on my chart, not yet counting the days. On February 12 I had 2000 miles to go while averaging about 150 miles a day. There were exceptions on the low side: "Rain, gloom, and fog with very light winds." And also confusion: "Second day of fog, or is it the third?" I had brought out my light-weather sail inventory. I also see a cheery entry that *Fantasy* and *City of Dunedin* to my south had east-northeast winds at 25 knots. I was not above wishing a little adversity on my friends.

> *February 16.* Breaks in the clouds in late afternoon revealed blue sky of the most appealing shades I can recall—lucky for this log I am no poet!

And that is the truth. Most of us cannot express these scenes with words, and the world is spared. On this day Philippe was passing Cape Horn. I ventured to note in the log he was setting a pace that would be hard to beat in future races if the rules remained the same. I was safe in this because they changed the rules, raising class lengths to 60 feet and 50 feet. At the same time I was very wrong in that I didn't anticipate the rapid strides in design and technologies that have now resulted in those racing machines, the "BOC Boats," and their matching skippers.

At this point I had 1270 miles to go. That was the way I thought—as if the 2000 miles from Cape Horn to Rio didn't count. I wondered if, like Moitessier, I had been living under the stars too long. He thought he could predict gales by the nature of their twinkle. Was it the cosmic winds, or the Jet Stream? I wasn't sure. Had he been reading Yeats? "Him who trembles before the flame and the flood / And the winds that blow through the starry ways . . ." I had developed my own distrust of the stars, which I now fixed into Stokes Law: Bright stars appearing in an otherwise black night are a warning to get out there and shorten sail. A few years later the sailing vessel *Marques* went down in a violent squall north of Bermuda with loss of half the young crew. The oncoming watch had just noted *bright stars* overhead. There are other examples.

Two nights later: "Stars came out in full splendor. I immediately went on deck and pulled down the jib. Sure enough, we averaged seven knots under double-reefed main alone for the rest of the night, with a continual parade of squalls." The stars were not the only clue here, since the barometer had been sinking slowly over four days and was now at 989 millibars, which is low but not a scary low for this latitude. The following night there were heavy snow squalls. I tried to make the first snowball as we were plastered with fat flakes luminous under the deck light. I was now at 55 degrees south, 89 degrees west, with the course south of east. I wanted to reach Diego Ramirez, making my landfall on these small islands before turning northeast for the last 60 miles to Cape Horn. I was counting down the last miles—still measured in days—while the weather was hardening. On the afternoon of the 22nd, wind came in from the south at 40 to 50 knots. I thought the seas would build dangerously and was afraid I would have to run off. I was intent on holding my course because there was still southing to make. I sat in the cockpit for a long time, watching waves with my hands freezing in this wind off Antarctica. There was a difference; these seas were large but well spaced. Now a shackle holding the mainsheet tackle to the traveler sheared. I carried on with just the storm jib and was slow to jury-rig a substitute in a case of congealed will. There was gradual easing through the night as we made fair progress eastward and even a little to the south. Some sun the next afternoon encouraged me to think this weather system was clearing out. But not so. Strong gale winds set in again from the south and southwest at dark. I secured galley drawers with screws and stowed potential flying objects. There was acute awareness of heavy seas on the beam, unseen in the darkness. For a time I sat braced on the cabin sole—I wouldn't call it cowering, though it might have appeared so to a neutral observer. Thus I slogged through the night and the next day, taking time to write down a list of birds sighted—an eclectic list of seabirds, I thought, for any sailor from New Jersey:

Gray-headed Albatross	Schlegel's Petrel
Light-mantled Sooty Albatross	Cook's Petrel
Wandering Albatross	Dove Prion
White-chinned Petrel	Wilson's Storm Petrel
Sooty Shearwater	Black-bellied Storm Petrel
White-headed Petrel	Skua

On February 25 I was truly counting miles. I had penciled in both Diego Ramirez and Cape Horn on my plotting sheet, with anticipation building. It was continuously overcast, though I had confidence I knew where I was. We were sliding and rolling along in style with west winds of 20 to 30 knots. I was moved to record this scene of Cape Horn gray and crawled forward with Chris Knight's movie camera. Wedged at the bow, I filmed until the lens was hopelessly fuzzed by rain and spray. Then I turned a camera on myself with disastrous results. We would pass south of Diego Ramirez in the morning by my dead reckoning. The sat-nav slept and had produced nothing for several days.

Sunday, February 26. A long day, but ultimately the most rewarding of this voyage or even my life.

I have yet to improve on this day; the long tension, and finally, sudden fulfillment on attaining the goal of many miles, or years—Cape Horn. I awoke to rain, fog, and occasional snow with visibility a mile or less, but this had to be the day. With no sun for two days I had been keeping a dead reckoning track. At daylight I set a course of 50 degrees, still aiming for the islands. After three hours of nervous staring into fog it seemed wise to bear off and pass south. All this time I thought the depthsounder should easily find bottom—I had installed the instrument precisely for this time, in fact—but it showed nothing. Four more hours passed with nothing seen and no change in the thick weather. Surely we had passed the islands now; I turned northeast toward Cape Horn, thinking to gain the lee of Tierra del Fuego and losing hope of sighting anything. Surprise was total when the mists suddenly parted in late afternoon to reveal a high, dark island. I was five miles due south and close enough to see details of the rock. I don't know if excitement or confusion was the greater. What was I doing here, 20 miles ahead of my carefully kept DR position? I fumbled with camera and chart, not totally convinced this was the Horn until the familiar profile showed itself as we moved east.

There was a sudden voice on the VHF: "Welcome to Argentine Territorial Waters." We had been told of a possible Chilean boat, but no matter, here was a friendly Argentine captain offering assistance, which I declined with thanks. I watched this patrol craft move out from the shelter of the Wollaston Group. The international boundary between Chile and Argentina among these islands is somewhat moveable, I gathered, but my mind was overflowing with other thoughts just then. They accompanied me for about an hour as it was growing dark.

There is an immediate change when you pass the Horn. *Mooneshine* was running easily in nearly flat water with the Pacific swell suddenly absent. I felt the weight of accumulated anxieties carried for six weeks through the Southern Ocean drifting away, left behind with those swells. Whenever I experienced gales I knew that Nature, insensibly and without effort, could have produced much worse. You pass through these waters in a small boat with tacit permission of the winds. Now I was looking at my chart trying to identify islands to my left, and the massive teeth guarding Isla Deceit rose from the water like fearsome sentinels. I was almost sorry to leave this brooding place, thinking I would never return. I felt an urge to talk to someone and tried to call Dick McBride, but now the Kenwood refused, its transmit switch suddenly cranky from salt water. Never mind, there was a relaxed sense of accomplishment on *Mooneshine*. I believe the skipper took a little nip while watching the Horn Islands fade into darkness on the port quarter.

I was wonderfully rewarded to have seen Cape Horn, for it is a monumental rock, a physically satisfying terminus to the American continents. Beyond that it bears all the baggage and mystique of seamen's tales since Drake. Later, Guy was heard to say, "Now I can die happy; I have seen Cape Horn." There is truth in that. Among possible earthly rewards there are few I would trade for this day. Fortune had been with me also because later, when I retraced my course from Argos positions received the next day, it seemed I had passed north rather than south of the Diego Group, which spans about six miles north to south. Current had set me well to the northeast of my calculated track. I will never know how close I was to those fog-shrouded islands.

North to Rio de Janeiro

I WATCHED STATEN ISLAND slide by the next day as the wind went light, and a more jagged, unwelcoming profile I have never seen. This island is not to be confused with the jewel of the same name in New York Harbor, served by ferries from Manhattan. I was thankful for the Cape Horn current that was taking me clear to the east and aware of my exaggerated perception of rocks after weeks of empty ocean. The Sailing Directions added their alarming descriptions of tidal action. But all of this was just background to a day of gentle ease, even sunlight. A reaching breeze set in as I moved well clear of the threatened overfalls off Cabo San Juan, and the following day was spent in unbelievable comforts of a warm sun and absence of swell. I was in a new world already, with West Falkland just over the eastern horizon. There was the strange sight of two southbound cargo ships; one is curious of their destination and business here. I watched the small Magellan Diving Petrel, the strangest bird I have ever seen— it literally flies into and under the water, and emerges on the wing, like a submarine-launched missile. Evolution follows many paths, but one wishes these energetic creatures luck.

Two weeks pass quickly when alone on a small boat, but in that span I was trading the darker pleasures of Tierra del Fuego for the sun and warmth of sub-tropical Rio, and cannot say it wasn't welcome. March 1 found *Mooneshine* galloping north with north-northwest winds and clear of West Falkland. Dick McBride was nursing damaged headstays and made the unlucky choice based on expected weather to pass the Falklands eastabout. We had a regular radio net and on March 2 Richard was there, bright as usual, with one big difference—he was on the rocks near the southernmost point of East Falkland. It was a devastating surprise, but what can you possibly say that is helpful or of cheer to a man with his ship and prospects on the rocks? Richard had built his boat with his own hands with no clear long-term plan. When the BOC Race was announced he and his boat found their joint agenda. In the days that followed the contrast in our situations became more marked. On *Mooneshine* I had shed the Helly-Hansens and was soaking up sun as it grew warmer every day. Reports from the Falklands sounded dismal: "*City of Dunedin* lying on her side with waves washing over her" on March 4. "High on the beach . . . Haven't given up yet" on March 5. But the cold southwesterly gales kept coming. Once again I thought how hard it is to see ourselves in another's place. Our worlds were growing farther apart as I could not give up my easy warmth to put myself, even figuratively, on Richard's bleak ledge. A less determined skipper and any yacht other than the steel-hulled *City of Dunedin* would not have weathered this ordeal. The rest of us had been languishing in the easy pleasures of Rio for two weeks when word finally came that she was afloat at last, and that was with the gracious and massive help of the Royal Navy. Through this episode Richard left his mark on the map of the Falklands— "Dick's Bay" is now located on Craigylea Point, East Falkland.

I was making good daily runs; there are few complaints in the log for a change. *Crédit Agricole* crossed the finish line in Rio on March 5 while I was still 1180 miles out, too far to count the days, especially as we neared the latitudes of uncertain winds. Although this course led us 300 to 400 miles from the coastline, the usual absence of pronounced swell presented the illusion of the South American continent as a benevolent protection. I had read of the Pampero, but this was still summertime in the South Atlantic and I was sailing north. I considered it a small affront and unnecessary roughness when the wind came from the north-northeast at 30 knots on the night of the 7th. The sea was turned into a giant washboard, but the barometer yielded no clues. I tacked on imagined windshifts with small success. Later I found the day's run had not suffered as much as feared, since a favorable current had boosted me along just as it had made a mess of the ocean.

Nike II had become *Nike III* in ceremonies in Sydney—I believe Richard Konkolski, and *Nike,* symbolically, were becoming citizens of the West. After his delayed start from Sydney, he had made a prosperous run across the Pacific and passed Cape Horn a few hours behind me. I could not reasonably hope to keep up with the faster *Nike,* but we held a daily radio schedule comparing notes on weather and many things. Occasionally his weather seemed remarkably at variance with mine, though we were not far apart: "60 knots on the nose. Unbelievable!" Actually, I had thought the weather quite good. He told me how the generator installed in Fremantle had almost ended his voyage when the exhaust line parted. Like Admiral Byrd at Little America he was nearly eliminated by carbon monoxide. In Rio I saw the broken rod headstay which he had spliced using rusted bulldog clamps. *Nike* sailed all the way to Newport in this fashion, in what I saw as the tenacious make-do style of his Iron Curtain period. Sailing was not the way up and out of Czechoslovakia in those years as compared with, say, professional tennis.

Now I saw flying fish, the first in many miles. A small finch came aboard and accepted my offering of oatmeal. Again I worried—did he know his way? The nearest land was 400 miles to the west. Who cares for these small land-based lives so far from shore? Petrels and the Black-browed Albatross were here in abundance, but this is their home. Efforts at the shortwave radio that night brought a log entry: "From the chaos of the airways came Alfred Cortot playing Chopin's D-minor prelude . . . A thread of continuity in our civilization and a reminder of things past." I was recalling Hurd Hatfield and George Sanders in the 1940s movie "The Picture of Dorian Gray," and this dark tale told in D-minor. Thus the singlehander spends a quiet evening.

Light airs on the 9th were followed by the threat of gale the next afternoon. I sat in the cockpit as the wind increased wondering if it was the real thing. I should have known for the sky had turned brassy and pale toward the southwest. At midnight I had reduced sail to storm jib in a wretchedly bumpy ride while I debated my conscience over more sail. In morning light I could see the problem—the sea was best described as lumps rather than waves. The skies were relentlessly gloomy that day. I had escaped easily, but as I suspected, Dan Byrne behind me was directly in the gale's path and had taken a beating. His mainsail track was coming loose from the mast, which would add a fatigued air to *Fantasy* on Dan's arrival in Rio. I wasn't doing very well myself as I was beset by layer upon layer of heavy cloud. I thought I had worked with unusual diligence to keep us moving, but produced only 65 miles that day. Two ships were noted in the log, a startling reminder of civilization. I began to display navigation lights. Rio was now 430 miles ahead; I had logged 7800 miles since Sydney.

Now came three days of blessed tailwinds—patience rewarded by unexplained luck. I made a note in the log: "*Fantasy,* perhaps 250 miles south, reports a 20-mile day. My own luck holds, and I will have one of my best day's runs. So it goes, Dan." And so it does. It is common in ocean racing that a boat ahead catches the wind while those behind are shut out by shifting weather patterns. You can find the same concept in the Bible—though in a different context: "To him that hath, more also shall be given." I was also visually blessed: "There was a stupendous sunset display last evening. No camera could do it justice because it covered so much of the sky. Another image to store in my mental file."

At noon on March 16 I was sitting becalmed 17 miles from the finish. I had been sitting for seven hours, in fact. *Nike* had finished early that morning. "A cold beer today now seems remote," says the log. But I had forgotten the afternoon seabreeze that came to my rescue by mid-afternoon. I set my red and white spinnaker and aimed at the finish, reading and re-reading our finishing instructions and the warnings of rocky islets to avoid. A shoreside radio watch had been set to accommodate us and circumvent our language deficiencies. I wasn't sure that my radio contact had been truly established, but now a red and white towboat was approaching, and there was Barbara Lloyd, who had faithfully followed our race for *Cruising World* magazine. *Mooneshine* posed for pictures while I was overwhelmed by sights, all new to me, of the approaches to Rio Harbor. There were brightly painted and often overcrowded fishing boats and the familiar profile of Sugar Loaf Mountain; I saw curving white beaches and the green of tropical vegetation; and high above all the stern concrete Christ figure on Mount Corcovado surveyed a city of wealth and squalor. It was visual overload for one alone at sea for 60 days and 8200 miles.

I did have my cold beer, and another. Yukoh had beaten me by nearly three days, but I would think about that tomorrow.

Rio and Newport

OUR STAY IN Rio de Janeiro was a near month-long Brazilian holiday, since the start of the return to Newport was set for April 10. It was thought awkward if we should arrive too early in the slow New England spring. Since we were being hosted by the Yacht Club of Rio de Janeiro I don't think any of our ragged party objected. That we were accepted by the club at all was due to the early and diligent work of Jim Roos. No organized yacht racers had been welcome here since crewmembers from an earlier Whitbread Race had partied and danced into the swimming pool one evening. We would be accepted only on personal recognizance and assurance of decorous behavior. Since our group was now only nine this seemed a reasonable condition. A lapse was brought to my attention one day when Richard Broadhead and I were sitting with our butts parked on a second floor window ledge, insensitive to our spoiling the view from below. Many hours were spent on the elegant veranda which overlooked the harbor and which was conveniently close to the bar and an espresso bar which never closed. My language skills progressed sufficiently to order two glasses of draft beer or breakfast. Needless to say, time slipped away charmingly with the soft breezes. If there was work to be done, surely it could wait until tomorrow. Thus the sailor's work ethic was shown to be a fragile thing.

The club had access to a fleet of matched towboats. I learned early that these were fast and powerful when I accepted a tow through the harbor entrance that first afternoon. *Mooneshine* surged forward repeatedly on the incoming swell and then fell back heavily against the towline, threatening the bow chocks and pulpit. My wildest gestures were ignored by the launch driver, who seemed oblivious and intoxicated with diesel power. Yukoh had done worse upon his arrival three days before in a driving rainstorm. There was the language barrier as he was instructed to await the tow after finishing. Through misunderstanding, he attempted to enter on his own by radar and found himself on the rocks of Ilha da Lage, a low fortress, some say prison, which guards the harbor entrance. I wish I could say I had been at the club that night to witness his cheery arrival by launch. A welcoming party was followed by sober reflection and a salvage operation was mounted by Philippe, naturally, with the official backup of Admiral Roberto Monnerat, rear commodore of the club. Philippe organized the setting out of anchors, and *Koden Okera* was eased off its rocky ledge with the tide. The damage was not serious except to the pride of the singlehanders; this was the third of our number to find a resting place on the rocks.

I was gathering surface impressions of the pace of Brazilian life, and enjoying it. A doctor came to check my passport and papers but not until I had been there for two days. This kind man bent close to see my documents for he was quite blind. I loved the pell-mell anarchy on the wide boulevards as long as I didn't have to drive. One wondered why there weren't more accidents until later I discovered there were indeed terrible wrecks. We stayed in a small hotel fronting Copacabana beach. A few mornings I attempted a lame jog on the curving black and white tiles bordering the beach itself, though I was quickly drained of ambition by the hot sun. Besides, it was more profitable to observe the life around me. Rio citizens soak up a great deal of sun; this wide beach was a focus for life in its wonderful variety. I liked the easy thumbs-up greetings exchanged on the street. I was seeing a tiny part of a vast country and forming impressions, however myopic.

You accept hospitality it is impossible to repay. A day was spent among the islands of Baia da Ilha Grande at the invitation of Admiral Monnerat. We lunched and swam on idyllic white sand beaches amidst tropical vegetation. *City of Dunedin* still rested on the cold rocks of East Falkland, but we lay about as if in the original Garden. We spent nights of gluttony at various *churrascurias* where the object is to eat meat until you drop. There was an evening at the French consulate in a vast apartment overlooking Guanabara Bay attending a ceremony put on by the French Navy. Jacques de Roux by this time was back in France, but Richard Broadhead received the symbolic *Bouche de Fer* for his rescue, since Jacques was a former French Navy commander. A resplendent captain came to do the honors. It was a fine thing, and of course, we were well fed. I engaged the wife of the consul in conversation about her life and the many diplomatic stations they had seen. And the languages—the opportunity now to know some Portuguese. "Oh, why bother," she said. She was tired of the life.

Vaguely, we reminded ourselves of the work to be done. Neville Gossen, especially, needed some serious welding on *Leda*. We had watched his track by Argos moving eastward away from Rio when he should have been sailing west, not knowing he could sail his crippled boat only on port tack. He did well to arrive at all, and that was earlier on the same day as my finish. Guy had followed me by two days, and Dan Byrne finally arrived on the morning of the 23rd after experiencing maddening periods of no wind, alternating with thunderstorms in the final days. Some of us sought to improve this occasion in the very early morning by venturing out on the shining black water off Copacabana in search of *Fantasy*. The lighted statue of Christ looked down; there were a few dots of distant white light from boats on the water, but no Dan. At dawn we were out again and visually urged him on as he coaxed his boat away from rocks and to the finish in the near calm. Dan and *Fantasy* were both mighty tired, and back at the club I helped once more with sails and lines. I know the feeling—Tony was to do the same for me in Newport.

The smaller boats could take advantage of the club's travelift facilities for a haulout. I used this chance to clean the hull and do just enough wet sanding on the bottom to give me a psychological boost, if nothing else, since there was little more needing attention. *Voortrekker* was beside me, with her hull in the area of the keel showing the strain of years and many miles. Yukoh was busy now adding fairing to his plate keel in hopes of improving light-air performance. I, of course, was hoping for the opposite effect because I was playing catch up—Yukoh had a lead of two and a half days.

We had let time slip away; now it was growing short, but something had happened to the lift. There was trouble with clutch and brake on one of the motors and nothing could be done because this was the long Easter weekend. I fretted against local ways in vain, but with the weekend over, the lift suddenly became operable. I produced two bottles of whiskey (inexpensive) for the lift driver and was first back in the water with a day to spare. From time to time I would look in on *Nike* where Richard was rebuilding the Volvo engine that had been damaged many miles ago in the Indian Ocean. Now this engine was flat on its back amid an appalling clutter of black diesel parts spread throughout the cabin while Richard poured new bearings with the help of another Pole without a country. Luckily, Miki Konkolski wasn't there to see her former living quarters. Also, at this late date they were unloading a large quantity of superfluous items, even household goods from the old country, that were to be shipped to Rhode Island by container. *Nike* would show her speed on this leg, but it was too late for his overall class standing. Work continued late into the night before the start, but *Nike* was ready.

There was a final evening send-off at the club. We had accepted many favors from the people there; I can only hope they felt repaid in some way. We were towed to the start the next afternoon, past Yukoh's Ilha da Lage, past leaning Sugar Loaf, and out to the start area off Copacabana. This was an easy occasion of light winds, sunbathing spectators, and skippers pleased to be on the way home. There were no lumps in the stomach as in earlier starts. I concentrated on Yukoh this time, and worked to a small advantage shortly after the start, but somehow Dan Byrne had found more wind, and I had to watch that ample Valiant stern pull away. His big genoa was working better than mine, but I was busy trying to keep moving and lost track of the others as the tropical night fell. The next morning I was sailing rather ineffectively in choppy waters somewhere off Cabo Frio—not knowing where I was, or anyone else—but headed home.

The coast of Brazil trends gently north-northeast for 1200 miles from the strangely named Cabo Frio—Cape Frigid—before bearing sharply away to the west. Not surprisingly, we were greeted by uncertain north-northeast winds and also current flowing south along this coast. I would have ample time to appreciate sailing in the tropics once again. First, there was a frustrating day weathering Cabo de São Tomé. This gentle Cabo resisted my efforts with an opposing current and light air, and to make it seem slower, I thought I saw one of our number ahead of me and escaping. I finally took a long tack offshore, taking advantage of an opening betweeen two thunderstorms. By morning there were smooth seas, tradewind clouds, and plenty of sunshine—but no tradewinds. The ancient Sailing Directions advised going well east to find the southeast trades, but none of us took that very seriously. I was hoping that Yukoh might go out there and become lost, and for a little while he really was moving east. Yukoh was of special interest at this time because there was a small pot of gold waiting in Newport for the class winner.

It is hard to race desperately in the tropics. Progress was slow, but I was enjoying the life. *Mooneshine* had logged only 575 miles in the first five days. Sunsets were brief but spectacular; I had forgotten how clear the air and sharp the horizon could be. Rising stars might be mistaken for a ship on the horizon. By day I watched row upon row of clouds marching way beyond the visible horizon, perhaps 40 miles in all directions, and stretching perception of distance. I could be looking at 5000 square miles of sky. In southern latitudes the Milky Way is more clearly defined. I would watch it revolve overhead through the night. The Southern Cross is snared in the Milky Way and it, too, revolves. In the early morning hours it was upside down, reminding me of the "tail-less dancing kites" of my youth. Actually, the Southern Cross waves a vestigial tail. The truth is I was tired of Crux and eager for the first glimpse of Polaris. I could already see the Big Dipper, which looked enormous lying low on the northern horizon.

Despite my usual complaints in the log the daily runs were improving. I began to look toward the doldrums and expectations of picking up the Northeast Trades north of the Equator. By April 22 I had passed Recife and was nearing the point we could bear away to the northwest. I had been on the radio with Bertie Reed on *Voortrekker* who was some six degrees of latitude ahead. He had passed easily into the Northeast Trades with hardly a missed mile. A few days later when it became my turn, I wasn't quite so lucky. I was sensitive about this because I had worked out a lead of 180 miles over Yukoh in the days of light and uncertain headwinds. I knew it wasn't enough once we were in the steady tradewinds, where he would have boatspeed on me. I would enjoy the lead while I had it and kept busy racing. My navigation books are filled with make-work in this period—many sun sights by day, and stars and planets morning and evening. Canopus, Regulus, and Sirius are in there, just as if I had confidence in this uncertain business. If I had luck with the stars it was owing to easy conditions of the tropics. I was never motivated to shoot the stars in colder waters.

By April 27 I was five degrees north of the Equator and still grumbling, but the complaints had been heard. Daily runs were now stretching out and over the next week *Mooneshine* covered 1200 miles, probably her best ever, with a little help from ocean currents and northeast winds. The trouble with the tradewind belts is that once entered, they are so quickly transited and left behind. I'm not sure if the Sargasso Sea has defined boundaries, but it aptly describes that weed-infested body south of Bermuda with its light winds and thick bands of sargasso weed that somehow arrange themselves into endless windrows. It is no wonder that early navigators got out their sounding leads. No opportunity in nature is wasted or simple; gulfweed provides shelter or sustenance to a web of ocean life spreading over the Atlantic basin.

My course was taking me west of Bermuda, but the daily runs had dropped to 100 miles or less. Yukoh was now east of Bermuda and nearly even in miles from Newport. I would never make up the two and a half days I needed, but these were home waters for me. I had done the Bermuda-Newport run several times, and I was receiving the familiar Coast Guard weather broadcasts from Portsmouth, Virginia, with Gulf Stream coordinates. I scribbled forecasts into the radio log, always waiting for those final words: "Warnings for non-tropical disturbances . . . none." On May 14th I was slogging against a hard wind from the north-northwest and into a looping southerly meander of the Gulf Stream that was raising waves so steep that *Mooneshine* occasionally elected to butt through them. Water sluiced from the bow, over the cabin and into my cockpit. Why this, and so close to home? I struggled with the sextant and flying spray for longitude sights, hoping to find if I could tack to the west and escape this mess. It was the very worst of times with the sextant, the ones they don't discuss in celestial navigation courses. Then I watched as a large vessel moved east across my bow; this ship, the *Branco,* seemed serene and unmoved by the chaos around me. I resumed my private, wet bash, but felt a certain envy.

The next morning, May 15, I was becalmed. The log read 4907 miles run since Rio. Three hours later it showed 4909. Argos that morning reported *Mooneshine* with 227 miles to go; Yukoh at 229. With nothing better to do I got out the camera to record us going absolutely nowhere. I was now listening to the weather with extra interest. A front would pass and a low form on that front, possibly bringing northeast wind the next day, veering east at 25 to 40 knots; another forecast mentioned north winds. I had to position myself for a reach to the finish before it all went into the northwest and in my face. I had the advantage of familiarity with the area and also the language. Just this once I would put my trust in the weatherman and held to the east to take advantage of forecast winds.

In the gray first light of May 16 the wind was fresh from the northeast. So far, so good. A flock of tiny dovekies scattered away from the port bow in a blur of rapid wing beats, like mosquitos. A radio bearing put me on a line southwest of Nantucket Light buoy. I would be using RDF all the way in, but you have to be patient. Block Island has only 20-mile range while Brenton Tower itself was so weak as to be useless. The wind was strengthening with intermittent rain; it was going to be a long day—and no time to goof up. I had to allow for leeway, but how much? It would be a finish after dark; I brought the Honda generator to the cockpit, propping it against heel angle with one cushion while sheltering against rain and spray with a second. The Perkins engine starter had died a couple of days earlier, but I intended to arrive with proper navigation lights and would pump up the batteries. This wasn't Cape Horn—just Newport, but the anticipation was welling up. Friends, family, successful completion of the voyage, just tying the boat to a dock—simple things, but it all looked very good to me.

The weatherman had been exactly on target. By noon the wind was 30 to 35 knots. I had a beam reach with just the storm jib and reefed main but was sailing at seven knots. In mid-afternoon the wind reached 40 knots, still northeast. *Mooneshine* was now overpressed; I wasn't sure what to do and actually had my hand on the main halyard waiting for inspiration. The inspiration finally was that it would be really stupid to shorten sail now, practically under the lee of Martha's Vineyard. And not much later I thought I saw the low, dark outline of the Vineyard about five miles to starboard. I tried to call Goat Island but couldn't get through. Later, I heard them calling me but still couldn't make myself heard and could see a foul–up coming. I had passed my position to a ham operator early that morning. Now ham contacts were not possible because of the short range. I didn't realize that the good people from Goat Island were actually going out in this rotten night to see me over the line at Brenton Tower.

I have finished many races at Brenton Tower, but none can equal the special joy that night on *Mooneshine* upon sighting this rather weak flash. There was still light enough to distinguish the ungainly structure itself from four miles out. Rhode Island Sound now dealt a final indignity with a dollop of water squarely into my open hatch, almost the cruelest lump of the voyage, and not far from the spot where the New York Yacht Club was to lose the America's Cup to Australia later that summer. *Mooneshine* was aimed straight at the finish of her world adventure and crossed the line with hardly a hitch in the course. Several powerboats were there waiting in driving rain and cold; friends and family were on board, but I couldn't distinguish them in the dark or express gratitude. It was no place to show the appreciation I felt. I took half measures to get my boat under control, thinking mistakenly I would sail her in. I was standing on the plunging bow when a Coast Guard 41-footer came up expertly, offering a tow bridle. Everyone would be happy to get back to the Pub, obviously. Inside the harbor the tow was changed to an alongside format. Tony came aboard to assist with lines; I stood in the cockpit as if transfixed by the competent activity around me as we were secured at the Goat Island Marina. It was raining hard and blowing; fresh from the tropics, I thought it might snow. A small crowd was waiting at the gas dock for *Mooneshine* and her crew. It was one of those fleeting, special times. We hurried toward the warmth of the Pub.

June 7, 1983 marked the end of our BOC Race. Early that morning a tired *City of Dunedin* crossed the finish line at Brenton Tower, the tenth of our number to close the circle. Her port side was battered like an old ferry and her interior stained by Falkland tides. Richard had made a brief stop at Stanley for the most essential repairs followed by a short layover and restart from Rio de Janeiro, and finally the long haul north through the Atlantic. There remained only the last barbecue and party that evening under the Goat Island tent as fog drifted in. It was a celebration with some sadness as we knew it was time to go our separate ways, and that ours had been a unique race that could not be repeated.

Epilogue: Full Circle

YUKOH CROSSED the finish line the following morning; he was towed to the Goat Island dock and arrived with a smile that matched the sun of this bright northwest day. He had spent one more night at sea but had beaten me around the world by a cumulative 35 hours. Later, at the final awards, he would hoist high the pot of gold, actually a piece of negotiable paper, that was the prize for first in Class II. It was a sum that would have repaid my doubting banker but would be scorned by most professional athletes seen on TV these days. As in ancient Greek games and the America's Cup there was nothing left for second-place finishers. It is useful to reflect that although most of our days are spent sweating, scheming, or enduring for the sake of money, there are other times in our short lives when, even briefly, you may see with a certain clarity things beyond money. Recent winners in BOC races have pocketed more; there have even been leftovers for second- and third-place finishers. The winner still takes home considerably less than your local Congressman for his year's labor, to be sure, but who will have the greater sense of accomplishment at the end of that year? I have watched the finishers of the later BOC races and seen the contagious glow that goes beyond their tans, and thought of Joshua Slocum on his return, writing of those who said, "Why, Slocum is young again!" I don't recall any such remarks on the skipper of *Mooneshine*, however.

Four of us in that first race were in our fifties—Neville, Dan,

Yukoh, and Stokes—and none would admit that age had diminished our effort. When Richard Giordano, chief executive of the BOC Group, announced to applause at the final dinner that there was to be a race sequel in 1986, all but one of these elders vowed to be at the starting line. Dan Byrne launched a magnificent effort to build a 60-footer to be called *Spirit of Los Angeles*. I reminded him of another of his vows, which I had recorded in my radio log: *Never Again!* That was Dan's reply to a ham radio query after a bad night off Cape Town, though he subsequently denied it. Neville's efforts fell victim to the Australian economy; *Leda* was sold and later graced Newport waters with freshly painted hull and spars. Yukoh succeeded in some shorter races, and then brought a new 50-footer of his own design (which he called the "Yukoh 60") to Newport for the start of the third BOC Challenge in 1990.

The laggard elder in these efforts was Stokes. At 57 I had just experienced what I considered was the best year of my life, and that was so, except that you must not only look back—this present year, whatever that is, must be your best. But I could see the changes coming, and the need for a sponsor with all that entails. You go with the times, and it was time for me to bow out. *Mooneshine* was sold, rendered obsolete by rule changes anyway. Later, I bought a J/35 sloop, which became *Sparrow*, for one more transatlantic race, as if in an effort to ease out of the life by stages. I am not sure that my body has forgiven me for that one, but so be it. Others are made of tougher stuff and come back time after time.

These changes were no more plainly seen than on the misty evening in August 1986 when Philippe Jeantot arrived from France in the new *Crédit Agricole*. The tide was high as Philippe brought his vessel to the dock at Goat Island, making her powerful hull loom even larger. Maximum length for Class I had been increased to 60 feet, in line with the new OSTAR rule, but these were big 60-footers as designers worked to cram in maximum speed and power. It was assumed that single manpower would meet the challenge of these boats, and that has been the case: with some notable exceptions, the skippers are younger now, or so they appear to me. I have long thought of the OSTAR-style of handicapping yachts by overall length alone as the definitive racing rule for distance events; i.e. your goal is to reach home first, but you can't win if you don't finish, and that is through everything the wind and sea may cast in your way. This concept of the open class must be valid, to judge by changes evident in BOC yachts in just eight years, and in their performance. Recent winning boats were averaging 10 knots through the long Southern Ocean legs with frequent 300-mile days.

In 1982 *Crédit Agricole* was the only boat to employ a water-ballast system wherein special tanks port and starboard can be filled with seawater as conditions warrant. The effect is the same as having a beefy crew sit on the rail to keep your boat upright while carrying more sail, but with the enormous advantage that this is a crew you dump overboard when not needed, and their noisome presence is avoided at all times. The concept was not new in 1982, but with Philippe's success it was quickly adopted by shorthanded sailors everywhere. The BOC Race Committee has placed a limit of 10 degrees static heel at the dock with maximum ballast loaded, and with this reasonable restriction, water ballast does not introduce undue risks. Your lead keel system is still there and doing its job. *Sparrow* performed admirably with her modest water-ballast arrangement, and I would go further and recommend it in many cruising situations where a more upright ride and smoother motion are always welcome.

Other common characteristics of the later BOC racers have been the nearly plumb bow for maximum waterline length, and a broad transom with flat run aft for best off-wind speed. Some have twin rudders for control; Warren Luhrs has employed a horizontally pivoting rudder for fullest bite while heeled. Roller-furling headsails have proven themselves on the big boats and are nearly universally used. Asymmetrical spinnakers (variations of which used to be called cruising spinnakers) are increasingly used in place of regular spinnakers because they are effective in light-air reaching, and also because they are simpler to handle, with or without a pole. The experimentation with hulls and rig is ongoing as new materials such as carbon fiber and the various composites become routine construction method with some designers and builders. Lighter and stronger is the goal as in aerospace; we may have even learned something from the millions spent on the America's Cup.

In 1990 we saw a number of extraordinarily wide hulls, i.e. 20-foot-plus maximum beam on a 60-foot hull. Waterline beam was considerably narrower, giving them a skimming dish appearance and arousing fears for their ultimate stability. These yachts all did well, with the exception of John Martin's *Allied Bank,* which had the bad luck to strike ice deep in the Pacific Ocean and was subsequently abandoned when it seemed in danger of breaking up. Martin was plucked from his liferaft in horrendous conditions by countryman Bertie Reed, making it an all-South African affair, and illustrating once more the interdependence of the racers in those waters. But some boats of comparatively narrow beam also did well, and so the debate continues and probably will never be truly answered. I have marveled at the varied configuration of seabirds in adaptation to their life—and how they float perfectly on their lines when at rest. It used to sound wise to say that moderation in all design parameters made for a good sea boat, particularly one headed for the deep Southern Ocean. This good boat in the traditional sense probably will not be the one to win the race these days, however. And the word "seakindly" will not be heard around the BOC docks.

In what might be called the Jacques de Roux Rule, watertight compartments were required for the BOC beginning in 1986. Jacques' aluminum hull had been holed as he tried to free his fallen rig in the Pacific in 1983. Then, wet and exhausted, he had bailed for his life for 60 hours until rescued by Richard Broadhead. It seemed logical that with proper flotation he might have awaited rescue in relative comfort. These designated compartments must be so located forward and aft that, in theory, your boat will float with any one section flooded, and some have gone further and added extra bulkheads. It has proven difficult in practice to bulkhead stock boats effectively, and thus another hurdle is in place for would-be entrants. And even with these precautions, it is easier to recall vessels lost in spite of them, beginning with the

Titanic, than those saved. Dick Cross' *Air Force* struck an unknown object in 1986 and went down; later, Guy Bernardin's 60-foot BOC yacht, *Biscuits Lu,* was lost off Cape Horn in another case of an aluminum hull being punctured by a fallen mast. Guy had attempted a solo record from New York to San Francisco to better the 89 days set by the clipper ship *Flying Cloud* in 1852. He was picked up from his emergency raft thanks to modern electronics, leaving the way open for Warren Luhrs and his crew of two in *Thursday's Child,* who set their own record of 81 days in 1989. This has since been eclipsed , and the quest goes on. One is inclined to think of another challenge for our times: Build a true clipper ship and sail that around the Horn. Part of your crew might be layabouts dragged from the Marina Pub.

Philippe Jeantot was first again in the 1986-87 race. He had run the course in 134 days and had cut nearly 25 days from his previous time. What was to be done now? A new race, of course, and he set about organizing the solo, *non-stop* event that became known as the Globe Challenge and later as the Vendée Globe Challenge. Comparing this grueling event with the BOC Race and its three intermediate stops makes the latter seem pleasant indeed, but veteran racers, led by the French, took on the job. Titouan Lamazou won the first race in 109 days, at an average of nearly 9.5 knots over the 24,900 miles. Other BOC veterans took part besides Philippe: Bertie Reed, Guy, and Mike Plant. Except for Guy, these men were back in Newport by the fall of 1990 for the start of the BOC Race and yet another solo circumnavigation.

Mike Plant's story is now familiar to many, even in a nation that assumes that any real sport must involve a ball and slow-motion replays. I first met Mike in 1986, when he had set himself the task of building a 50-foot racer to enter the BOC that year. With little or no corporate sponsorship at that point, he was doing most of the work himself, and resin fumes had made him ill. But he persevered and went on to win Class II, arriving back in Newport to a big welcome in May, 1987—America's first round-the-world winner. It had not been easy, and had included a capsize in the Indian Ocean. By the fall of 1992 Mike had already made three solo voyages around the world, and was on his way across the Atlantic to his fourth, the Vendée Globe Challenge, leaving from Les Sables d'Olonne on the Bay of Biscay, when he was lost. I like to believe that he found respite and pleasure in being once more at sea and alone after all the shoreside pressures before he left, although the October Atlantic is not likely to give one much rest.

> *A lonely impulse of delight*
> *Drove to this tumult in the clouds.*
> *I balanced all, brought all to mind,*
> *The years to come seemed waste of breath,*
> *A waste of breath the years behind*
> *In balance with this life, this death.*

Thus Yeats imagined his "Irish Airman." Perhaps Moitessier alone among solo sailors would admit to the poet's license in this manner. Most grunt and go about their business, but with the implied understanding that each is driven in his way and for his own reasons. One definition of wisdom might be knowing when to accept with grace what lands on your plate. For some reason, Mike's plate overflowed.

Would he have approved the costly and probably futile effort to locate him? Most of us don't have an honest opinion of our own reaction until the time we find ourselves in the same straits. It probably doesn't matter, because this is what we do when someone who has inspired imaginations is lost. We launch these search efforts as much for ourselves as for the missing. Yes, he should have registered his special locator beacon, and it should have been mounted so as to float free and give a continuous signal. These were among a myriad of projects left to complete during final preparations in France. That is the way it often is, and we are left to wonder for ourselves when reaching becomes over-reaching, and about the fine differences between familiarity and overconfidence. It seems most likely that the sudden, catastrophic keel failure would have given him little chance in any case.

It is always awkward when we sailors, who think of ourselves as exemplifying independence and self-reliance, have to call on others for help. And especially so if we are calling on others to place themselves at risk on our behalf. I have had my own pretentions to personal responsibility, but there have been strings attached, except in my earlier voyages, in the form of radio and Argos. Now new possibilities in instant communication via satellite links are being tested that will be used in future races—the space and computer ages taking aim on the lone sailor; gentle Peter Dunning in the unlikely role of Big Brother. When Robin Knox-Johnston wrote the story of his 1968 circumnavigation he called it *"A World of My Own,"* and it certainly was. The intervening years have wrought these amazing changes which we call progress. But the new modes of communication, combined with GPS navigation, become a natural ingredient when you have specially bred yachts with their competitive skippers and sponsorship out there in a wild scramble to win. This is the logical future in races like the BOC Challenge, the Vendée Globe Challenge, and the Whitbread Race. The ham radio links will still be there as backup channels and human contact; otherwise, you may be looking at your computer screen.

A successful related aspect of the BOC has been the Student Ocean Challenge, wherein classrooms around the country have followed the race or "adopted" skippers; the students are encouraged to learn some geography, or think of wider horizons. And who knows what idle sparks might have found their mark? When I was very young I would reenact shipwreck with small boat models or exhibit other rebellious behavior which some might say I returned to in later life. This marginal activity must have been inspired by books; future sparks may come via satellite with equally unpredictable result.

Safety also is incrementally promoted with every advance in electronics. The Argos system and the 406-MHz locator beacons have come to the aid of many a seafaring wretch who probably doesn't have a clue how they work or what holds those satellites up. These have been important in keeping the sport relatively safe despite a laundry list of potential mishaps and the unexpected that may not yield to instant communications. The loss of Jacques de

Roux in 1987 was such a case, when he simply disappeared from *Skoiern IV* off Australia, just one day short of rest in Sydney.

Jacques had returned to Newport in 1986 with a new 50-foot yacht; he was there to finish the job he had left incomplete four years before. As always, Jacques and his boat were organized and immaculate, showing the personal discipline that had carried him through his brush with death in the Pacific. He was leading Class II when he was lost, but must have been extremely fatigued in those final miles after severe knockdowns and loss of self-steering in the Indian Ocean. It is assumed he went on deck to attend to something minor since his foul-weather gear and safety harness were left in the cabin. His death was especially ironic and remains a mystery covered over by the sea.

In this way accidents can happen to the very best, and I think of Rob James, the supremely experienced and skilled ocean sailor who was lost from a trimaran while entering Salcombe Harbor near Plymouth, and Alain Colas, lost during the Route du Rhum race in 1978. These are deaths that serve to keep the rest of us humble.

Yukoh Tada became my ham radio partner as we moved down the Atlantic in 1982. In the course of that race his English improved far more than my Japanese. If my instructions on baking bread were unsuccessful, neither did I improve my diet with rice and certain morsels scavenged from the sea. Yukoh, who called himself the "Tokyo taxi driver," arrived in Newport in 1982 with his paints, saxophone, Buddhist priest, and laughter. There was his early kamikaze training—"not so good!"—and the hand crippled by an incendiary. He did not join the restart from Sydney in 1991 after a bad crossing of the Indian Ocean and disappointment with his boat. Despondency led to suicide, leaving us to wonder at darker mysteries of the human spirit. One respects Yukoh, who grasped life's highs and lows better than most, and left his unique memory with fellow racers.

In the course of sending us away in 1982, Robin had said his only regret was not to be sailing as one of us. At the time I thought this was rhetorical flourish meant to encourage our weaker hearts. After all, what did this experienced sailor, author, and Commander of the Order of the British Empire have yet to prove? Nothing, except that he loved the oceans—and he has continued sailing, sometimes in racing catamarans and sometimes pushing old *Suhaili* slightly beyond her limits. Recently he teamed up with Peter Blake, the Whitbread-winning New Zealander, as co-skipper aboard the 85-foot catamaran, *Enza New Zealand.* They were joining the wild quest for the *Trophée Jules Verne,* to be the first yacht to sail "around the world in 80 days." They were 26 days and 9000 miles into the course, on schedule, when a crash with a wave or with an object in the black Southern Ocean night opened one hull and cracked both centerboard trunks, forcing a lame return to Africa. A few days earlier the 89-foot French entry, *Charal,* skippered by Olivier de Kersauson, met a similar fate and was also sailing slowly back to Cape Town. These craft are like giant, high speed playpens; they may fracture themselves but are reluctant to sink. (Olivier is one of the middle-aged men of the sea now, but I picture him boiling past *Mooneshine* in *Kriter VI* at the start of the 1980 OSTAR, which seems such a long time ago.)

Bruno Peyron and his crew in *Commodore Explorer* had better luck, crossing the imaginary finish line in the English Channel in 79 days, with just hours to spare, like Phileas Fogg. Robin Knox-Johnston and Peter Blake tried again in 1994 and broke the record by approximately four days, sailing around the world non-stop in 75 days. So now the globe has been sailed in under 80 days; the world shrugs, and we move on to the next challenge. Chichester was right: it's the effort that will be remembered; success itself may be short-lived as others take aim.

Whatever it is that drives the men offshore also drives women. Florence Arthaud, the French "Superwoman des Mers," persisted after her earlier disappointments and won the Route du Rhum in 1990. She has also held the West-East Atlantic multi-hull record. In 1990 Isabelle Autissier sailed the 60-foot ketch, *Ecureuil-Poitou-Charentes* to seventh place in the BOC despite a dismasting off Australia, and became the first woman to complete a solo race around the world. She entered Sydney Harbour with spinnaker flying from the still-standing mizzen mast and to a tremendous welcome, which must be a good argument for sailing a ketch. I remember *Ecureuil* as a slender 60-footer with virtually no protection in the cockpit for the skipper.

The major round-the-world races now follow one another in breathless succession. The Vendée has fueled tighter competition with new designs, better equipment and strategies that show up in the next BOC Challenge, and vice versa. In this way we have come an amazing distance in a few years with the magic mix of human creativity and money. You could see it as a mini-Renaissance in sailing, with a variety of technologies coming together just as the Southern Oceans were perceived as a vacuum by singlehanders who rushed to fill the void. Frontiers are scarce in this modern world.

I always enjoyed the rationale for singlehanding as the kind of sailing you could enter at almost any level, choosing the style that suits your means and your goals. That is no longer the case in the world races, where it takes a major commitment just to get to the starting line. These may be endurance contests of a peculiar sort, but they have quickly become races start to finish, where equipment, preparation, and planning become more exacting with every race. That is the way of life at the top for the world sailor, provided you think of being wet, freezing, sometimes battered, and occasionally frightened as any life at all. But when they return you will see that the life must be agreeable afterall; you may even envy them. I have seen the same sense of accomplishment in the faces of sailors returning from Bermuda. You set your own goals, and it is all relative.

I once won the Ancient Mariner award in the Bermuda One-Two, and that was some time ago. That year it was a bell that tolled, and it was awarded to the most elderly duo on the double-handed return. Yet you don't have to be that ancient to have sailed through the changes in ocean racing between Robin's 312-day voyage in the Golden Globe of 1968 and the *Trophée Jules Verne*. It would have taken a science-fiction view in 1968 to guess at developments of the next 25 years. You cannot look ahead with any assurance; we may tire of pushing ourselves around the world under sail and look for other goals. Progress does not like a straight path.

These may not be the best of times; you may think a country that requires warning labels on beer cans has seen its noblest days. Some would like to see us licensed so we can be removed from the water if we don't heed that label. The Coast Guard is hard pressed to carry out a social and environmental agenda along with its more traditional roles. (Do they realize that some of our most advanced racing craft have eschewed the MSD in favor of the primitive bucket?) You dwell on things of this nature at your peril—it may drive you off the water; or you may dream seriously of the freedom farther offshore. My most successful dreaming has involved oceans, and it led first to England and eventually around the world.

I have grumbled and protested in my time, but the world tires of cranky Age and is happy to move on. I am grateful to Francis Chichester, the greatest complainer of them all, for he showed the way into the Southern Ocean in small boats. Now I think of the 40s and 50s in southern latitudes as an enduring frontier, a special "last place" where man goes infrequently and leaves no tracks. You watch your vessel carve endless links of foam wake through dark seas, only to see them swallowed by the next wave. These are the most beautiful oceans on Earth; the loneliness will always draw a few singlehanders to take their chances among the whorls of depressions that dance around Antarctica. A sailor on his small boat feels vulnerable, perhaps like a solitary hunter in an empty landscape eons ago. There is wisdom in the physical reality of it; you know beauty and harshness go together; that the inscrutable albatross and the mollymawks may have your eyes before you sink if they find you struggling in the water; and that this body, like it or not, is our bond with Nature.

APPENDIX

VALIANT 40
Designer: Robert Perry

LOA	39'10"	Sail Area:
LWL	34'0"	100% foretriangle 761 sq. ft.
Beam	12'4"	
Draft	6'0"	
Displacement	22,500 lbs.	
Ballast	8,400 lbs.	

Mooneshine I has the standard interior plan of the early Valiants with aft cabin and open main saloon area which is hard to improve upon for the voyager. The sturdy cutter rig is still my preference for ocean sailing. Alas, I was too conservative or born too soon to take advantage of the wonderful roller-furling and roller-reefing headsail gear now available.

One reason for this cruising boat's relative success in distance racing was that she was kept light; that is, little gear was added to her factory newness. That is somewhat harder to do these days as race requirements and intriguing gadgetry complicate life at sea.

Water ballasting of yachts was not unheard of in 1976, but it certainly was not something that came to most minds when preparing for an offshore race. Looking back now I see the Valiant as an obvious candidate for a built-in water ballast system. The rather modest sacrifice of interior volume would pay off in comfort and speed to windward as well as more power on a reach. These happy advantages apply to the cruiser just as for the racer. As I look back on the many hard windward miles in the OSTARs of 1976 and 1980 I think, too late, of water ballast.

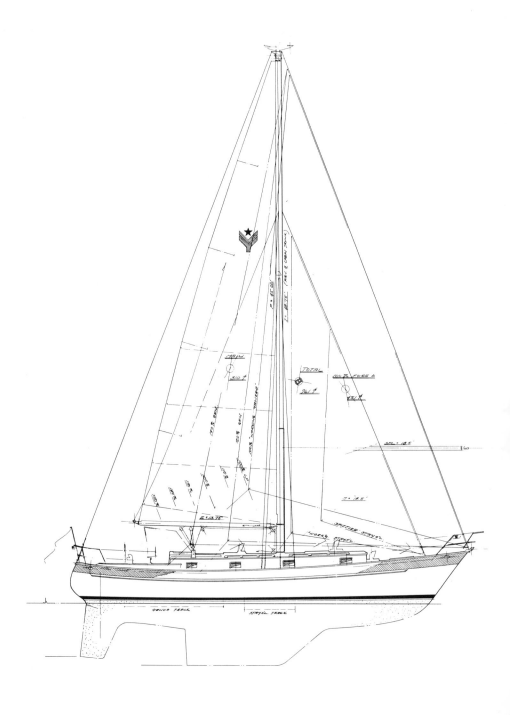

FAST PASSAGE 39
Designer: William Garden

LOA	39'6"	Sail area:
LWL	33'6"	Main 356 sq. ft.
Beam	11'2"	Staysail 227 sq. ft.
Draft	5'6"	Yankee 379 sq. ft.
Displacement	22,000 lbs.	
Ballast	7,500 lbs.	

I find these comments on *Mooneshine II* in a letter I wrote to William Garden shortly after the BOC Race: "My best day's run doesn't compare with the larger boats. Mine was 190 miles on two occasions, once in the Indian Ocean and once coming home in the northeast trades. Both times there was some assist from ocean currents. Worst day's run was 25 miles, also with assist from current. No records here. I found I did better relative to the larger boats in lighter going. I could consistently keep up with boats like *Gypsy Moth V,* and she didn't pass me until well south of the Equator on the first leg Newport to Cape Town. I am sure that the 39 is very effective in the light going despite its being a true cruising design. My largest sail was a 140% genoa (besides spinnaker), and all sails were 1 oz. heavier than usual practice, e.g. the mainsail and staysail were 9 oz. dacron.

"The 5'6" draft seems to work well downwind in those more anxious times. I believe I was knocked around less severely than most of the larger boats for a couple of reasons, besides luck. Moderate draft allows a boat to slew sideways if caught wrong by a wave instead of tripping. The other factor is the directional stability and fast response to the rudder to keep her square to steep waves coming up astern. I used an Aries vane which could spin the wheel over quickly when knocked off course. When that was broken the Alpha autopilot handled it quite well. The boat seemed directionally stable when surfing. There was never any thought of towing anything to maintain control or slow her down.

"I couldn't go upwind in heavy air with the bigger boats. She makes a lot of leeway if the angle of heel is greater than 20 degrees. For this reason I used small headsails going to weather, often a 135 sq. ft. storm jib and the staysail with double reefed main. She likes two small headsails working together. In sailing alongside a Valiant 40 I would tend to shorten down quicker but always went as fast . . ."

This *Mooneshine* had the simplest of instrumentation. Wind-speed and boatspeed were Swoffer analog meters with duplicate readouts at the navigation table. These are self-powered, requiring no ship's battery. The associated log readout does use a tiny amount of 12-volt power. Ten years later these meters are still on the job, and the log is still clicking every 60.8 feet. My other sailing "instrument" was the masthead Windex. I relied heavily on this for apparent wind direction at some cost to muscles in the back of my neck, and was also jealous to guard it from damage in knockdowns.

My comments on water ballast for the Valiant would also apply to the Fast Passage—and many other cruising boats.

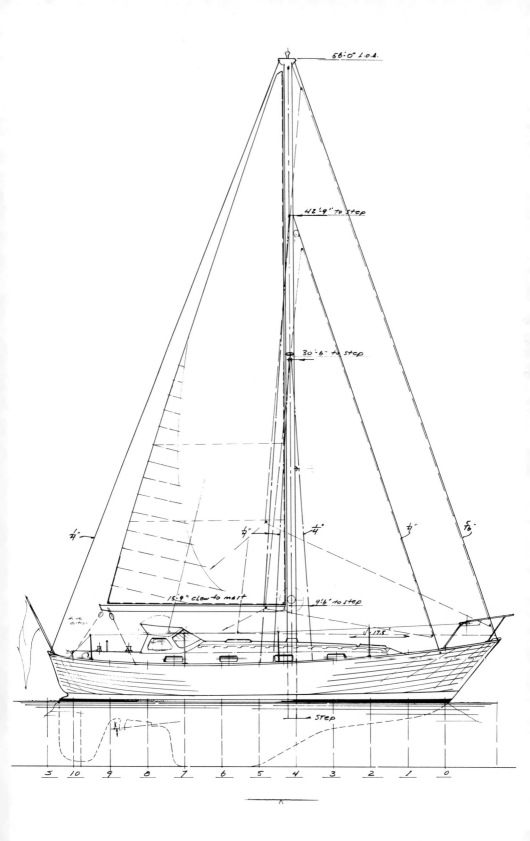

56'-0" L.O.A.

42'-9" to step

30'-6" to step

15'-9" clew to mast

9'-6" to step

17.5

step

5 10   9   8   7   6   5   4   3   2   1   0

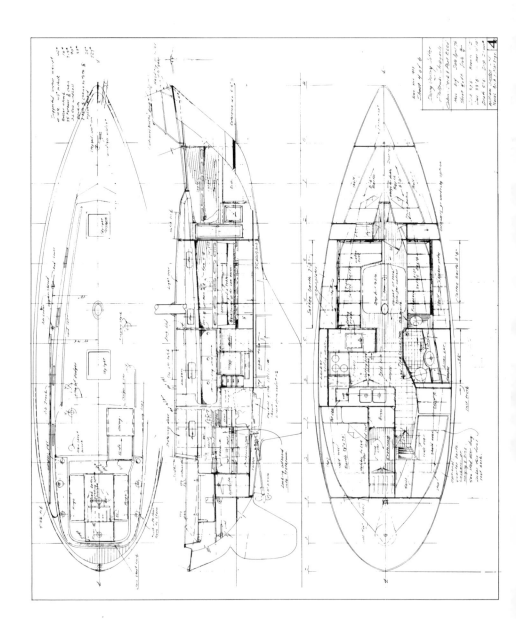

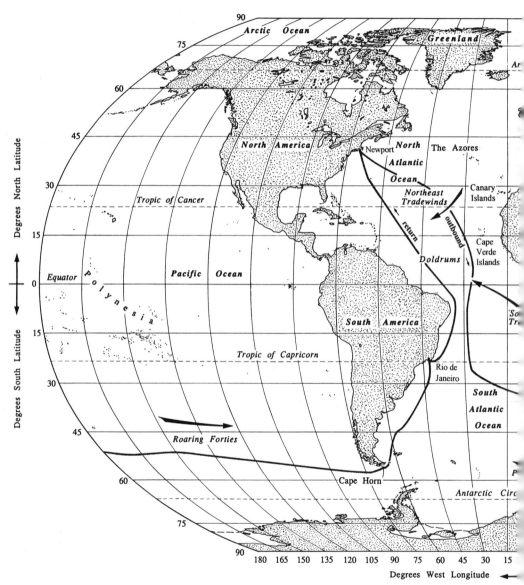

Map prepared by Eric W. Sponberg, naval architect
Sponberg Yacht Design Inc.
Newport, Rhode Island